MEMORIES:
The Murrieta Schools

Compiled and Edited by Jeanne Nelson

First Edition

ISBN-10 150088007
ISBN-13 978-1500788001

Createspace, North Charleston, SC

Table of Contents

PART ONE: The Story Unfolds

PART TWO: The People Who Helped Make It Happen

Acknowledgements

This history could not have become a reality without the help of some remarkable people. Thanks to those who graciously told their stories, it is a far richer history than it might have been. Their stories are an irreplaceable treasure of information on how things used to be. Sadly, some of these people have passed away.

Several people helped with fact checking and editing, sharing memories and stories that did not all make it into print. Donna Brantly, Karen Robertson, and Gary Farmer spent hours reading drafts, and I can't thank them enough. They were wonderful at catching typos, misspellings, time/place/name/fact errors, and encouraging me when I got frustrated.

Dave Hutt sent a large box of material and shared memories of the most challenging times in the District history, even though he knew he was fighting a losing battle with cancer.

Guy Romero helped catch some early errors, and provided support and encouragement during the first iteration of the book.

John Richardson gave technical advice and guidance in getting a book published, with tips on formatting software.

Many others answered questions, helping sort out what really happened, way back then. Karen Briski, Karen Michaud, Robin Haigh, Judi Rightmire, Judy Gould, Margi Wray, Karen Parris, Brenda Brandley, Sherry Wyman, Lynn Farmer, Barbara Hughes, Joann Dailey, Julie April, Ron Peace, Cheryl Dufresne, thank you for your insights, memory for details, and willingness to help!

Guy Romero's retirement in 2014 provided motivation to finish the book, and present it to him as a memento of his contributions to the success of the district.

Thank you all.

Preface

It hit me one day, in the early 21st century, that Murrieta school district's history was exciting, dramatic, and the kind of story that should be written down and shared. However, nobody was writing it down. After nudging various people to do this, it dawned on me that if I wanted to see this story written down, I'd need to do it myself. Disclaimer: I am not the best person to do this. But I care enough to want the story told.

There were two places to begin this project. First was locating school district history that has already been published. There are books about the community of Murrieta: *Murrieta, My Children's Home*, by Arlean Garrison, and *Murrieta, Old Town, New Town*, by Mary Alice Rail Boyce, and both include information about the school district. More recently, photos provided by Tony Guenther were included in a photo history, *Murrieta Hot Springs*, with authors Rebecca Farnbach, Loretta Barnett, and Marvin Curran. Loretta Barnett and Rebecca Farnbach also wrote *Images of America: Murrieta*, with photos from E. Hale Curran's collection. Reporters John Hunneman and Carl Love chronicled school district history through newspaper columns and articles about school happenings over the years.

To give people in the district a chance to contribute, I invited everyone to write down their memories of working there. A number of people wrote and sent stories, I added my own memories of what happened, and the book was begun.

Each person told their story as they remember it, and each remembered different things. Sometimes people's memories disagreed on what happened, and it will not surprise anyone that each person feels their telling of the story is the correct version.

After compiling a chronology of the schools, it became clear that this was not the entire story, not by far. So much of the history that impacted the school district was left out, and the history of those who worked supporting the district was also missing. This led to more research, adding stories that make the history come alive. With the Internet now available as a resource, correcting details was easier.

Many stories are not included and not everyone who contributed to the district is named, because there were so many people. Some stayed only a short time, but for others, their first job was with the school district and they stayed until they retired. This history is intended to remind the people who lived those stories about that time, now so long ago.

The story does not stop, nor will it ever be done. But it needs a stopping point, and someone else will have to write the sequel or tell "the rest of the story."

Introduction

Murrieta schools by the numbers

The Murrieta Valley Unified School District has had an exciting history, led by determined and visionary people dealing with some incredible challenges. This book attempts to capture some of that excitement by telling the story of the people who made it all happen, ranging from former students to the superintendent.

And what a story it was! For many years Murrieta was a small community of people who all knew each other, with one small school that educated their children in kindergarten through grade eight (and did it well, thankyouverymuch!).

Then came the most tumultuous time in the district's history, starting in 1989, when the community became a city almost overnight. In the space of two years, the school district grew from one elementary school to five, and at times experienced more than 100% growth.

Student enrollment numbers show how dramatic this change was. In 1885, there were 14 students waiting for the first school to be built. By 1918, student numbers had increased to 49 and it became necessary to build a larger school. In the 46 years from 1916 to 1962, the number of students increased to 74, including kindergarten students from Temecula.

Then, in the ten years between 1978 and 1988, 725 new students arrived, bringing the total number of students to 1,036. In the next ten-year period from 1988 to 1998, the district population exploded, from 1,036 students to 10,376 students.

Here are some of the enrollment figures* during those incredible growth years;

Year	Number of Students (% Growth)
1988 (K-8)	1,036 (70%)
1989 (K-8)	2,443 (139%)
1990 (K-9)	3,990 (61%)
1991 (K-10)	5,229 (31%)
1992 (K-11)	6,216 (19%)
1993 (K-12)	7,043 (13%)
1994	7,873 (12%)
1995	8,399 (7%)
1996	9,111 (8%)
1997	9,688 (6%)
1998	10,376 (7%)
1999	11,279 (9%)

* Student numbers are fluid numbers—new students arrive, other students leave all year long.

Murrieta students attend high school...but where?

When Murrieta was a small rural K-8 district, the community's students went to high school in Elsinore. Later, when a high school was built in Temecula, Murrieta students attended high school there. When Murrieta finally built its own high school, most—but not all—students finally attended school K-12 in their own community.

Why not all? Because, as the city of Murrieta grew, its boundaries expanded to include parts of surrounding school districts. Some Murrieta residents found themselves living in the Perris Union High School District boundaries, and their children went to high school in Perris. For a brief period of time, some Murrieta homes were even within the Hemet School District boundaries. To make things more confusing, some families learned that they lived in the K-8 Menifee Union School District, so even though they lived in the City of Murrieta, their younger children would attend school in Menifee.

The district enjoyed such a good reputation that it attracted students from surrounding communities. To attend Murrieta schools at the time, students from other districts had to get permission from their home school district to transfer to Murrieta, and from Murrieta to accept them.

By the 2003-04 school year, there were 15 schools in the Murrieta district, 17,480 students, 797 teachers, and 593 classified staff. Compare that with ten years prior, in the 93-94 school year when there were 8 schools, 7,043 students, 282 teachers, and 212 classified staff.

By 2013, there were 23,032 students in eleven K-5 elementary schools, four 6-8 middle schools, three comprehensive high schools, one continuation high school, one independent study school, and one adult education program. What an adventure it was, creating the district that exists today.

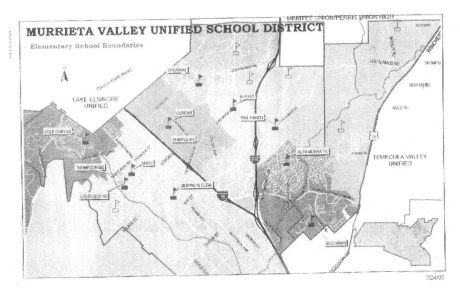

Map of the Murrieta Valley School District

PART ONE
The Story Unfolds

The story of the Murrieta school district was
many years in the making

History of the Murrieta Area

To understand the story of the Murrieta School District, it helps to know some history of the city of Murrieta and the area around it. This story begins more than 10,000 years ago with the people who lived in this area at that time. Their legends say that life on earth began in the Temecula valley. They called it "Exva Temeeku, the place of the union of Sky-father, and Earth-mother." These early people called their home Temeekunga— the place of the sun (from the Pechanga Band of Luiseño Indians website).

San Luis Rey Mission

When Mission San Luis Rey de Francia was founded in 1798, the Spanish missionaries established ranchos in the Temecula valley on land that had been home to native villages, and the natives became the forced labor of the mission.

Because the villages were on land claimed for Mission San Luis Rey, the native Indians became known as San Luiseños, later shortened to Luiseño. There are six bands of Luiseños in this area: the Pechanga Band in Temecula, the Soboba Band near San Jacinto, the Pauma Band in Pauma Valley, the Rincon Band near Valley Center, the La Jolla Band near Palomar, and the Old Pala Band at the Pala Reservation.

Some of the Murrieta schools' names are taken from Indian words. Avaxat (Ah va' ha), which means "cottonwood," was the name of the Indian village in the Murrieta area, and was used for the second elementary school in Murrieta. Shivela (Sha vay' lah), which means "sycamore," was the name given to Murrieta's first middle school. Tovashal (Toe' vah shal) Elementary School's name comes from the Indian word for "white oak." Tenaja (Ta nah' ha) Canyon Academy's

1

name is the Indian word that means pond or small lake.

By the late twentieth century, circumstances had changed dramatically for the Luiseño Indian bands, especially the Pechanga Band. Indian casinos brought in millions of dollars and the Pechanga Band has been generous to local schools, donating more than $2.7 million dollars since forming a school-funding program in 1998. As of 2010, Murrieta Valley High School has received $400,000.00, Vista Murrieta High School $270,000.00, and Murrieta Mesa High School $30,000.00.

Juan Murrieta

While Temecula's name has a long history, it wasn't until the middle 1800's that Murrieta got its name. Eighteen-year-old Juan Murrieta arrived in California from Spain in 1863 with his two brothers. The three brothers originally settled in the San Joaquin Valley, where they raised sheep.

Seven years later, with three partners, Juan Murrieta moved into the area that now bears the Murrieta name. Mr. Murrieta and his partners purchased 52,000 acres of the Temecula and Pauba Ranchos for $1.00 per acre, and brought 100,000 sheep from Merced to their new ranch. They were hard workers and were successful in this new business. Mr. Murrieta eventually moved on to Los Angeles, selling his ranch and sheep. He died in 1936 at the age of 91.

There was another famous Murrieta character who was no relation to Juan Murrieta. This was Joaquin Murrieta (also spelled Murieta, or Murietta), who became a bandit in Southern California. Many stories were told about his robbing and killing. California State Rangers killed him in 1853.

Murrieta becomes a town

In 1882 the California Southern Railroad Company built a railroad line across the valley, providing access to the area. Two years later the

Temecula Land and Water Company was formed and purchased 14,500 acres of land from Juan Murrieta. They subdivided it into lots on the eastern side of the railroad and named it Murrieta.

That same year the Murrieta train depot was built and the town began to grow. Land sold for as little as $5.00 an acre and attracted families from other areas. In 1885 the Fountain House Hotel and the Post Office were built. The Murrieta School was built a year later. By 1890 the town's population had increased to 800 and the community was thriving.

Most of the people who moved into the Murrieta area in the 1890's were interested in agriculture and ranching. The abandoned grain elevator in Murrieta serves as a reminder of that time. Farmers and ranchers grew alfalfa, wheat, barley and oats, and planted fruit, nut and olive orchards. Cattle ranches joined the sheep ranches as part of the economy.

The railroad and flooding

Engineers who were not familiar with weather in this area and ignored warnings from the locals about flooding had planned the San Diego to San Bernardino railroad. Sure enough, the following year it rained and rained. Then it rained some more! The Temecula Canyon portion of the railroad washed out, leaving a train stranded. Over four weeks, a series of storms brought over 40 inches of rain. The railroad company, facing huge losses, was able to rebuild the tracks, and trains ran again in 1885.

But 1891 was another wet year and the railroad through Temecula Canyon washed out again. The railroad company decided they could not afford to rebuild it, and that was the end of trains between Fallbrook and Temecula. The trains continued to run north from Temecula to Murrieta, going on through Lake Elsinore, Perris, and Colton.

The train was an important part of the life of the new town of Murrieta, bringing visitors and taking crops and livestock to market. It also took students to high school in Lake Elsinore daily. Murrieta and Temecula did not have high schools at that time and would not for many years.

The last train ran in March 1935, and Murrieta students started riding a school bus to high school in Lake Elsinore. That year the railroad station closed and the Fountain House Hotel, a Murrieta landmark, burned. The end of the trains also marked the end of Murrieta's boom years.

Flooding continued to be a problem. Streets in the original business district of Murrieta (later called Old Town) turned into small rivers for a few days each year and there were many road closures. In 1994 Old Town Murrieta flooded for the last time, with an estimated $210,000 in damages. Work began on two flood control channels that finally solved the problem of the annual flooding in Old Town.

Murrieta Hot Springs

The Murrieta Hot Springs were an important part of the local economy for many years. In the late 1800's Juan Murrieta and other sheep ranchers used the hot springs to bathe sheep. After the railroad was built the hot springs became a Chinese laundry, with laundry shipped to and from San Diego.

The Guenther family purchased the Hot Springs in 1902 and built the Murrieta Hot Springs Resort. By the 1920's this had become a famous vacation spa, attracting many well-known visitors. The Guenther family owned it for 67 years. After they sold it in 1969, a series of owners tried unsuccessfully to manage the beautiful resort. During that time the facilities deteriorated and the need for repairs was evident everywhere. It was finally purchased in 1995 by Calvary Chapel and restored for use as a conference center and Bible College.

Fire Department

Fire has always been a serious problem in Southern California. Neighboring Perris, 20 miles away, originally provided fire protection for Murrieta. By 1947 Murrieta had a population of 1,200 people and the residents voted to form their own fire protection district. They purchased

4

a fire truck for $1,400.00 and staffed the first fire station with volunteers.

That first station was located behind the Murrieta Machine Shop. In 1965 Murrieta residents voted for a $30,000 bond measure to build a new fire station on land across the street from Murrieta Elementary School. This fire station became the current Fire Station #1.

The Murrieta Fire Department and the school district have had a close relationship over the years. Marvin Curran served as Chief of the Fire Department from 1972 to 1992, and was also a school board member and the first school bus driver for the school district. Teacher Karen Robertson's husband Barry became a fireman.

Dorothea Tiss, who worked in the Murrieta Elementary school library for many years, kept a radio scanner in the school library so she would know when there was a fire. When that happened, she would go across the street to the Fire Department to help direct volunteers. Two of her children would work for the Fire Department when they grew up. "I want to be a fireman when I grow up" was a reality for a number of Murrieta youngsters.

The Fire Department has held an annual "Old Fashioned Pit Barbecue" each April, beginning in 1948. That first barbecue was attended by 300 people who enjoyed 300 pounds of barbecued beef. Murrieta residents have always enjoyed good food!

In 1993, the new City of Murrieta took over the 46-year old Fire Protection District. The Fire Department continues to be a source of pride for the community and works closely with the school district to teach fire prevention skills and safety to students.

Town Hall Association

Any community needs a place where the citizens can get together for business or entertainment. Murrieta residents met in the school, the Fountain House, or the Historical Hall, which burned in 1924. Another building replaced it, but by the late 1930's there was little interest in maintaining a building for meetings and in 1946 the building was sold.

From 1946 to 1954 there was no building for community meetings. In 1956 the Murrieta Valley Town Hall Association was formed to start planning a new community center. That year Mrs. Inez Hunt donated her house and five acres to be used as a Town Hall.

Mrs. Hunt's property included a large cement slab. In the summers there were activities on that slab every evening. These included square dancing, movies (projected on the wooden back wall), volleyball, western dances, and roller-skating.

Dorothy Renon led the effort to build the new community center, which would be located on the area where the cement slab had been.

In 1981 the Association built a new Town Hall on the Hunt property using community development block funds. Murrieta finally got their long-awaited community center for town events. However, the Town Hall Association charged a fee for use of this facility, and this ended the free summer evening community activities. When Mr. van de Wetering retired, his retirement celebration was held in this building, the only building in town with room for the many people who wanted to congratulate him.

The Hunt property also included a small arena where youngsters could ride their horses and where the community held gymkhanas for adults and children. Some members of the community wanted to see this space used as a baseball field, and sixty-five people showed up in the little Town Hall building to argue baseball vs. horses. As a result, the baseball field was built and a piece of Murrieta's western culture disappeared.

Murrieta Public Library

Library service in the Temecula/Murrieta area provided another challenge for these new cities. Riverside County had a county library system, managed by the City of Riverside, that provided bookmobile service to Temecula and Murrieta. When Temecula began to grow rapidly in the 1980's, citizens there began working to get a library, and opened a tiny library facility in a storefront building. They were able to raise enough funds to get a matching grant through the County Library System and build a permanent library. The County, in an effort to provide library services for Murrieta and Temecula, located this library as close to Murrieta as possible, but still within the Temecula City limits.

As Murrieta grew there was increasing interest in getting a library located in Murrieta. Carol Kravagna and Dorothy Renon formed a Friends of the Library group, saying that Riverside County provided Murrieta no library services. Through their efforts the city was able to negotiate the withdrawal of Murrieta's tax base from the County Library System. Using these funds, Murrieta opened its own library in 1999 in a former bank building on Los Alamos Road, just off the 215 highway.

Diane Satchwell, Murrieta's first library director, submitted the successful grant application for state funds that would pay for a new 12,000 square-foot library. The grant application included a partnership between the city and the school district. When Mrs. Satchwell left, Loretta McKinney replaced her and oversaw the construction of this long-awaited library, which opened in 2007.

Rapid growth

In 1890 the new town of Murrieta had 800 residents, but by 1970 this number had dropped to 542. When the state completed the stretch of Highway 15 from Riverside to San Diego in the 1980's, this provided increased accessibility to Murrieta and a housing boom followed. Young families were attracted to country living and affordable homes. Most houses and businesses in Murrieta were built after 1987. When Murrieta became a city in 1991, the population was approximately 19,000. In the period between 1990 and 1999, the city grew 107 percent and by 2011 Murrieta was home to 105,857 people.

Here's what that looked like:

YEAR	POPULATION
1890	800
1947	1,200
1970	542
1980	2,255
1985	3,000
1990	19,101
1995	24,596
2000	51,799
2005	84,418
2010	103,466
2011	105,857

Cityhood!

On November 6, 1990 Murrieta voters approved cityhood by an 81 percent margin. Murrieta officially became a city on July 1, 1991, with Jerry Allen elected as the first mayor. The first city council was composed of Joe Peery, mayor pro tem, and councilmen Gary Smith, Fred Weishaupl, and Dave Haas. Jack R. Smith was hired as the first city manager. In 1992 Murrieta formed its own police department.

For a while the Murrieta School District Office and Murrieta's City Hall shared a building on Beckman Court, but soon outgrew that building. The school district moved to its own building on McAlby Court, while City Hall moved to their new building in Town Square, the site of the new library and other city buildings.

The school district and the city continue to work together on projects that benefit the children of the community.

Murrieta Schools: The first hundred years

In the late 1800's students in Murrieta attended school in Temecula, Fallbrook, Lake Elsinore, Perris, Riverside, and Murrieta, depending on when schools were built, and what grades were included. If students wanted to go to high school and Riverside had the closest high school, that was where they went. In those days, students were lucky if they were able to finish elementary school and 'graduate' from eighth grade.

The first area schools

Temecula opened the first school in the Temecula/Murrieta/Elsinore area. San Diego County records note that in 1873 nine boys and two girls were enrolled in school in Temecula and that the average daily attendance was seven. Temecula had the only school in San Diego County with enough money to keep school open eight months of the year. Riverside County did not exist at the time; both Temecula and Murrieta were in San Diego County.

Other schools in the Temecula area soon followed. Pujol School District was formed in 1882, holding classes in the Welty Boarding House in Temecula until 1888, when they built the Pujol School at the northern end of Temecula. Santa Gertrudes School District was formed during this time to provide education for students along Winchester Road, but no school was ever built.

In 1882 the Pechanga Indian Reservation was formed and in 1885 the federal government built the first Pechanga Indian School. The original adobe building was replaced by a frame building that burned in 1891. A larger school was built, with a room for the teacher to live in. In 1894 Mary J. Platt, the Pechanga Indian School teacher since 1890, was murdered and the reservation's schoolhouse was burned to cover up the crime. The schoolhouse was rebuilt that year and then remodeled in 1911.

In 1884 the Lake Elsinore School District was created with the construction of Elsinore Grammar School, teaching students in grades one through eight.

A school in Murrieta-- 1885

The Temecula Land and Water Company laid out the new community of Murrieta in 1884. With fourteen school-age children, the residents of this new community wanted their own school. Daniel N. Buchanan, a skilled carpenter, fixed up Marcus Hedges' barn near the southeast corner of Washington and Ivy to use as a temporary school until a school building could be built.

On July 15, 1885, a lot on 2nd Street was designated for the school and construction began. Mr. Buchanan was hired to build this one-room school, which cost $2,200.00. The school had a baseball field and track, and a small stable where students who rode to school horseback could keep their horses during school hours.

By the end of October, the school was completed and ready for students, with one teacher teaching all students, first grade to eighth grade.

The school bell

The school bell rang for the first time on October 28, 1885. Students in those early days took turns ringing the bell, and it was considered quite an honor to be allowed to do this. The bell was rung for the entire community for emergencies and to signal important events.

When Murrieta Grammar School was built in 1920, the old school bell was moved into this new school and continued to serve the community.

Peggy Goffman said that they rang the bell when her house burned down in 1947 to recruit help to put out the fire. Seventh and eighth grade students helped save her possessions from burning.

In the early 1980's, the bell was put in a bell tower at Murrieta Elementary School to keep students from ringing it, and new electronic bells were installed at the school. The new bell tower was on the corner of Adams and B Street and looked pretty bare, so the Murrieta Livewires 4-H Club landscaped the area around it.

The first area high school

In the late 1800's, students in the Temecula/Murrieta/Lake Elsinore area attended high school in either Fallbrook or Riverside, going to school by train. Lake Elsinore residents wanted a high school in their community, and in 1891 they formed the Lake Elsinore Union High School District.

The first high school class of 17 students met that September in a room at Elsinore Grammar School. Lake Elsinore's high school classes were held in various places until the new Elsinore High School building was completed in 1911. Students from the entire area attended this high school, including students from Murrieta.

Murrieta students would attend high school in Lake Elsinore, and later Temecula, until Murrieta Valley High School opened in 1990.

Murrieta Grammar School-- 1920

By 1900 there were enough students in Murrieta that an addition had to be built onto that first one-room school building.

The community continued to grow, and by 1918 there were forty-nine students in Murrieta and they needed a larger school. In 1920 the old school was torn down and a new school, Murrieta Grammar School, was built on the same location on 2nd Street. Students attended classes in the Murrieta Methodist Church while their new school was being built.

This new school introduced a new educational concept: different grade levels and several teachers. The school also featured indoor plumbing, a controversial topic at the time. The school board members who oversaw these innovations were T.R. Wickerd, Amos Sykes, and Walter Thompson.

Murrieta Elementary School — 1958

In 1956 the 36-year-old Murrieta Grammar School on 2nd Street was declared unsafe. The community needed a new school and passed their first school bond for $60,000. This, combined with $200,000 from the state, allowed them to build a larger school on Adams Avenue. Architect Bolton Moise was hired to plan this new school, which opened in 1958. This new school selected the community's first mascot, a jaguar, with school colors of red and white.

When the new school was completed, the old Grammar School building was sold to an artist, who used it as his residence. It burned in 1984, and its owner narrowly escaped the fire himself.

The new Murrieta Elementary School opened with four teachers: Barbara Stilwell, primary, Eunice Cain, three/four, George Contreras, five/six, and teacher/principal Gordon Harmon, seven/eight. Almost ten years later, in 1965, there were 79 students and still four teachers: George Contreras, Edith Lambert, Ethel Holl and Gordon Harmon, who was still teacher/principal.

Mrs. Cain taught from 1952 to 1965, when she retired. Her husband died in 1967 and she returned to teaching second and third grade until 1971.

Support staff in the new school building included Cora Stoller, school caretaker, Bonnie Swain, part-time custodian, and Carolyn Donoho, part-time bookkeeper and clerk.

12

In 1965 Mrs. Donoho was diagnosed with cancer. She recommended Donna Brantly as her replacement, a good choice. When Mrs. Swain retired in 1966 Marvin Curran was hired to replace her, becoming the first full-time custodian.

Mr. Harmon retired in 1966 and Ethel Holl became the teacher/principal. That year, Mrs. Goodhope taught grades six/seven/eight, Rod McQuillan four/five, Principal Ethel Holl two/three, and Edith Lambert kindergarten and first grade.

The Board was composed of Ann Miller, Carroll Anderson, and Marvin Curran. At a meeting when the Board voted to make the custodian position full-time Mr. Curran abstained from voting. The measure passed and he resigned from the Board to apply for the job as custodian. Mr. Curran was replaced on the Board by Curtis Thompson. Marie Curran was hired in 1968 as playground supervisor and Jackie Shield was hired as a clerk in 1970 to help with the increasing workload.

Dorothea Tiss started working at Murrieta Elementary July 1, 1970 and for four years she did just about everything, including cooking lunch for the 100 students and working as a teachers' aide. She said, "I did everything but drive a bus, and they even asked me to do that." When the school library was created, Mrs. Tiss would find her niche.

Mr. van de Wetering hired as principal

Charles van de Wetering was hired as the new principal of Murrieta Elementary School in 1971, when there was a staff of four teachers and 150 students. They desperately needed another teacher and the board hired a fifth teacher, Karen Fountain (Robertson), to teach a three/four class. A school district with five teachers was large enough to have a superintendent so "Mr. Van" became Principal/Superintendent, and the first superintendent in the district.

The teaching staff consisted of Ethel Holl, kindergarten, Edith Lambert, grades one/two, Karen Fountain (Robertson), three/four, Russel Love, five/six, Verdell "Satch" LaValley, seven/eight, and Joan Watson, special

13

education.

As more students moved into the community, additional teachers were hired. Mr. McQuillan left and was replaced by Greg Lockett. Carl Lyons, Carmen Stratemeyer, Charlie Riendeau (first as Mrs. Stratemeyer's aide, later as a teacher), and Mr. Lyon's wife Sally were added to the staff and almost all of them stayed until they retired.

Murrieta fights unification with Elsinore

Mr. van de Wetering was hired at a time when the K-8 Murrieta district was threatened by a unification election which would have joined Murrieta, Temecula and Elsinore Elementary districts with the Elsinore Union High School District to create one unified K-12 district. The Murrieta residents wanted no part of this! Temecula was also a one-school elementary district at the time, and like Murrieta, happy to remain so.

A group was formed composed of Mr. Van, board members Curt Thompson, Kenny (Kennadine) Turner and Mike Devitt, staff members Donna Brantly and Marie Curran, and many parents and community members. They were led by realtor Dave Turner in a campaign to defeat unification with Elsinore.

On the day of the 1972 election, there were 278 registered voters in Murrieta, many less than in Elsinore. However, when voting results were announced, Murrieta had won!

The old Murrieta school bell was rung in celebration when the community realized they would not be part of the Elsinore School District. Eunice Cain, long-time teacher, was given the honor of ringing the school bell this time. She pulled the rope, the bell rang, the rope pulled back up, and Mrs. Cain flew up in the air! She was quite shaken, but not hurt.

14

School and community events

Murrieta Elementary School in those days was close-knit and everyone knew everyone else. Mr. LaValley, the drama teacher, held fashion shows each year that were popular and well attended. Teachers and community members modeled his collection of antique Hollywood clothing that had belonged to famous movie stars. Being one of Mr. LaValley's models was quite an honor and Marsha Kempf, clerk at Murrieta Elementary, was always one of the models.

Mr. LaValley was also well known in the community for directing student performances at Christmas. He wrote a new script for each show and included every class in school as part of the cast. These were annual events that everyone in town looked forward to with anticipation. As the school grew Mr. LaValley had to add an afternoon matinee and two evening performances so everyone in town could attend.

In this small community, there were a number of annual events that were popular and well attended. The Halloween Carnival was held at either the Fire Department or Murrieta Elementary. The Dime-a-Dip dinner, similar to a potluck, was a fund-raising event. Like a potluck, people brought food to share but paid a dime for each dip of food they took. A family of four could eat a large meal for under $3.00.

In the 1970's there was a big concrete slab where the community center is now located. There was no movie theater in Murrieta, and many nights this slab was the center for evening entertainment. These included skating, square dancing, movies, volleyball, western dancing and auctions.

All this changed when the community center was built on that concrete slab. To maintain the facility, there was now a charge to use it, so those evening events came to an end.

Employees form unions

Prior to the 1970's there were no written contracts for Murrieta employees, though there was a district-adopted salary schedule. In 1974 Marie Curran was instrumental in forming a classified union in Murrieta, a chapter of the state Classified School Employees Association (CSEA). Mrs. Curran served as the first Murrieta chapter president from 1975 to 1983.

During these early years, the superintendent negotiated raises for the teachers, since the teachers had not yet organized as a union. Karen Robertson recalled that in the late 1970's negotiations consisted of two teachers, Mrs. Robertson and Mr. Lyons, attending a board meeting and simply asking for a raise for the teachers. The board members would discuss this for a while, and either agree to the request or counter with an offer of a few percent less. Negotiations were usually completed in just a few minutes.

This changed when a new teacher, John Jacobsen, was hired sometime in the early 1980's. He had union experience and presented the school board with a 65-page document to form a teachers union, a proposal that upset many members of the community. Angry community members showed up for the board meetings when this was discussed, and teachers were advised to stay away until things calmed down.

This was the start of the Murrieta Teachers' Association (MTA) in Murrieta. The relationship between the Board and MTA was sometimes contentious. Board member Dave Hutt recalled issues arising when the Board decided to change the teachers' salary schedule and implement a performance-based pay structure (merit pay). This lasted three years, and no teacher received merit pay. When the contract was renegotiated the former pay schedule was put back in place.

Later the Board, attempting to create a more positive relationship with the teachers' union, added a board position for an MTA representative. This was a non-voting position, but the representative received the board information packet and could participate in discussion.

16

Playground activities during lunch period

Mr. Van enjoyed being with the students, so he was often out helping supervise the playground during lunch. He started intramural sports during lunch period and loved refereeing, umpiring and getting out in the sunshine.

Mr. Van used wresting as a method for solving disputes between boys. He simply had them wrestle out their disagreement. He started a wrestling program that proved popular and grew rapidly. The wrestling room at Murrieta Valley High School is named for Mr. Van because of his long-standing support for the sport.

The first school library

There had been a library in the old Murrieta Grammar School, but it was a room where books were stored and there was no librarian. Thanks to Mr. Van, a library was added to Murrieta Elementary School with Marie Curran managing it. This new school library occupied the stage in the multipurpose room, with shelves built by Ellis Holl, who had been a principal at the old Murrieta School. Books came from a library in Perris that had closed.

In 1974 Dorothea Tiss took over management of the school library and Mr. Van purchased the first "real" library furniture, including shelves and a desk. Mrs. Tiss worked in the library until her retirement in 2001.

Over the years Mrs. Tiss increased the original collection of books with donations. When there was money she bought more books, until there were almost 15,000 books for students to check out. The Murrieta Elementary library also served as a community lending library since there was no other library in the area. Zane Gray westerns and Agatha Christie mysteries could be found among the children's books, and parents checked out books for themselves when they dropped off or picked up their children.

For many years there was also a Riverside County Bookmobile that came by once a week to let students check out additional library books.

Special Education support

Carmen Stratemeyer was hired in 1974 as a special education teacher and resource specialist, and stayed with the district until she retired 18 years later. She was recruited by Mr.Van , who persuaded her to break her teaching contract with Fontana School District and come to Murrieta.

In 1975-76 the special education program was a joint program with Menifee, whose students were bussed to Murrieta. A Special Day Class (SDC) was added in 1980, with Mary Godfrey as their teacher.

Flooding is an annual problem

For years flooding was a problem in Murrieta during the rainy season and almost everyone had a "flood story" to tell. For example, one day when it rained heavily, flooded streets blocked Mrs. Stratemeyer's way to school. She shouldered her book bag and started wading through the running water. When it got too deep she used a fallen tree as a bridge to get across, finally getting to the school.

When she entered the school office, totally drenched, Mr. Van turned to her and said, "No electricity. No school." Mrs. Stratemeyer broke down in tears, because she had tried so hard to get there.

One hundred years, 1885 to 1985, and still no high school

While flooding would continue to be an issue, dramatic changes were coming for this small school district. Murrieta was ready for its own high school.

The District Grows, 1980 to 2000

In 1981 there were less than 300 students in the Murrieta School District. The teaching staff at that time included Satch LaValley, Sally Lyons, Lois Shumway, Susan Reynolds, Kathaleen Quinlan, Carol Gurulé, Rudy Gurulé, Sharon Gunrud, Donna Reid, Karen Robertson, Carmen Stratemeyer, Guy Romero, Mary Godfrey, Jan Wilson, Charlie Riendeau and Carl Lyons.

Bridget Fitzwater, Patty Julian, Val Whisenand, Jessee Carter, Dorothea Tiss (in the library), Marsha Kempf, and Diane Light worked as instructional aides. Cindy Crismon and Marie Curran handled secretarial duties, while Donna Brantly served as superintendent's secretary and business manager.

More students start arriving

Starting in the mid-1980's Mr. Van and the Board saw the beginning of the tremendous growth that was coming. The number of students increased steadily, and in 1985 the school district had a high initial enrollment of 420 students, which warranted hiring additional teachers. Elizabeth Ellsworth, Constance Gray (Youens) and Patricia Lagger (Beal) were hired that year.

With more students and teachers, Mr. Van needed some help handling it all. Susan Reynolds, kindergarten/first grade teacher, was the perfect choice for the district's first assistant principal, and she also became

19

District Project/Curriculum Coordinator. With a final count of 375 students and 18 teachers, for the first time Murrieta Elementary School had to add portable classroom buildings.

A new multipurpose building!

The 1984-85 school year was exciting for the district in another way. The Board learned that Murrieta Elementary School would receive $855,098.00 from the state to construct a new multipurpose building and remodel the old multipurpose room to create two new kindergarten classrooms.

Architect Wendell Harbach was hired to design the building that would be a "cafetorium," a combination cafeteria and auditorium with a complete kitchen, walk-in freezer, dishwasher, and storage space. The plans also included a shaded outdoor patio. The state funding formula at the time allowed ninety percent of the costs to be paid by the state and ten percent paid by the school district.

District childcare program

With new families moving into the community, Assistant Principal Susan Reynolds saw a need for more child care. There were not enough local options for children to be supervised before and after school while their parents were working. Many of the newly arrived parents were commuting to jobs elsewhere, and often both parents worked. With characteristic determination, Mrs. Reynolds started the district childcare and summer camp programs in 1985.

As the program evolved, the childcare program at each of the school sites varied according to their needs and the personality of the person in charge, resulting in different fees, hours, and services. It needed consistency and coordination, and Karen Robertson took over management of this program in 1992, working with Coni Stevens.

At that time, there were five childcare centers and four of them were operating at a deficit. Thanks to Mrs. Robertson's efforts the program became financially sound, paid staff salaries, and was even able to purchase buildings for child care centers.

When Mrs. Robertson retired five years later, the child care program became part of Family Services.

Mr. Van becomes full-time superintendent

In 1986, Mrs. Reynolds was promoted to principal of Murrieta Elementary, a position she would hold until 1995. Mr. Van became full-time superintendent with an office in a trailer at the school, and Donna Brantly continued to work as his secretary and also handle the duties of business manager.

Additional district leadership

Mr. Van and the Board knew that more families would be moving into the area from the number of housing tracts that were approved and starting to be built in the community. Becoming a large district would mean leadership in hiring teachers, building schools, managing an increasingly complex budget, and providing curriculum and instructional materials for the many students that were expected to move into the area.

To meet this need, four assistant superintendents were hired in 1988: Tom Tooker, Assistant Superintendent of Facilities Services, Dr. Karen Lynch, Assistant Superintendent of Instructional Services, Dr. Arvo Toukonen, Assistant Superintendent of Personnel, and Donna Brantly, Assistant Superintendent of Business Services. Mrs. Brantly was the only one of the four who already worked for the school district, serving previously as the school business manager and superintendent's secretary. Her promotion meant that Mr. Van needed a secretary, and he hired Chris Hanson.

The first District Office building

Space was needed for the newly hired district office personnel to work. The small office trailer at Murrieta Elementary School no longer served the purpose, and there weren't many options. A building on the corner of Ivy and Plum (the current Murrieta Day Spa building) was available, and became the first District Office. This was an older building and during earthquakes the entire building shook alarmingly, especially in the upstairs conference room.

The school district was not the only tenant in the building. A hairdresser occupied part of it, and when she gave a customer a "perm," everyone could smell the chemicals.

Unification and the bond measure

The following year, 1989, was a major turning point for the school district. That November there were two crucial items on the election ballot: Murrieta School District unification and a bond measure to build the first high school. Architect Ralph Allen, hired to design that high school, recommended that it be built for 3,000 students. He estimated that $44 million would be needed to build a high school of this size. The Board was not sure the community would vote for such a large amount, and decided that the high school would only need to house 2,400 students. With only 279 high school students in the district at that time, a school for 2,400 students seemed enormous. The cost for a 2,400-student high school was $38.5 million, which was set as the bond amount.

There was a lot depending on that election because Murrieta planned to start teaching high school students the following fall. The community showed their support by approving the $38.5 million bond to build Murrieta's first high school. Measure P, unification, also passed and Murrieta finally became a unified K-12 district. The newly named Murrieta Valley Unified School District started with about 1,000 students.

That same year, 1989, the district added three more elementary schools, for a total of five. Alta Murrieta School opened first in February as a K-8school, led by Principal Buck DeWeese. In September Rail Ranch Elementary School opened with Principal Al Ross, and E. Hale Curran opened with Principal Charlie Riendeau. This was an exciting year, district-wide.

Planning for the future

The Board of Education members who oversaw these dramatic changes were Patty Julian, Dave Hutt, Austin Linsley, Peter Lemke, and Evelyn Henning. They felt their new district needed clear direction if it was to be successful. During many board and staff meetings, district retreats, and presentations by experts, a plan was developed to guide the district through the next 15 years. The Murrieta Plan was developed with Board member Dave Hutt as chief architect and Principal Guy Romero helping to guide the process with his insights and suggestions.

Mr. Van and the Board had no experience in building new schools—this hadn't happened in Murrieta since 1958. They looked for experts to help them with the huge task of planning new schools for the students who were moving into the district daily. Marshall Krupp, of Community Systems Associates, was the best choice for this job, and was hired.

Food Services

Another area of dramatic change was Food Services. This had been a fairly simple operation when the district was small. As the district grew they needed to provide hot lunches for students at many schools, and the schools with portable buildings did not have kitchens. To solve this problem, lunches were prepared at Murrieta Elementary School which had a kitchen, and taken to the other schools in vans.

When MVHS opened in 1990 with a large modern kitchen, the Food Services staff relocated there to prepare the lunches for the district. Oversight of the program was moved to the District Office as part of the

Business Services division. Penny Beaulieu was selected as the Director of the Food Service Program, in addition to her role as Director of Technology. Robin Haigh was hired to take over the bookkeeping and accounting for this new program.

Ms. Beaulieu and Mrs. Haigh soon learned that there were problems with how funds were being handled. As a result, oversight of the collection and deposit of money was also moved to the District Office to ensure proper checks and balances were being followed.

Combining Technology and Food Services, each a full-time job, was overwhelming and didn't work very well. Ms. Beaulieu left the district and Technology and Food Services became separate departments, each with its own director.

The first counselors

As the district grew, counselors were hired for each of the elementary schools. Betty Nead joined the staff at Murrieta Elementary, Butch Owens at Alta Murrieta and Gary Farmer at E. Hale Curran. Candyce Julian would become the counselor at Avaxat and Bonnie Cringan at Rail Ranch. The counselors would often serve as assistant principals because there was so much to do.

New computers for students to use

As part of planning for the future, Mr. Van and the Board wanted to provide computers for students and teachers. There were a few computers in use already, but the Board wanted all students to be able to learn how to use these new tools. In August 1989, Karen Robertson became the district's first Computer Coordinator. She ordered, installed, and trained teachers and students to use 350 new classroom and computer lab Apple IIGS computers. These computers were very high tech then, with 528K of memory.

When construction of new homes in Murrieta slowed in the early 90's,

24

so did the funding for computers. By the time there was technology money again, the district decided to replace the durable little Apple computers with PC's, which were more widely used.

The district librarian is hired

In November 1989, Jeanne Nelson was hired as the first District Librarian. Mrs. Nelson oversaw the ordering of library books and library furniture for the many schools that would be built, providing input into the design of each new library. Initially, these new libraries opened with paper card catalogs in large cabinets, but as technology evolved, the schools changed over to new digital library catalogs. Getting all the information from the old card catalogs entered into a database was a huge project.

These new libraries shared a room with a computer lab, and a "library/lab technician" supervised both sides of the room. Classes were scheduled regularly for both computer and library time.

Planning secondary schools, classrooms for many new students

Families were moving into the new homes being built in Murrieta and there were not enough classrooms on the five elementary school sites for the incoming students. The district needed more classrooms and decided to open another school, which ended up being a middle school. All sixth, seventh and eighth graders from the K-8 elementary schools would be moved to the middle school, freeing up elementary classroom space.

The last 8th grade class at Murrieta Elementary, before it became a K-5 school in 1989-90, became the first graduating class at Murrieta Valley High School.

In 1989 Lucinda Brouwer was hired and given the task of planning and opening Shivela Middle School. In early 1990 Dan Burch was hired to start planning for the opening of Murrieta Valley High School. Mrs. Brouwer and Mr. Burch began hiring teachers, thirty for Shivela and fifteen for MVHS.

Classroom space had to be provided until the middle school could be opened, and double sessions were one solution. Alta Murrieta/Rail Ranch (sharing the Alta school site) and E. Hale Curran Elementary Schools opened that year with double session schedules. Alta Murrieta students went to school early in the morning and Rail Ranch students attended school starting in the afternoon. At E. Hale Curran, two sessions were held for kindergarten through sixth grade students and one overlapping session for seventh and eighth grade students.

Avaxat and Murrieta Elementary schools were able to remain single session. Except for Murrieta Elementary, these schools were all in portable classroom buildings.

Murrieta sues Riverside County

The School Board and the Superintendent, desperate for money to provide space and materials for the deluge of new students, filed a petition to sue Riverside County for "failing to plan adequately for new schools to serve the growing community."

The grounds for the lawsuit were in the South West Area Community Plan, adopted by the Board of Supervisors in November 1989. The school district wanted and needed twice as much in developer fees as had been allocated by the county. Murrieta won the lawsuit and as a result, developers were required to pay additional fees to the Murrieta school district.

Changes at the District Office

When Assistant Superintendent of Curriculum and Instruction Karin Lynch left in 1990, her position was restructured to a directorship, and Principal Guy Romero was promoted to Director of Curriculum. Assistant Superintendent of Personnel Arvo Toukonen became Assistant Superintendent of Personnel and Educational Services.

Mrs. Donna Brantly, Assistant Superintendent of Business Services, retired in June 1990 after 25 years with the district and was replaced by Dr. Roland Werner. Dr. Werner formed the first District Budget Advisory Committee, composed of district staff, site administration, parents and teachers. This committee's charge was to provide input into the budget process.

Dr. Werner also planned a district warehouse and reprographics department for cost-savings and convenience. Materials could be purchased more cost effectively in large quantities and stored in a warehouse until they were needed. Printing in-house would also be less expensive and printed materials could be sent out to the schools rapidly. At this time there were few options for having materials printed in the Murrieta area.

Plumbing becomes a problem

In 1990, 564 students attended Murrieta Elementary school and by 1995, there were 905 students. At the time Murrieta Elementary School was built, residents of Murrieta relied on septic tanks, and so the school was built with its own septic tank. This worked for a small school but when the number of students grew to 900 in the 1990's, the septic tank adventures began. Any puddle on campus was suspect, and students had to be monitored so they would not play in standing water.

Mrs. Brantly recalled one such septic problem, an emergency for a school, and a plumber was called. He fixed the problem with a pump-out, but when the bill arrived, Mrs. Brantly and Mr. Van were shocked with how high it was. They called the plumber to see if they could get the charges reduced. In response, the plumber offered to return the contents of the septic tank. The bill was paid.

This ongoing plumbing issue was solved with the connection to city sewage, when that became available.

A series of new principals at Murrieta Elementary

Murrieta Elementary School had a series of principals during the 1990's. Karen Michaud was hired as Assistant Principal in 1993, working with Principal Susan Reynolds. When Mrs. Reynolds became the District Title I Program Facilitator/Reading Specialist in 1995, Buck DeWeese became Principal. Mr. DeWeese was promoted to Director of Human Resources at the District Office in 1997, and Ms. Michaud became Principal.

Murrieta Elementary School celebrates Murrieta cityhood

On July 1st, 1991 when Murrieta became a city, it was a cause for celebration for long-time residents of the community. Dorothea Tiss, Murrieta Elementary School's librarian, had been actively involved in the cityhood effort. She decorated the Murrieta Elementary School library with newspaper clippings, flags and balloons, sharing the excitement with each class of students that came to the library. Like so many other Murrieta residents, she was happy that this dream had finally come true.

Murrieta got its first traffic light in June of that year, at the corner of Los Alamos and Hancock. Murrieta was becoming a real city.

Schools begin year-round multi-track scheduling

In order to get elementary and middle school permanent building applications approved for funding by the state, the district had to change to year-round multi-track scheduling, which was implemented in 1991. A lottery drawing was used to assign students to one of four tracks. Every effort was made to keep families on the same track, but in some cases this was not possible.

The increased number of students had an impact on the Transportation Department. Supervisor Chuck Depreker requested 15 additional school buses in June of 1991 to transport all these students on a year-round basis.

At the start of the next school year, it was projected that 2,300 of the 3,800 students in Murrieta would need bus transportation.

At the high school, year-round multi-track scheduling posed problems and MVHS went to single track (S Track), but still year-round scheduling, on July 1, 1992.

Mr. Van retires, Dr. Parker becomes superintendent

Mr. van de Wetering was superintendent until 1991 when he retired. Dr. Tate Parker who had experience working in Chula Vista, a much larger school district, replaced him.

Dr. Parker knew that the school district would need a much larger district office. They soon outgrew the small building at the corner of Plum and Ivy, even with rented office space in other parts of town.

District offices were scattered around town. The Purchasing Department and warehouse were located in a small industrial complex on Hobie Circle, just off Jefferson. The Facilities Department occupied a house on Ivy Street. Transportation and Maintenance had a mobile home near the intersection of Jefferson and Ivy, close to the Windmill Restaurant. The mobile home was not designed for this use, and Chuck Depreker's staff learned that a shower stall makes a good storage place for the many rolled-up blueprints and plans. Just don't turn on the water!

The buses parked behind this mobile home in a dirt parking lot, which caused problems with dust and mud, depending on the weather.

Dr. Parker and the staff found a new home for the district office on Beckman Court, located in a new industrial building area close to Temecula's city limits. The school district would share this building with the City of Murrieta, which was also growing and needed space for City Council meetings and the many services provided by the city.

Tom Tooker, Assistant Superintendent for Facilities, left the district and Chuck Depreker was promoted to become the next Assistant Superintendent of Facilities. For a while the department was called

MOTC—Maintenance, Operations, Transportation and Construction. Construction was a large part of the work they did during this time, building a new school almost every year, and sometimes more than one.

Improving district communication

Dr. Parker saw a need for more communication between the school district and the community, and between the district office and the schools. To help accomplish these goals, he hired the district's first public relations person, Ellen Larson.

He oversaw the creation of district-wide committees, such as the Budget Advisory Committee, so that the entire district had input into budget planning. Other committees included the District Advisory Committee, composed of parents, teachers, site administrators and district staff. Administrative Council, which had been primarily a principals' meeting, was expanded to include representatives from the departments.

Dr. Toukonen left the district for another position in Adelanto and Dr. Ruth Lander was hired to replace him, becoming the Assistant Superintendent of Personnel and Educational Services. In 1999 Principal Shari Fox was promoted to Director of Curriculum and Instruction. Guy Romero became the Director of Assessment, and formed the Assistant Principal Council. Norma Cunnington served as Dr. Lander's secretary, and when she retired, Karen Parris replaced her.

During this time the school board was composed of Shauna Briggs, Alan Christenson, Austin Linsley, Judy Rosen and Margi Wray.

Parent-Teacher Clubs/Parent Teacher Associations

Murrieta Elementary parents formed a Parent Teacher Club (PTC) early in the history of the school, deciding not to be part of the national Parent Teacher Association (PTA) organization, which levied dues. Their reasoning was that all the funds they raised should go to support students.

As the district grew, newer schools formed PTA or PTC groups. The choice of PTA or PTC was often made as a result of the new school's student and teacher population. If most of the students and teachers came from a PTA school, the new school became a PTA school; if the original school had been PTC, the new school formed a PTC group. Over the years, all the schools' parent-teacher organizations became PTA's.

Ellen Larson, an active PTA member, was instrumental in forming the Murrieta Valley Council PTA in 1992. Mrs. Larson served as the first Council PTA president from 1992 to 1994. The superintendent, Dr. Parker, supported PTA as a way of providing better communication between the school district and the community. He attended PTA meetings and conferences and encouraged principals to attend Council PTA meetings.

Through the years, the PTA/PTC groups raised many thousands of dollars to support the schools. The school libraries, in particular, have purchased large numbers of books using PTA funds, and the PTA members annually hold book fairs at most of the schools.

The hard work of the Murrieta PTA's has been recognized at the state level. The Rail Ranch PTA was named California Outstanding PTA in 1996. The Murrieta Valley Council PTA was chosen California State PTA Outstanding Council in 1994, 2000, and 2001.

The Parent Center

In 1994 the Parent Center was added to programs supported by the Board and the Murrieta Council PTA Parent Involvement Committee, and Kate Van Horn (Hamaker) was hired to create it. Board members had attended a California School Boards Association conference where there was a session on how a parent center can provide support for parents and their children, and the Board loved the idea. They provided seed money to get it started, with the idea that the program would become self-supporting.

31

In 1997 the district childcare programs were added to the Parent Center's offerings. Coni Stevens and later Pam Blood began working with Mrs. Van Horn (Hamaker), overseeing the childcare programs at each of the elementary schools. They also implemented new programs and activities as the Parent Center expanded.

Initially, the Parent Center occupied classrooms at each site, but as the district enrollment grew, these rooms were needed for classes of students. The permanent staff of the Parent Center had to relocate several times.

Some of the Parent Center activities included classes on parenting, small parenting conferences, an obsolete textbook give-away to parents, and a Parent Advisory Council. Courses on first aid and CPR, and support groups such as Alanon are also available there. One year the Parent Center staff put on an elegant and well-attended Valentines Day dance to raise funds. The Parent Center also set up a small library of parenting books and videos, available for checkout to parents.

After Tovashal elementary staff and students moved into their permanent buildings, the portable buildings they had occupied at Avaxat became available for the Parent Center, later renamed Family Services, providing a long-term home for the program. One of the more recent programs added is a State Preschool Program, providing yet another valuable resource for students in Murrieta.

Permanent school buildings

From the opening of Avaxat Elementary School in 1988 to the completion of permanent facilities at Tovashal Elementary School in 1999, new schools in Murrieta opened in rented or purchased portable buildings, often sharing facilities at another school site.

Murrieta Valley High School was built in phases and construction was finished in 1993. Beginning in 1994, permanent buildings were completed for the four elementary schools still in portable buildings: Alta Murrieta, Avaxat, E. Hale Curran, and Rail Ranch. Alta Murrieta was the last of these to move into their new permanent school, in 1996.

Shivela Middle School's permanent buildings were not completed until 1998, the same year that Creekside Alternative High School's buildings were finished. Tovashal's permanent buildings were ready to move into in 1999, and Thompson Middle School's permanent buildings were completed in 2000.

Finally having "real" school buildings district-wide was a big accomplishment for the district. Teachers, parents, students and administrators celebrated each school dedication with a mixture of gratitude and pride.

Dr. Francisco, the third superintendent, is hired; more changes

There were a number of changes in 1997. Dr. Chet Francisco was hired as Superintendent to replace Dr. Parker, who had left the district for a position as superintendent in Simi Valley. New people were added to the Murrieta school district "family." That year Duane Coleman was hired as Principal at Murrieta Valley High School, replacing Shelley Weston.

Dr. Ruth Lander became Assistant Superintendent of Educational Services, a position that was re-created from the combined Personnel/Educational Services Assistant Superintendent position, which she had previously held. Buck DeWeese was promoted to Assistant Superintendent of Human Resources.

Students get access to the Internet

Technology in the 1990's was changing dramatically. Computers were starting to be used to manage complicated tasks and were replacing typewriters. Penny Beaulieu was hired to oversee work- related computers, including those in business services, attendance, payroll, student records, discipline, scheduling, and counseling. Tom Paulson, the first computer tech in the district, worked with Ms. Beaulieu.

Karen Robertson had served as district Computer Coordinator, overseeing the Apple IIGS computers used in classrooms and labs but as

33

technology changed, PCs replaced Apple computers and the Technology Department took over management of all district computers.

The computers at this time had limited memory storage space and to solve this problem, data was stored on large floppy discs. As technology improved, small hard-shelled disks that held much more information replaced these. These in turn became obsolete as new computers were built with hard drives that held increasingly more information. Additional access to information such as databases and video could be purchased in another new format, the CD-ROM. The World Wide Web and the Internet provided yet another new portal to information, if there was technology to access it. That meant not only computers, but also communications wiring.

To provide this Internet access and network all schools in Riverside County, the Riverside County Office of Education obtained grant funding for their Riverlink project. The project included planning, purchasing and installing new digital hardware and wiring, and training the people who would be overseeing and using this new resource. As part of the plan, each school was provided with two Internet connections, one to the school library and another of their choosing. This project was completed in 1997.

In 1998, Bill Olien was hired as Director of Technology for the Murrieta school district, replacing Penny Beaulieu.

And more students kept arriving....

Students still kept arriving in ever-increasing numbers, requiring more schools, teachers, programs, and district support. It was starting to seem like a never-ending cycle, building a new school and hiring a new school staff every year.

The District Enters the 21st Century

Technology provided a dramatic change in how work was done and allowed rapid communication and access to data. More students arrived, new schools were built, curriculum changed, and the district worked to provide a world-class education for their students.

Technology changes

Dr. Francisco's decision to hire Bill Olien as Director of Technology would impact the district in ways no one could have predicted. One of Mr. Olien's first tasks was preparing the district for "Y2K" or "Year 2000." It was widely predicted that computers, which were not set up to handle the turn-of-the-century date numbering change, would crash and result in techno-chaos. Mr. Olien put together a plan and sent computer techs out to every computer in the district, making sure all of them were ready. It worked, and when Y2K happened, there were no problems.

Computer servers were installed at the school sites and networked to computer stations. This posed a new problem: where to put these servers? The schools had not been designed with this technology in mind. Servers ended up in closets and storage rooms. Before long, the Technology Department was able to install and network computers to servers located in the District Office, making it much easier to maintain them.

Mr. Olien formed a District Technology Committee, which helped create an updated District Technology Plan. This Plan would determine what technology would be purchased and how it would be used. As a result, computer courses were offered for district teachers, new computer labs set up for students, and standards developed for the kinds of programs that would be used on these computers.

The school libraries were now using database programs to circulate library books and to check out textbooks to students. The Technology Department worked closely with the library staff and often the site technology person was housed in the school library.

Administrative changes

Dr. Francisco made some other key personnel decisions at the district level. Stacy Coleman was hired in 2001 to replace Sherryl Avitabile, Assistant Superintendent of Business Services. Dr. Ruth Lander, Assistant Superintendent for Educational Services, left the district in 2002 and Shari Fox, Director of Curriculum, was promoted to that position.

Guy Romero became Director of Assessment and Research. One position did not change: Chuck Depreker continued as Assistant Superintendent of Facilities.

The third district office

By 2001, the school district staff had outgrown the building on Beckman Court, as had the City of Murrieta. The City planned to move to what would become the Murrieta Town Square complex and offered the district space for the district office at this location. This seemed like an ideal site for a permanent school district office building, but negotiations between the city and school district on pricing failed to reach an agreement. Assistant Superintendent of Facilities Chuck Depreker said the issue was cost, that building in the Town Square would cost the district an estimated $7 million.

The alternate plan was to build offices on McAlby Court in a building originally planned as the district transportation facility, for an estimated $5 million. Without any other good choices, that plan was implemented. As a result the Facilities Department gave up office and warehouse space to the other departments.

The move to the new District Office, renamed the District Support Center, was the most complicated move the district had yet made. The warehouse, with pallet racks and countless boxes, had to be moved into a new and smaller warehouse area. Office furniture, filing cabinets, boxes and boxes and boxes of 'stuff,' and computers all had to be moved and set up again. Wiring for phones and computers had to be installed, and equipment connected and programmed. Julie April, the Purchasing Agent, planned the move and helped design the arrangement of offices in the new building.

Transportation

The new Support Center gave the buses their first real home, with a paved parking lot, offices, a lounge for drivers, and covered areas for mechanics to work on buses. In 2001, the Transportation Department transported 3,600 students daily to school and back home, in addition to field trips and sporting events, with a fleet of 34 buses. According to Dave Kempf, Director of Transportation at that time, Murrieta buses had never been involved in a major accident.

The Murrieta Public Library

Another major event during Dr. Francisco's tenure with the district involved the city library. The city had started planning a public library building and applied for a grant from the state to fund the construction. One of the requirements for this state funding was an agreement with the school district on shared programming.

Dr. Francisco, working with Board members, approved a 20-year agreement that allowed the city to proceed with their application. As a result, they received the funding and the new city library was built across the street from Murrieta Elementary School, as part of the Town Square complex. This property had been pasture (with cows and flies) for many years.

Murrieta Elementary School remodeling

In 2002, Murrieta Elementary School was remodeled. Included in the remodeling were the administration area and the school library. The school library had occupied various rooms for many years and finally a new, 'real' library would be built. Long-time librarian Dorothea Tiss had retired for health reasons and passed away before she could see this beautiful new library. Mary Shufford had worked with Mrs. Tiss and was hired to manage the library.

Mrs. Shufford's first challenge was moving more than 10,000 books.....to somewhere. But where? The classroom that housed the old library was needed for classes and it would be a while before the new library building would be finished. Mrs. Shufford spent a crazy year boxing and unboxing and moving library books from the old library to a temporary room beside the stage, and then finally to the new library.

The School Bell

As part of the remodeling, the 117-year old school bell was moved out of the old tower and placed in a new one at the front of the school. On May 24th, the bell was rung after 20 years of silence and former students were there to enjoy it, including Alice Vose, Minnie Norris, Pauline Michaels, Diane Snider, Peggy Goffman, Leonard Michaels, Larry Collins, Jim and Mary Kean, and Donna Keskila.

New titles for administrators

Under Dr. Francisco's leadership, the district continued to evolve. To better describe some positions and events, some titles were changed. For example, the annual district leadership retreat became the "Advance." Assistant Principals became "Learning Directors," and while this title may have better reflected what they did, it confused parents, students, and people from other school districts. More confusion came from changing the Counselors' title to "Learning Coordinators." The name of the District Office was changed to "District Support Center" and fondly referred to as the DSC.

Another change occurred in 2004 when Chuck Depreker, Assistant Superintendent for Facilities and Operations, left the district. Mr. Depreker had been involved in the construction of every permanent school in the district except Murrieta Elementary. Bill Olien, Director of Technology, was selected as his replacement.

Dr. Francisco leaves

Superintendent Chet Francisco left the district on September 9, 2005 for a position in Chico. During his eight-and-a-half years in the district, the number of students increased from 9,680 to approximately 20,000. When he was hired, there were ten schools, and when he left there were sixteen.

After Dr. Francisco left, Dr. Buck DeWeese served as interim superintendent while the Board, composed of Ken Dickson, Margi Wray, Robin Crist, Paul Diffley, and Kris Thomasian, conducted a search for his replacement.

The District hires Dr. Scheer, the fourth superintendent

On July 1, 2006, Dr. Stan Scheer became the district's fourth superintendent. Dr. Scheer felt the superintendent should be visible and available to the district and the community and he could be counted on to attend most area events.

Dr. Scheer's cabinet when he arrived consisted of Assistant Superintendents Buck DeWeese, Human Resources; Bill Olien, Facilities and Operations; Stacy Coleman, Business Services; and Guy Romero, Educational Services. Dr. Scheer could tell that this was a good team and so the only change he made was promoting Dr. DeWeese to a new position, as Deputy Superintendent. Pat Kelley was promoted to the newly vacant position of Assistant Superintendent in Human Resources.

The state and national economy tanked soon after Dr. Scheer arrived. The district, along with every school district in California, faced severe funding cuts for several years. Dr. Scheer kept the district focused on maintaining staffing despite financial issues, while other districts across the state were reducing or eliminating counseling, art, music and library positions. Murrieta was able to maintain these positions, thanks to positive negotiations with the teachers and classified unions.

Dr. Scheer was very angry about California politics and the lack of vision that would allow school funding, and therefore programs that impact children, to be cut so drastically.

Building Mails and McElhinney schools

Building new schools during a financial crisis was no easy task. The construction of Lisa J. Mails Elementary School and Dorothy McElhinney Middle School was especially challenging. They were located close to each other in a rural area with no paved roads, water, or sewer hookups.

Dr. Scheer and Bill Olien, Assistant Superintendent of Facilities and Operations, came up with a plan to solve each of these problems, allowing Lisa J. Mails to open, ready for students, on the first day of school. McElhinney opened two years later, though classrooms were being used before their formal opening day.

Building Murrieta Mesa High School

The district's third high school, Murrieta Mesa, was in the planning stage when the economic recession hit. As a result, construction bids for the project were lower than expected. This was good news, but there was bad news, too. The State of California did not have the money to provide its share of the construction costs. The superintendent and Board, working with Stacy Coleman, had to figure out some way to keep construction going while they waited for the State funds, and they found a way. Murrieta Mesa High School was completed on time.

Dr. Scheer leaves and Pat Kelley is appointed superintendent

Early in 2012, Dr. Scheer left for a superintendent's position in his home state of Colorado. He had promised when he was hired that he would stay for five years and he kept his word.

October 1, 2012, Pat Kelley became the district's fifth superintendent. Mr. Kelley had a long history with the district. He started working in Murrieta as a teacher at Shivela Middle School in 1991, then became the district's first Coordinator of Child Welfare and Attendance.

When a position opened as Assistant Principal at Rail Ranch Elementary School, he was hired, working with Principal Shari Fox. Mrs. Fox left to become Director of Curriculum and Mr. Kelley became Principal of Rail Ranch. When Daniel N. Buchanan Elementary School opened in 2001, Mr. Kelley took this opportunity to open a new school and serve as the first principal.

After two years at Buchanan, he was promoted to Director of Human Resources and returned to the District Support Center. When Dr. Scheer was hired in 2006, Mr. Kelley was promoted to Assistant Superintendent of Human Resources. In 2012 Dr. Scheer left and Mr. Kelley briefly served as Deputy Superintendent. That fall he was appointed Superintendent by the Board of Education.

Mr. Kelley would be working with Board members Ken Dickson, Kris Thomasian, Paul Diffley, Robin Crist, and new board member Barbara Muir. His cabinet members were Assistant Superintendents Guy Romero, Educational Services; Stacy Coleman, Business Services; Bill Olien, Facilities and Operations; and Pamela Wilson, Human Resources.

41

The Schools, 1988 to 1999

Earlier chapters told the story of the entire district. In this chapter, each school that opened between 1988 and 1999 is profiled individually. When it opened, who designed it, the mascot and colors, how it was named, and who the administration and some of the teachers and staff were. There were so many teachers hired rapidly as the district grew that all of them cannot be named, nor can the many support staff who kept things going while teachers were in the classroom and students were learning.

Avaxat Elementary School—1988

Designed by architect Wendell Harbach, the Avaxat school name comes from the Luiseño Indian word for "cottonwood." Polly Filanc, local journalist, suggested the name to the school board. It was the Indian name for the Murrieta area before Juan Murrieta arrived. The school mascot was originally a warrior, which was discontinued and replaced with an alligator in 2012.

Staffing the new school

Guy Romero, hired as a teacher in 1981 at Murrieta Elementary, was selected to be the principal of the district's second school. He opened Avaxat in 1988 in classrooms at Murrieta Elementary School, with five teachers--Sally Lyons, Maureen Lorimer, Donna Reid, Robin Vaughn, and

Nancy Lashley (RSP/SDC) and 77 students. At this time, there were 525 students in the entire district. Avaxat's classified staff during this time included school secretary Lorna Benson and clerk Charlene Stone (Boone).

Moving to the permanent site

The new portable Avaxat classrooms were not ready until October, and even then there were problems that could put off the opening of the school. Students and staff were excited about moving into their new school. Mr. Romero's philosophy was to get things done, so the staff and 85 students moved into eight portable classrooms on their permanent site, ready or not!

There were two huge problems: no water and no electricity. How can you have school without water or power? Avaxat provided a model for many future schools in the district, solving seemingly unsolvable facility problems. The first problem was water, because there wasn't enough water pressure for toilets to flush. The solution was portable toilets and bottled water. The other problem was electric power, also easily solved. A generator was brought in to provide electricity until the power lines to the school could be completed.

Things settled down and by the end of the first year there were 127 students attending Avaxat. However, over the summer some 300 additional students moved into the neighborhood. That meant ten more classrooms and ten more teachers would be needed. It also meant combination classes which were usually K/1, 2/3 or 4/5. For many years most Murrieta elementary schools had combination classes. These are more difficult to teach because there are two textbooks and curriculums for each subject in the same room.

The school library opens...and closes...and opens again

In addition to regular classrooms, during that first year Avaxat had a library in an 'extra' classroom, with books from the Murrieta Elementary library. But new students kept arriving and the school soon needed another classroom. The library was closed, the books were put in boxes, and the room became a classroom again.

The library was not forgotten, however. Lee Titford was hired in November, 1989, as the school's first Library/Lab Technician. The library was reopened as a library/computer lab in December 1989 in another portable classroom. Half of the room had tables, chairs and bookcases and the other half held a U-shaped computer lab with enough computers for an entire class.

In 1990 rapid increases in the number of students meant the cafeteria/day care center, housed in a portable classroom, had to give up their room for a second afternoon kindergarten. After-school day care was moved to the school library and sack lunches from the Murrieta School cafeteria were provided for students who wanted them.

Permanent school buildings!

By 1990, 598 students attended Avaxat, still in portable classrooms. In 1994 students and faculty moved into their new, permanent school buildings with more parking spaces, though there would never be enough parking. The rapid growth of the community continued and by 1995 there were 827 students at the school.

Changes in administration

When Principal Guy Romero was named Director of Curriculum in 1990, Butch Owens became principal at Avaxat. Karen Briski was hired as Avaxat's next principal in 1996, staying there until she left to open Antelope Hills Elementary in 2005. The next principal of Avaxat was David Ciabbatini.

Avaxat was named a California Distinguished School in 2004. This award is given by the California State Board of Education to public schools that best represent exemplary and quality educational programs. Approximately five percent of California schools receive this award each year following an extensive selection process.

Alta Murrieta Elementary School--1989

Alta Murrieta Elementary School opened in portable classrooms in 1989, and permanent buildings were completed 1994. The design of the school mirrors that of Avaxat, both designed by architect Wendell Harbach. The school was named for the Alta Murrieta sub-division that surrounds it and the mascot is a mustang.

In January, 1989, Buck DeWeese was hired as Alta Murrieta's first principal. When Butch Owens was hired in September as the school counselor, the similarities in their names, Buck and Butch, often caused confusion.

Moving into portable classrooms

Alta students began the school year attending classes with Avaxat students, planning on moving to their new school site when it was ready mid-year. The school would be housed in portable classrooms on the permanent school site. However, rain delayed the move by a few weeks. By February, 1989, excited students and staff finally moved into their new school.

Double sessions

The following school year, Alta Murrieta shared their classrooms with Rail Ranch Elementary school, operating on double sessions. The Alta students arrived early in the morning and the Rail Ranch students arrived at noon, when the Alta students went home. The afternoon students were very quiet, having worn themselves out playing all morning before going to school.

First teaching staff

Some of the first Alta Murrieta teachers included Charlie Riendeau, Bonnie Cringan, Laurie Poliska, John Brown, Donna Fuller, Rudy Gurulé, Lori McKenzie, Bev Monroe, Greg Baird, Russ Murphy, Ron Pickrahn, Tom Kuzma, and Mary Godfrey.

Also teaching at Alta during those early years were Steve Geresy, Randy Hintz, Kristin Marney, Diane Welsh, KristinTinsman, Stacy Small, Loretta Houston, Diane Burlison, Wendy Chiri, Barbara Miller, Catherine Kerr, Debbie Wolfe, and Debbie Saldivar.

The library is slow to open

The school library did not open immediately. Books had to be ordered and they needed someone to manage the library. Judi Rightmire was hired in November, 1989, and the library/computer lab opened in January, 1990 for the 643 students to use. During that first full year, Rail Ranch Library/Lab Technician Susan Fralick worked in the Alta library, ordering books for the Rail Ranch library in the morning. Rail Ranch books were packed in boxes for the anticipated move to their own school site, and students from both schools checked out Alta Murrieta's books. By the end of the school year, those books were well-worn.

Groundbreaking

The groundbreaking ceremony for the permanent campus was held on November 10, 1992, with Dr. Tate Parker, Superintendent, and Mrs. Shauna Briggs, Board Member, serving as featured speakers. The school choir sang the school song, written by teacher Donna Fuller for the occasion, and the Murrieta High School Band played the National Anthem.

Permanent school buildings

In 1994, students and faculty moved into their new permanent school buildings. By the next year, 1995, 869 students attended Alta Murrieta Elementary School.

Focus on bilingual education, technology

For several years Alta Murrieta served as a district bilingual school, with Spanish-speaking teachers and classes in Spanish at every grade level. Even the textbooks were in Spanish.

Another focus for Alta Murrieta was technology and for a while the school was known as the Technology School, proudly proclaimed on a banner that hung on the front of the school. Counselor Bonnie Cringan was instrumental in getting grant funding for the many computers that occupied the school's study pods. Alta Murrieta was also one of the first schools to have their own website, created and maintained by Mrs. Fuller.

Several principals, one school secretary

There were a series of principals at Alta Murrieta over the years, but Secretary Judi Husband, the first school secretary, has remained in that position. Buck DeWeese opened the school, and was followed by Jeanne Longerbone, Shari Fox, Hector Rivera, Ron Hess, Randy Rogers, Terry Picchiottino and Brent Coley.

Mr. Rivera was principal at Alta Murrieta when the school first became a California Distinguished School in 2000. The school was named a California Distinguished School two more times, in 2004 and 2010.

Rail Ranch Elementary School—1989

Rail Ranch Elementary School opened in portable buildings on the Alta

Murrieta campus in 1989. Permanent buildings were completed 1994. Designed by architect Ralph Allen, the school was named for the pioneer Rail family's farm. Donna Brantly told the Board that the Rail family farm had been on the land where the school would be built and Patty Julian, board member, requested that "ranch" be in the name of the school. Nathaniel Cardenas, a sixth grader at the school, designed the black, white, and red sketch of the Red-Tailed Hawk which became the school mascot.

The school opens with double sessions

Principal Al Ross and Counselor Bonnie Cringan opened Rail Ranch in 1989 with 352 students in kindergarten through grades six. At first the Rail Ranch students shared classroom space at Alta Murrieta Elementary, on double sessions, until the Rail Ranch school site could be set up with portable classroom buildings. By the end of that first year, 597 students attended the school. Seventh and eighth grade classes were added in 1990.

First staff

Teachers Karen Michaud, David Koltovich, Jane Smith, Wendell Oshiro, Yvonne, Kazmierowicz, Sandra LeBaron, Anna McCandless, Jim Davis, Carla Greenhalge, Erin Bawcombe, Bea Highlen, Barbara Carlisle, and Catherine Kerr were among the first faculty at the school. Jan Danker served as the first secretary, and Kathryn Barnett, Cristy Wood and Sandra Brown were instructional aides. Mrs. Barnett and Mrs. Wood went on to become teachers in the district.

School library

The school library did not open until the school moved to their permanent site. Library/Lab Technician Susan Fralick, hired in November

1989, spent her first year in the shared Alta/Rail library processing and ordering books for Rail Ranch in the morning, and checking Alta books out to Rail Ranch students in the afternoon.

Rail Ranch moves

In January, 1991 Rail Ranch students and faculty could finally move to their permanent school site with portable classroom buildings. By 1994 permanent school buildings were completed and the school moved once again, though not so far this time. The move was an event that included district office staff, board members, parents and teachers, moving classroom materials over plywood ramps that covered muddy paths. By 1995 there were 685 students in attendance.

Changes in administration

Over the years there were changes in leadership at the school. Principal Al Ross left to open Creekside Continuation High School in 1992 and Shari Fox was hired as principal. Mrs. Fox was promoted to Director of Curriculum and Pat Kelley was selected to replace her. When Mr. Kelley left to open Buchanan Elementary School, Jennifer Tan became principal of Rail Ranch. Mrs. Tan left to move to northern California and Kerry Wise became principal. When Mr. Wise left, Tammy Hunter-Wethers became principal.

The sixth grade returns to Rail Ranch

By 2011 all four middle schools had large student enrollments. Many parents of middle school students wanted their youngsters in a smaller school and the district tried to accommodate them. Working with the District Office, Mr. Wise had developed a plan that would add grade six at the Rail Ranch campus, creating the small school option that parents had requested.

E. Hale Curran Elementary School—1989

E. Hale Curran Elementary School opened in portable classroom buildings in 1989, and permanent buildings were completed in 1994. The school plan mirrored Rail Ranch Elementary School, designed by architect Ralph Allen. The name was suggested by Murrieta Elementary School teacher Satch LaValley, who wrote a letter to the Board recommending that the school be named for long-time Murrieta resident and historian E. (Emma) Hale Curran. The mascot is the cougar and school colors are green and gold.

Curran opens with double sessions and rapid growth

Principal Charlie Riendeau and Counselor Gary Farmer were hired as the first administrators. Mr. Riendeau had worked in the district for a while, teaching at Murrieta Elementary and Alta Murrieta Elementary School. E. Hale Curran School opened in September 1989 with nine classrooms, double sessions, and 360 students. In October seven additional portable classrooms were added, and by January enrollment topped 500 students.

There was a period of time when the school added a classroom of 30 students and a new teacher each week, and the district experienced 100% growth in student numbers! Each new class of students needed textbooks, and other materials for classes like science, and each new teacher needed teaching materials. There were no maps, projectors, computers, all the things teachers expect to find in their classroom.

School Library

The school library didn't open until January 1990. For Library/Lab Technician Robyn Norland there was a lot of preparation before it could open for students to check out books. At that time books had paper checkout cards and students used a card catalog with cards in drawers to find the book they wanted.

That year, Eagle Scout Christopher Gharda selected the empty shelves at E. Hale Curran's library as his Eagle Scout project, conducting a book drive throughout the community. His goal was 600 books, but thanks to his hard work he delivered 1,200 books to the library when the project was completed.

The mural, "Unto Everything There is a Season," in the new permanent library was painted in 1994 by parent Pam Barrett, who later became a teacher in the district. Parent Chuck Washington provided computer expertise, helping to upgrade library computers. The Curran PTA actively supported the library, and by 1994 had donated $16,000.00 to purchase books.

Student growth continues

New students kept coming, and in May 1990 the school added six more portable classrooms. In one year, the student population at the school increased from 360 to more than 750 students.

The following September, enrollment dropped because the seventh and eighth graders had moved to newly opened Shivela Middle School. This was also the year that the district ended double sessions and eight more portable classrooms were moved in. But new students kept arriving and by November, there were 662 students attending E. Hale Curran Elementary School.

Teachers were hired rapidly as the school grew that first year. Cecilia Zavestoski, Kerry Wise, Leslie D'Arezzo, Kevin Hitchcock, Laura Pechin, Sandy Oliphant, Jeanne Cusack, and Robin Westphall were among the first teachers at the school. In rapid order, Jamie Barnett, Peggy Field, Diane Joyce, Janet Spivey, Melody Whitley, Cindy Brisendine, Vicki McKnight, Kim Wiseman, Doug Highlen, Leslie Schuda, Mike Lorimer, Marsha Lutwen, Kim Holt, Elizabeth Seaman, Deena Cortus, Patricia Skeans, Lauren Greenberg, Debbie Tuley, and Sharon Rodak were added to the teaching staff.

51

A unique facilities problem

Growth was not the only problem facing Curran Elementary School. The earth moved! There were problems with the soil compaction at the site, discovered when sidewalks started cracking, and the cracks got larger. Portions of the school were sliding slowly downhill in an area that included the library. Classes in these rooms were relocated to more stable rooms, and until the problem was solved, Mrs. Norland took library books on carts to each classroom to provide library time for students.

Groundbreaking

Groundbreaking for the permanent school was held on November 9, 1992, with Dr. Tate Parker, superintendent, and Margi Wray, board member, as featured speakers. Curran students contributed items to a time capsule. The Murrieta High School Band under the direction of Bryan Boos provided music, followed by a performance by the high school flag team directed by Sherri Allred.

Mr. Riendeau left for another school in 1993. The next Curran principal would be Melinda Bossenmeyer. Ms. Bossenmeyer brought a passion for safe school playgrounds, and always wore a beautiful scarf around her neck. When Ms. Bossenmeyer left, Sandi Whitlock became principal. She left after only one year and David Koltovich became the school's fourth principal.

By 1994, students and faculty moved into their new permanent campus. By 1995, 1,012 students attended E. Hale Curran Elementary School.

E. Hale Curran Elementary School was named a California Distinguished School three times, in 1995, 2000, and 2006.

Shivela Middle School—1990

Shivela opened in 1990 in portable classrooms and permanent buildings were completed in 1998. The school was designed by the architecture firm of Nickoloff & Associates. The school name comes from the Indian word for "sycamore." Ron Wickerd, a native of Murrieta and former journalist whose mother was a Tarwater and a member of an early settler family, provided a list of suggested Luiseño Indian names to Donna Brantley for board consideration. Shivela's name came from this list. The school mascot is the panther and the school colors are teal, black, gray and white.

First district middle school

Shivela was originally planned as a K-8 school, but parents felt that the district needed a middle school. They attended board meetings to present their case and the board agreed to make this change. This meant shifting sixth, seventh, and eighth grade teachers and instructional materials from the five elementary schools. Some of those teachers transferred to the new high school, others moved to open elementary positions, and some went to the new middle school.

The first Shivela administrators were Principal Lucinda Brouwer and Counselor Loretta Houston. Shivela and MVHS shared an assistant principal, Shelley Weston. Administrators and staff felt like pioneers embarking on a new adventure and worked long days, sometimes working into the night, to get everything ready for students.

Middle school and high school share the campus

Like many district schools before it, Shivela opened sharing their portable classrooms with another school, the long-awaited Murrieta Valley High School. Initially there were not enough portable buildings, so two classes taught by teachers Maureen Lorimer and Stacy Tumlin

(Swenk) shared the school library until more buildings could arrive.

Most of the teachers at Shivela were first-year teachers, many of them recruited from Ohio or Minnesota. There was a lot of homesickness among these young teachers and many left after one or two years. One couple experienced their first earthquake before they even started teaching and immediately went back home. California was not for them! The staff changes and inexperienced teachers led to some discipline problems during those first years.

When the high school staff and students moved to their permanent campus, Mrs. Houston, the counselor, went with them and was replaced by Betty Nead.

When Shivela opened there was no grass, trees or shade structures on campus. The priority was putting classrooms where they were needed, district-wide, to meet the influx of students. Landscaping was a lower priority. Shivela students ate lunch out in the sun or in the shade of the buildings, standing on dirt or sidewalks. Their parents, who had come from places where there were large trees and plenty of grass around schools, expected grass, trees and shade structures around this new temporary school. They attended school board meetings and expressed their displeasure. Soon sod was laid, trees planted, and shade structures built.

A combined school library

Cheryl Brummett and Cheryl Dufresne staffed the joint middle school/high school library on this campus and their first task was to sort huge stacks of textbooks and materials that had been sent from the five elementary schools. Textbooks were stacked all around the large portable room that would be the library and many of the stacks were four feet high or higher. Their next task would be getting library books ready for students to check out and figuring out which library books would go to the high school and which would stay at Shivela.

Among the materials that came from the elementary schools was a human skeleton from the science classroom at Murrieta Elementary. A skeleton is fragile, so it was decided to move it in a car instead of a truck, and the skeleton was set up on the seat. Going around a corner, the skeleton tipped over and its arms were thrown around the passenger in the car, providing a few moments of sheer terror!

Student numbers increase

In 1990, 654 students attended Shivela Middle School and before Thompson Middle School opened in 1994, there were around 1,800 students on campus. When the students were all outside on break, it seemed like twice as many! By 1995, the number of students attending Shivela had dropped to 1,346. That seemed small compared to the number of students who had been there before Thompson opened.

Administrative changes

Frank Passerella succeeded Mrs. Brouwer as principal. Gary Farmer became assistant principal in 1993 and when Mr. Passerella left in 1995, Mr. Farmer was appointed principal, a position he held for fifteen years, retiring in 2010.

Permanent facilities

In 1998, permanent facilities at the school were completed. The first permanent building to be completed was the gym, in 1996, a decision made based on a vote of the faculty. They felt that the gym would provide room for classes, assemblies, and athletics, providing more benefit for students than any other building.

Shivela was named a California Distinguished School in 2001.

Murrieta Valley High School — 1990

Murrieta's first high school was designed by architect Ralph Allen, featuring many curved walls, typical of his building designs. The school mascot is the nighthawk, and according to the first principal, Dan Burch, "I came out to the school site one day and there was a nighthawk perched on one of the surveying stakes. No one believes me, but it's true." School colors are red and black.

Mr. Burch, Assistant Principal Shelly Weston and Counselor Candyce Julian were the first administrators.

This first and long-awaited high school opened with ninth grade only and 279 students, sharing the facilities at the Shivela Middle School campus. Before this school opened, Murrieta students had attended Temecula Valley High School, which was also new and added one grade a year, ending with the 12th grade in 1989. Before TVHS was built, Murrieta students attended high school in Lake Elsinore. Murrieta parents were happy to finally have their high school students going to classes in their own city.

Groundbreaking ceremonies

Groundbreaking for the permanent high school was held in December 1990. The district was excited about this new school and spent $9,938.12 for the opening ceremonies, which drew criticism from the community when the newspaper publicized this. (This money purchased the following: $3,134.50 for the design and printing of 5,000 invitations; $2,889 for mailing tubes and labels; $250 for bulk mail; $1,820 for a rented canopy and chairs; $484 for red and black Nighthawk mascot buttons; $309 for stakes and signs marking the location of each building; $275 for speaker Vick Knight; and $1,026 for an audio system, security guards, and taxes.)

Superintendent van de Wetering said, "I think the community deserves it. Some of you who are new to the community may not know how much the high school means to the district. We wanted to do it with a little class and pizzazz."

Principal Dan Burch brought all 282 current students to the bare hillside where this new school would be built to take part in the ceremony. Sixteen students paired with teachers to dig the first hole to mark the start of construction. Stakes and signs were laid out to mark the future location of various buildings, so everyone could envision what the school would look like.

This was a dream come true for the district and the community. Murrieta would finally educate all their children, all the way from kindergarten through grade twelve.

Permanent buildings

MVHS opened in phases, building classrooms for each grade level of students who would be attending that year. The first group of buildings on the permanent Murrieta Valley High School site opened in 1991 with freshmen and sophomores. There were thirty-four classrooms, one of which was the temporary library and another used by the administration as an office. Classes occupied the row of classrooms facing Fullerton Street.

During that first year occupying the permanent high school site, heavy equipment operated within yards of classes in session and the site swarmed with plumbers, electricians, carpet-layers, carpenters, and other construction workers. It was noisy, but it was exciting for students and teachers to watch their school being built. This was an experience they would never forget.

This second phase of construction included additional permanent classrooms, along with the permanent gym, library and administration building. Parking was expanded from 50 spaces to 600 and the football field was completed. During the third phase of construction, beginning in 1992, the remaining permanent classrooms (math, science, computer center) were completed.

The rainy season always causes problems for the school district, with flooding, roof leaks, mud, and construction delays. MVHS's newly-laid gym floor was flooded by the first big storm that followed construction and had to be replaced. Mr. Burch took pieces of the scrap wood from the first gym floor and made name tags for the teachers.

First teaching staff

Some of the teachers who worked at MVHS during the first two years included Lou Bailey, Sharon Hatch, Linda Spoon, Stacy Tumlin (Swenk), Greg Baird, Greg Ireland, David Koltovich, Cynthia Erbel, Ramona DiBene, Lynne Rogers, Leslie Schuda, Gale Bjelland, Christal Fixen, Bill Ciancio, Doug Highlen, Bob and Carol Cape, Mary Walters, Jack Jones, Ed Diaz, Bruce and Sheri Erickson, Geniel Moon, Bryan Boos, and Todd Myatt.

By 1993, Mary Wulfsburg had been hired as a second assistant principal and there were three counselors: Jim Allured, Loretta Houston, and Candyce Julian. Teacher David Koltovich took on the duties of Activities Director and Geniel Moon and Brian Golphenee served as Athletic Directors.

Academics

Courses offered during the first year included geometry, algebra I, Math A, biology, general science, English, social studies, Spanish, French, computers, typing, art, drafting, journalism, PE and drama. Not too bad for a new high school!

The district focus was on providing classrooms, teachers, support personnel, and materials for these new grade levels. Newly hired Director of Curriculum Guy Romero's first task was creating course outlines and curriculum guides, working with teams of teachers in each subject area.

To continue providing a "small school" environment, the high school implemented a village concept, similar to what was being used at Shivela Middle School. Students were divided into four villages where they would be scheduled with the same teachers and classes. This evolved into a "Wing" concept, which was field tested with 120 juniors and four teachers during the 92-93 school year. The following year all students were scheduled into Wings.

In 1997, a Western Association of Schools and Colleges (WASC) review team found the Wing structure still in place for ninth and tenth graders. The College Preparatory Math program had just been adopted and three academies (business, communications, and health) had been implemented at the eleventh and twelfth grades. A fourth academy, engineering, was planned. Expected School-wide Learning Results (ESLR) were introduced into the common language of students and teachers.

Zero Tolerance and more programs

High school students from other areas brought new problems to the district, including drugs. A Zero Tolerance Policy was adopted by the Board and students learned that they would be expelled for a first violation of drug rules. This policy created considerable controversy and was replaced later on with alternative education programs to keep students in school, but still discipline them for using or selling drugs on campus.

These alternative educational programs were available on the MVHS campus and included the Learning Center, the Opportunity Program for freshmen, and Creekside High School.

As the MVHS increased in size, Junior ROTC program and ROP classes were added to the course offerings. Two SDC classes and two ELD English/language arts classes were also available, along with an RSP pull-out program. A LAB period added at the beginning of each day provided opportunities for students to receive additional tutoring.

Extracurricular activities

During the first years, MVHS had no place for dances, drama productions, and concerts. These were were held at Murrieta Elementary school in the multi-purpose room, which at that time had the only stage in the district. Murrieta's Town Hall was also available with a stage, but the fees they charged prevented most school district events from being held there.

One parent described picking her high school daughter up at Murrieta Elementary School after a dance. It was raining hard and she said a tall, slim man was escorting the students out to the waiting cars, holding an umbrella over them and in the process getting soaked hi.mself. She found out later that this was Principal Dan Burch.

Visual and performing arts

Music was always important in the Murrieta school district, and Bryan Boos was hired as the first MVHS music director. At the first district staff meeting of the school year, Mr. Boos was surprised to be asked to sing the National Anthem at the beginning of the meeting, a cappella! Which he did.

The music program expanded over the years to include a marching band, the Crimson Cadets. They are members of the Southern California School Band and Orchestra Association (SCSBOA) and compete in SCSBOA field shows, winning 2nd place in the championships in 2011.

The Drama Department was originally under the direction of French/English teacher Sharon Hatch. When she left, Shilind Wheaton was hired to teach drama and the theater group was given the name Theatrix. Drama students present an average of seven performances during the year. They have also competed in the annual Fullerton College High School Theatre Festival, where they have won in events such as Technical Olympics, Theatre Games (Improv), technical design, and dramatic and comedic monologues.

Athletics

When MVHS opened in 1990 sharing the Shivela campus, head coach Ken Hedlund worked with the first Nighthawk football team. In 1992, Coach Wally Clark was hired as head coach and MVHS became a charter member of the Skyline League, playing Beaumont, Rancho Verde, San Jacinto, Serrano, and West Valley, plus other schools in non-league contests and tournaments.

Other sports that year were football, volleyball, co-ed cross country, girls' tennis, cheerleading, boys' and girls' basketball, boys' and girls' soccer, wrestling, softball, baseball, co-ed track, boys' tennis, and co-ed golf.

Butch Owens and Arvo Toukonen put together the first sports schedule, so that incoming freshmen could compete with ninth grade teams from other schools on a "free lance" basis. There would be no pool or gym as part of the first facilities, so the school board recommended no gymnastics or swimming teams. A basketball squad could use outdoor courts and there were local tennis courts available. Soccer, football, cross country, golf, wrestling, and baseball were also proposed.

When MVHS opened on the permanent site in 1991, it included a baseball field, two softball fields, and eight outdoor basketball courts.

The coaching staff in 1993 included Russ Murphy, Ed Diaz, Ted Berry, and Del Helms.

Coach Clark retired in 2006, after fifteen seasons. Football successes during those years include four league championships, ten playoff appearances, advancing to the CIF-SS Division V semi-finals twice. Coach Clark was succeeded by Coach Lance Neal. At the end of the 2008 school year, Coach Greg Ireland took over as head coach. In five seasons Coach Ireland compiled a record of thirty-eight wins and twenty losses and led the Nighthawks to five straight playoff appearances.

The football stadium, the pool and a famous graduate

The football stadium was dedicated on October 2, 1993, and was built to seat approximately 3,000 fans, with restrooms and snack bar facilities on both sides. The school was unprepared for an unexpected consequence of home games: during the first well-attended home game, much of the year's supply of toilet paper was used.

In 1996, the MVHS pool was dedicated, the last facility to be built. Principal Shelley Weston formally presented the pool to School Board Trustee Margi Wray. This pool cost $900,000 and came from the original 1989 school bond funds. Annual maintenance costs were estimated at $77,000 for heat and pool chemicals.

In 1996, MVHS graduate Lindsay Davenport won a gold medal in women's tennis in the Olympics. Miss Davenport continued to win numerous other awards during her professional tennis career, including Wimbledon. She remembered Murrieta Valley High School fondly and donated tennis courts to the school.

Library

The permanent building housing the MVHS library opened in 1992 with Library Technician Cheryl Brummett supervising this new library. The library included shelving for 30,000 books and opened with only 5,000 books on these shelves. There were many, many empty shelves. Because the district was growing so rapidly and funding depended on the number of students from the previous year, budgets were always tight and it took a long time for those empty library shelves to be filled.

Deborah Jacobs was hired as the first certificated librarian at MVHS in 1994, working with Mrs. Brummett. In addition to managing the library, the library staff was charged with the storage and distribution of textbooks.

In 1997 the school library provided access to the Internet for the first time, thanks to a partnership with the Riverside Public Library System.

Through a computer and dial-up modem provided by the Library System, the school library was able to access the Internet and the public library catalogs. Interlibrary loan was offered to students and faculty. Other databases were available through a CD-ROM tower, and there were eight databases available for students to use.

In 2000, the school library added online databases for student use, replacing the CD-ROM databases that had been used previously. This meant instant access to constantly updated information. This was also a year when the State provided funding for school libraries and the MVHS library added $57,000 worth of new books.

First graduating class

In 1994, MVHS graduated its first senior class. Eleven of these students attended school in Murrieta starting in kindergarten: Sky Lovingier, Erin Archbold, Jeff Anderson, Heather Jordan, Nikki Richardson, Vanessa Farias, Jerrod Littlejohn, Maribel Alferez, Elodia Vasquez, Roland Addison, and Danny Gutierrez.

A souvenir program listing all the graduating seniors and showing a map of the campus was sent to every member of the community. Lisa Ricci and Stacy Androus were the Senior Class Co-Presidents, Salutatorians were Mark Nibbe and Keith Sanders, and Valedictorian was Heidi Schneringer. Miss Schneringer was the first of the Murrieta graduates to return and teach at the high school.

These students and the rest of the first graduating class left a memento to the school, personalized tiles embedded in the ground in an area known as "Senior Square." As the school grew and space was needed for portable classrooms, these tiles had to be moved, and in 1997 they were reset in an area near the gym.

Changes in leadership

Mr. Burch left before the first class graduated in 1994, but he was present at graduation ceremonies to celebrate their success. He was succeeded as principal by Shelley Weston, who had served as assistant principal. In 1997 Duane Coleman replaced Shelley Weston as principal at MVHS. After a year, Mr. Coleman left for a position closer to home, and Mark Johnson was hired as principal of the school.

When Mr. Johnson was promoted to Director of Educational Programs in 2003, Renate Jefferson became principal at MVHS and stayed for eleven years. When she retired in 2013, Eric Mooney was hired to succeed her.

California Distinguished School

MVHS was named a California Distinguished School in 1999, one of 64 schools so honored across the state. According to Mr. Johnson, "This is a real honor for our school to get this award, but it is not something that was one year in the making or one written application. It has been nine years in the making from the very beginning of the school's existence."

Continued growth

MVHS continued to welcome new students and add teachers and support staff. By the 1998-99 school year, there were 2,400 students, 103 teachers, 50 classified support staff, four assistant principals and four counselors.

The number of high school students continued to increase. By the 1999-2000 school year, there were 2,700 students, 128 teachers, and 57 classified support staff at MVHS. There were still four assistant principals, but one additional counselor had been added, for a total of five counselors.

The 2000-2001 school year found 3,270 students on campus and the school, originally planned for 2,400 students, maximum, was packed! The school scheduled two lunch periods and the lunch lines were still long. For that number of students, there were 137 teachers and 63 classified support staff, but still four assistant principals. The number of counselors had been increased to six.

In 2003-2004, MVHS Learning Directors (formerly assistant principals) were Robert McGonigal, Errol Garnett, Chona Killeen, and Mick Wager. The number of counselors, (now called Learning Coordinators) had increased to eight, and included Adriana Alarcon, Erika Bennett, Lisa Overshaw-Durhan, Dean Lesicko, Tom Petrich, Shani Santiago, Candyce Julian, and Rich Lockwood.

In the same year, the six-year WASC review of the school reported that there were a number of reasons to be "passionately proud" of the school. WASC findings showed a curriculum aligned to district, state and national content standards; highly regarded courses including a variety of electives; award-winning extra-curricular programs; and highly qualified teachers who enjoy working with students.

Creekside Alternative High School — 1993

Creekside Alternative High School opened on the MVHS campus in 1993, moving to their permanent site when it was completed 1998. The school was designed by the architecture firm WLC. Creekside was named for its location near Murrieta Creek. The mascot is the bulldog.

The first Creekside principal was Dr. Al Ross, working with teachers Charlie Riendeau, Bill Spivey, Pat Lagger (Beal), Kevin Hughes, and Tom Jabro to plan and open this new school. Betty Nead was hired as the first counselor and Rebecca Kelley, who had worked with Dr. Ross at Rail Ranch Elementary, became the first school secretary. When Mrs. Nead left in 1995, Chris O'Sullivan was hired as counselor.

Sharing a high school site

Creekside began classes on the MVHS site in classrooms at the southwest end of the campus. A chain-link fence separated the two schools and because bathrooms were not part of the four-classroom complex, the chain-link fence was extended to include the closest bathrooms. Two high schools with different schedules on one campus posed problems and everyone was happy when the Creekside students moved into their own permanent school in 1998.

At the permanent site, there was room to include the Esperanza program for pregnant and parenting teens.

The first two students graduated from Creekside in December 1993 and another thirty students followed in June 1994.

Finally, a library

The one thing Creekside did not have for a number of years was a library. Mrs. Jefferson fixed that, closing off part of the multipurpose room and turning it into a library in March, 2002. The library was named the Marcy Carri library after a popular English teacher who was passionate about libraries. Mary Shufford worked as the first library technician on a substitute basis, processing books and getting the library set up. She left in February for the library position in Murrieta Elementary School, and Laurie Smith was hired as the first permanent library technician.

Administrative changes

The first ten years saw many personnel changes. In 1996, Butch Owens became the second principal at Creekside, occupying that position until 2002, when Renate Jefferson became the third Creekside principal. When Mrs. Jefferson was named principal at MVHS in early 2003, Mark Johnson was promoted to Director of Alternative Educational Programs, which included Creekside, Adult Education, the Independent Study program (now formally named Tenaja Canyon Academy) and Home/Hospital Education.

Mr. Johnson retired in 2010 and Jared Rogers became principal of Creekside and Tenaja Canyon Academy, working with Tom Petrich, counselor.

Thompson Middle School—1994

Thompson Middle School was designed by the architecture firm Nickoloff & Associates. The school was named for the Thompson family that owned and farmed the area where Murrieta Valley High School and Thompson Middle School are located, and the mascot is the timberwolf.

Sharing the Shivela campus

Principal Manny Valdes and Counselor Mary Martin opened Thompson Middle School in 1994 with 270 sixth and seventh grade students sharing the Shivela campus in eighteen portable classrooms. At the time, Shivela had 1,600 students and there was a real need for a second middle school.

Moving to the permanent campus

By 1995, there were 310 students attending Thompson Middle School, and in January, 1996, Thompson students and staff moved to portable buildings at the new campus while the permanent buildings were being constructed. The move was scheduled for mid-year, which happened to be during the rainy season. There was lots of mud which meant wet carpets, damp boxes and muddy tracks in new classrooms, but teachers and students were happy to be in their new school.

As with the other new schools, it took awhile before sod was laid, trees planted, and shade structures in place. With its location on the west side of Murrieta, Thompson Middle School served a smaller student population and would stay small for a long time.

The permanent school was dedicated on May 23, 2000.

Library

When Thompson Middle School opened on the Shivela campus, the Thompson school library occupied its own portable classroom building and Library Technician Pat Raether was hired to start this new library. When students and staff moved to the permanent school site, the library moved into another portable classroom. Finally, when the permanent buildings were completed in October 1998 Mrs. Raether moved the library one last time into the new library facility.

Mrs. Raether retired in the spring of 2004 and Barbara Vogel transferred from Monte Vista Elementary School to take the library position. That was a year when the State provided Library Funding and Thompson received $46,000 for new books to help stock the new library.

Changes in Administration

Butch Owens became principal of Thompson in 2002, working with Assistant Principal Pamela Wilson. When Mr. Owens left in 2003 to become principal of Vista Murrieta High School, Dale Velk, assistant principal at Murrieta Valley High School, became the next Thompson principal.

Thompson was named a California Distinguished School in 2001.

Tovashal Elementary School—1996

Architect Ralph Allen designed Tovashal Elementary School, named for the Luiseño Indian word for "white oak." The name was selected by the Board of Education in November 1988, long before plans were drawn up and ground broken. The mascot is the tiger shark, from names selected and voted on by the students of this new school.

The permanent site was completed in 1999.

Sharing the Avaxat campus

Chuck Jones was the first principal at Tovashal, opening the school in 1996 on the Avaxat campus and occupying the portable classrooms left empty after the Avaxat permanent buildings were completed and occupied. The two schools shared the Avaxat library, multipurpose room, cafeteria, and playgrounds.

Tovashal opened as a two-track school when most of the district's schools were on four-track scheduling. School started in July of 1996 with 13 teachers, 240 students, a secretary, a half time attendance clerk/ half-time health clerk, two aides and one custodian. Over the next two years six classrooms were added and enrollment increased to 680 students.

Moving to the permanent school site

In September of 1998, after two months of school, the new permanent campus was finally ready and the school moved. Students took buses from Avaxat on the Friday before the opening to carry their books and personal belongings to their new classrooms. Teachers and staff worked long hours all day Friday, Saturday, and Sunday to get ready and provide a smooth opening of school.

Library

Jackie Katz worked as a volunteer in the Avaxat school library, and then as a long term substitute library technician for Tovashal, still in the Avaxat Library. When the school moved into permanent buildings, Mrs. Katz was hired full-time to manage the library.

Each spring Tovashal students and staff participated in Dr. Seuss-based reading activities, inviting guest readers, drawing pictures of Seuss characters, and even enjoying green eggs and ham, prepared by Mrs. Katz for the entire school. One memorable year Mr. Jones decided to read to students while astride a huge, rolling Horton the Elephant, created

69

from two-by-fours and paper Mache. It was an opportunity for a terrible fall, but fortunately, nothing happened, though getting on and off Horton was quite a feat.

Administrative changes

When Mr. Jones left to become the first principal at Monte Vista Elementary School in 2003, Assistant Principal Terry Olson took over as principal, with Assistant Principal Andy Banks. Mrs. Olson died unexpectedly in 2008, and Mr. Banks was appointed principal, working with Assistant Principal Leigh Lockwood. When he decided to step down, Mrs. Lockwood became principal, working with Assistant Principal Luis Ortiz.

In 2012, the school housed 800 students and included 41 classrooms, a multipurpose room, computer lab, library, cafeteria, administrative offices, staff lounge and two play areas; one for kindergarten students, and one designated for students in grades 1-5.

Tovashal was named a California Distinguished School in 2004.

A century ends, and a century begins...

So ends the story of Murrieta schools in the twentieth century. The district increased from one school to ten schools and almost all of that change took place in the last decade of the century. During those ten years, the number of students increased from 3,990 to 11,279. And there were more students coming....

The Schools, 2000 and Beyond

New families kept moving into the Murrieta area at the beginning of the twenty-first century, bringing more students to increasingly overcrowded district schools. The district placed signs at each school showing how many students the school was planned for and stating that overcrowding could be a problem. As new schools were built, students moved from overcrowded schools to the spacious new schools. Often teachers moved with their students, along with textbooks and teaching materials.

Cole Canyon Elementary School--2000

The first new Murrieta school in the twenty-first century, Cole Canyon Elementary was designed by architecture firm HMC. It was named for Cole Canyon, a nearby canyon, and the name given by the developer to the surrounding tract. The school mascot is the coyote and school colors are maroon and black. While the school was under construction, it had views of the surrounding hills in every direction. These views quickly disappeared as large houses were built around the school. Cole Canyon would grow as the community increased in size, eventually housing more than 1,000 students.

This school would be the first to open in permanent buildings since Murrieta Elementary School in 1958. Interestingly, the first two

71

permanent school buildings in the district (Murrieta School in1885 and Murrieta Grammar School in 1920) had opened with students in temporary buildings until their school was ready to use.

Karen Michaud, who had served as principal at Murrieta Elementary, was Cole Canyon's first principal. Luis Ortiz was hired in 2002 to serve as the first learning director (assistant principal). Linda Coleman was hired as the first secretary.

Dedication

Cole Canyon Elementary, with 560 students, was dedicated on September 20, 2000. Music was provided by the fifth grade band under the direction of Ed Wentz, and singers in the Coyote Choral Club, led by Diane Rehagen. Speakers included Superintendent Chet Francisco, Board President Judy Rosen, and Fred Weishauptl, representing Assemblyman Bruce Thompson. Students also spoke: fourth grader Sven Hurney read his essay, and fifth grader Cheyne Forgerson read his poem.

First teaching staff

Murrieta schools in the 21st century would open with more students and larger staffs. The first teaching staff at Cole Canyon included the following teachers:

In kindergarten, the teachers were Alicia Jaime, Natalie Rohwer, Jarilyn Parra, and Kristin Hanson. April Barns taught a kindergarten/first grade combination class.

First grade teachers were Debbie Phillips, Pamela Picchiottino, Ali Knights, Kathy Davis/Laurie Paysse (sharing a teaching assignment), and Arnette Jasperson.

Teachers for second grade were Kristina Murphy, Chrissi Levin, Diane Rehagen, Kathy Quinlan, and Tammy Hunter-Wethers.

Third grade teachers were Laura Hanson, Keri Hayes, Anne Hess, Mark McCandless and Lorrie Peterson.

Fourth grade teachers were Carol Hernandez, Scott Payne and Constance Youens. Fifth grade teachers were Kathy Ericson, Tricia Keller, Connie Sieber and Beth Szabo.

Ronda Smyth, shared with Murrieta Elementary School, taught RSP.

Academic achievement

Cole Canyon students performed well on California Academic Performance Index (API) tests and their test scores steadily increased, ahead of the other district schools, so there was soon a waiting list of students wanting to enroll. The school proudly states, "Our API test scores consistently place us as one of the top scoring schools in all of Riverside County."

Cole Canyon was named a California Distinguished School in 2006 and 2010.

Students support the school library

During the first year, fourth grader Brian Choi won $50 for a drawing he submitted to the Riverside County Credit Union Art Contest. Brian decided to give all the money to the Cole Canyon library. "Our school is new and the library doesn't have that many books. I wanted to give the money to the library so the kids could read," Brian said.

Scott Foster chose Cole Canyon's library as his Eagle Scout project, helping to organize all the new materials, including textbooks, and create a database inventory.

Debbie Foster was hired as the library technician at this school, after serving as a substitute in the position and helping to get the library ready to open.

Character Counts!

Mr. Ortiz was an advocate for the *Character Counts!* program, which promotes trustworthiness, respect, responsibility, fairness, caring, and citizenship. Thanks to his leadership, this program was implemented school wide at Cole Canyon. Other schools in the district soon followed suit. A research study of the *Character Counts!* program was conducted at a different Murrieta school and results indicated that behavior referrals dropped when the program was implemented.

Celebrating reading

A highlight of each school year was the annual reading event celebrating Dr. Seuss' birthday. Teachers and students read Seuss books, drew pictures, ate green eggs and ham, invited guest readers, and enjoyed a special reading recognition assembly. One year Mrs. Michaud, as a reward for the students' reading achievement, kissed a goat as part of the theme, "A goat in a boat." It wasn't easy to get the boat there, or get the goat into the boat, but the goat seemed to enjoy being kissed. Another year, Mrs. Michaud "danced a jig with a pig in a wig." The pig refused to be kissed, and the students loved it!

School facilities

The school has forty-seven classrooms, a multipurpose room with a kitchen, computer lab, library, an outdoor eating area, amphitheater, administrative offices, a health office, teacher workrooms, and two play areas, one for kindergarten students and one designated for students in grades one through five.

Daniel N. Buchanan Elementary School-2001

The architecture firm HMC also provided the design for Buchanan Elementary School. It was named for Daniel N. Buchanan, an early resident of Murrieta, who built the first one-room Murrieta School on 2nd

Street. The mascot is the "blazer" horse, which was shortened from "Trailblazers." That name was selected by a vote of students attending Alta Murrieta and Rail Ranch schools, who would be the first students at this new school. The school colors are slate blue and tan.

Pat Kelley, who had been the principal at Rail Ranch Elementary, was given the opportunity to open this new school as the first principal. Estelle Jaurequi was assistant principal and Cathy Diyorio was school secretary. Thanks to the teamwork between administration and staff, things went smoothly.

Dedication

The school was dedicated on September 13, 2001. *Californian* newspaper reporter John Hunneman spoke about Murrieta history and how the school came to be named. Superintendent Chet Francisco and Board president Austin Linsley also spoke, along with fifth grader Elecia Avonetti. The school song, written by Sue and Brad Ackley, was sung at the end of the ceremony.

Many of the teachers and staff at Buchanan transferred from other schools in the district, including Library Technician Jan Lauletta, who transferred from the MVHS library to open this new library. She said it took a while to get used to the change from tall high school students to elementary-sized students, but found she enjoyed working with the younger students.

Staffing changes

When Mr. Kelley was promoted to Director of Human Resources in 2003, Mike Lorimer became the Buchanan principal. He would stay at Buchanan for ten years.

Support and enrichment programs

Programs in addition to academics include tutoring, gifted and talented education, English Learner support, resource specialist services, Learning Centers for academic support, and speech. The school also provides enrichment opportunities through "Meet the Masters" art programs, choir, band, drama, running clubs, and after school classes such as art, chess, and science.

Buchanan was named a California Distinguished School in 2010.

School facilities

The school includes fifty-four classrooms, a multipurpose room with a kitchen, two computer labs, library, cafeteria, an outdoor eating area, amphitheater, administrative offices, a health office, teacher workrooms, and two play areas, one for kindergarten students and one designated for students in grades one through five.

Warm Springs Middle School — 2002

Architects from WLC also provided the design for this new school, named for nearby Warm Springs Creek, which actually comes from a hot spring. The mascot is a wildcat, chosen with input from the students, and the colors are blue and white.

Warm Springs Middle School was built in two phases. Phase One allowed the school to open on August 14, 2002 with 675 students in grades six and seven. The next year WSMS added eighth grade, and by the beginning of 2004, Phase Two of the school site was completed.

School facilities

The school opened with thirty classrooms, increasing to sixty-seven classrooms in 2013. There was also an administration office and food services building. By the time Phase Two was completed, the campus included a covered lunch area, library with a computer lab, multi-purpose room/cafeteria, band and choir classroom, science building, computer lab, a P.E. pavilion, athletic fields and a track.

Administration

Tim Custer, who had been assistant principal at Thompson Middle School, was hired as the first principal at Warm Springs Middle School. The school grew rapidly and teacher Joe Shaw took on the duties of learning director. Tracy King, learning director at Shivela, became the second learning director at the school. At the time, assistant principals were known as "learning directors."

Library

Brigid Nelson was hired to open this new library, starting in a portable classroom. With textbooks and library books in a classroom-sized facility, it was extremely crowded, but Mrs. Nelson made it all work. When the library moved into the permanent, large library room, there were many empty shelves for a while.

Additional programs

Programs offered at the school include Associated Student Body (ASB), Advancement Via Individual Determination (AVID), art, band, choir, drama productions, media technology, yearbook, intramural sports, and at-risk intervention programs.

Monte Vista Elementary School—2003

The architecture firm HMC designed Monte Vista Elementary School, which was named for the view of the mountains in the area. The mascot is the mountain lion.

Principal Chuck Jones took advantage of this opportunity to open a second school in the district and relied on his experience opening Tovashal to make opening this school smoother. However, with two schools opening in the same year (Vista Murrieta High School also opened), some things did not go as planned and it was a good thing that Mr. Jones knew a lot about school facilities. Construction lagged, a very rainy year held up progress, and things like carpeting in the office and sidewalks weren't completed until students arrived—and sometimes after.

Dedication

The School's dedication was May 27, 2004 and featured a presentation or song by each grade. Speakers included Superintendent Chet Francisco, Board President Ken Dickson, and Chuck Depreker, Assistant Superintendent of Facilities.

Administration

Sharon Seelman was hired as the first learning director (assistant principal). Mr. Jones left Monte Vista after one year for a position in the Facilities Department and Randy Rogers became the next Monte Vista principal in 2004, staying there until 2013.

Library

Barbara Vogel was hired as the Library Technician to open Monte Vista's library. After a year, she transferred to Thompson Middle School and Connie Kim was hired to take her place. Mrs. Kim was interested in becoming a counselor and when she left, Lynette Dodds was hired, bringing her creative talents to this position.

Each year Mrs. Dodds planned a different school-wide reading program. Among these memorable events was a school-wide letter-writing event, where every student in school wrote a letter to American troops fighting in Iraq. Another event was "Celebrity Book Readings" with firefighters, police officers, soldiers and race car drivers reading their favorite stories to the students.

School facilities

The school has forty-nine classrooms, a multipurpose room, speech and resource rooms, computer lab, library, cafeteria, administrative offices, staff lounge and two play areas. One play area is for kindergarten and the other is designated for students in grades one through five.

Vista Murrieta High School—2003

Architects at WLC also designed this school. On February 27, 1999, after hearing from the public, the Board of Education named the school based on their input. They selected the diamondback rattlesnake as the school mascot. This mascot selection didn't set well with the students and community and was soon changed to a Bronco. The colors are blue and gold.

Problems with land and butterflies

By this time, finding available and affordable property for a high school was not easy. The City of Murrieta owned land between Clinton Keith and Los Alamos Roads, east of Highway 215. The school district negotiated successfully with the City to purchase part of this property, which would be adjacent to a planned sports park.

Early issues included the discovery of the endangered Quino Checkerspot butterflies (*Euphydryas editha quino*) on the property, so mitigation to protect this species had to be included in the plans. While this was happening, construction of the high school was put on hold. The

Murrieta school district worked out an agreement with the Fish and Wildlife Service that included a district-funded laboratory to house a Captive Breeding Program for study of the butterfly and 114 acres of native lands for habitat.

Dedication

VMHS was dedicated on Saturday, October 9, 2004, with performances by Ben Cave, violinist, and the VMHS Chamber Choir, directed by Jennifer Page. Dr. Shari Fox, Principal Butch Owens, MVHS graduate Megan Miller, and Board member Austin Linsley were featured speakers.

Administration

Mr. Owens was given the opportunity to open this second, highly anticipated high school. He had extensive experience in the district, serving as counselor at Alta Murrieta Elementary School, principal at Avaxat Elementary School, principal at Creekside Alternative High School, and principal at Thompson Middle School.

By this time, there were over 4,000 students at MVHS and a second high school was desperately needed. MVHS had been designed for 2,400 students, and was terribly overcrowded.

Mr. Owens and his secretary, Tracy Spencer, were given an office in the MVHS administration building to plan for the school opening, hire staff, order supplies, furniture, and equipment, and much, much more. It was a daunting task, as many others had learned. Mr. Owens created the school motto, Character, Leadership, Attitude, Scholarship, and Service (C.L.A.S.S).

Mr. Owens' first administrative team included learning directors Darren Daniel, Michael Moore, and Pamela Wilson.

Coley Candaele was among the first group of teachers hired. He had a strong reputation as a football coach and would put together a successful football program. Ray Moore was the first athletic director, and Michael Pattison took on the duties of activities director.

School opens in two phases

The school opened with half of the campus completed, but all of it framed and the shell done. A chain-link fence down the middle of the campus separated the finished from the unfinished. The library was on the unfinished side, so for a year books were circulated from temporary quarters in teacher offices on the southwest corner of the school. That first part of the school included thirty-two regular classrooms, teacher office/workrooms, the interim library and food services, four technology labs and administrative offices. Athletic fields were ready for practice and competition on opening day.

Academics

VMHS opened offering a full range of academic and athletic programs, with many teachers from MVHS transferring to this new high school. New programs were added, notably college courses in partnership with neighboring Mt. San Jacinto College. Students could take these classes and get high school and college credits at no cost, and the program met with enthusiastic support.

Library

MVHS librarian Deborah Jacobs transferred from MVHS to open the new high school library, an exciting and challenging opportunity. In getting ready for the incoming freshmen and sophomore students, lots and lots of textbooks had to be bar-coded and made ready. Volunteers and library personnel started working on textbooks in the future dance classroom with no electricity, so there were no lights, air conditioning, or restrooms. A long extension cord brought power to run the computers, while a large open door provided light and some air circulation. Lights were added first and by the end of a week, restrooms and air conditioning were all working.

The second phase of the school, including the Aquatics and Athletic Stadium, were completed in 2004. The school's first class of seniors graduated in June, 2006.

Athletics

The school has received many awards and accolades including Max Preps Most Spirited School award for two consecutive years, four consecutive CIF School of Character Awards and 2012 Coach and Athletic Director magazines' Interscholastic Sports Program Excellence Award.

VMHS students have compiled impressive results in the various athletic programs. According to athletic director Ray Moore, by 2012 the school has had a fifty percent participation rate in athletics, impressive in a school of more than 3,200 students. More than 1,600 athletes participated in twenty-one sports and fifty-one teams at the school. The grade point average for varsity athletes is an impressive 3.3.

The sports teams are also involved in the community. In California, high school students must complete forty hours of community service before graduation. At Vista every sport selects its own community service project, which has included raising funds for cancer and coaching clinics for younger students. All students can be involved somehow. For example, approximately 1,000 student members of the "Bronco Bleacher Creatures" attend sports events to support the teams.

School facilities

VMHS was built on sixty-eight acres of land overlooking the City of Murrieta, in what was an area of brush and beehives before. The school grew to ninety-nine classrooms, including computer and technology labs, library, college career center, science facilities, a lecture hall, classrooms for ceramics, art, fashion and design, photography, and foods. There is a performing arts center with band, choir and drama classrooms.

The administration area includes offices for school administrators, staff, the school nurse, workrooms, an ASB office, and student store. Athletic facilities include main and practice gymnasiums, an aquatics facility, athletic stadium with an all-weather running surface, three competition baseball and softball diamonds, two full-size soccer fields, physical education fields and courts, a weight room with state-of-the-art equipment and classrooms for health, wrestling, and aerobics.

First graduates

VMHS's first graduating class, wearing sashes that read "It all began with me," graduated June 9, 2006. Valedictorian Anita Kalathil said, "What an amazing job we have done."

Tenaja Canyon Academy—2003

Tenaja was named for the Luiseño Indian word meaning pond or small lake. It shares facilities with Creekside High School.

An informal independent study program had been in place in the district for many years, providing extra support for students in grades K-8 who needed it. After Murrieta Valley High School opened, the district realized that more students needed an independent study option. Karen Robertson, district coordinator, took on this responsibility and met with each student in the program weekly, providing one-on-one teaching and support. Those students included a fourteen-year-old with a baby and a student who was so stressed by the traditional high school environment that he threw up each day before school.

When Creekside Alternative High School opened, that program met the needs of many high school students. There were still students who had special scheduling needs, including students who were professional athletes. During the 1998-1999 school year, before Tenaja Canyon Academy was formed, teacher Kelly Daly-Yee took over teaching an independent study program on the Creekside campus for grades 9 – 12.

The Academy opens

By the end of the 2002-2003 school year, the demand for independent study at all grades had increased and there was a waiting list of students wanting to enroll. In 2003 Tenaja Canyon Academy opened on the Cole Canyon Elementary school campus for grades one through eight, and at Creekside High School for grades nine through twelve. Cole Canyon continued to attract new students and an increase in student numbers meant the school needed all their classrooms. The independent study program had to be moved to Alta Murrieta Elementary for the students in grades one to eight. Overall, there were seventy-five students in grades one through twelve.

When classroom space at elementary schools was needed for incoming students, the entire independent study program moved to Creekside High School.

Early staffing

Shilind Wheaton developed and taught the early district K-8 independent study program, working with parents and students and providing weekly guidance on lessons in all subjects. The program also provided textbooks for home use, including teacher editions. Later on as the number of students increased, Loretta Chavez was added to the staff for grades one through five and Terese Clower for grades six through eight. An additional teacher, Ricky Ray, was hired for the nine through twelve Tenaja program.

Instruction

When the program was small, students met their classmates one day a week to receive direct instruction from the teacher. This time was also used for group projects, which included art projects and drama presentations. As the program grew it became more individualized.

Students continued to meet with the teacher weekly to receive instruction, take exams, and discuss the past week's assignments.

Tenaja students use the same textbooks and curriculum as students at the other district schools and are required to complete the same number of credits to graduate. To provide additional courses, students are allowed to take up to two classes at one of the MVUSD comprehensive high schools.

School facilities

The school shares a campus with Creekside High School and the Murrieta Valley Adult Education program, with sixteen classrooms, a computer lab, basketball courts, a library, administrative offices, and a staff lounge.

In April, 2006, there were eighty-five students enrolled in the program, which included fourteen students in grades three through eight and seventy-one in grades nine through twelve. This number would not change much and by 2013 ninety-eight students were enrolled.

Antelope Hills Elementary School—2005

Architect Brian Staton, of HMC, designed this school. The school mascot is an explorer and school colors are green and gold. The original name proposed for the school was "Old Antelope Road Elementary School," but this was changed to Antelope Hills by the Board of Education. The school is located by the former route of Antelope Road, which ran from Highway 15 to Highway 215 before it was rerouted and part of it was renamed California Oaks Road.

Principal Karen Briski and Learning Director Ken Goltara were selected as the administrative team to open this school. Mrs. Briski had been principal at Avaxat Elementary and Mr. Goltara had been Assistant Principal at Rail Ranch. Kim Smith was hired as the first school secretary.

Like most of the district schools, getting ready to open involved some scrambling to get everything ready. The staff was assembling furniture the day before school started, and office furniture didn't arrive until after school had been in session for six weeks.

Opening day and a new teaching staff

Antelope Hills opened with approximately 550 students and a "Join the Adventure" theme matching the school mascot, the Explorers. On the first day of school teachers dressed as safari guides to set the tone for the new school.

The first teachers included Julie Aves, Carol Ponce, Valerie Walters, Sally Lyons, Jennifer Dunaway, Kaeli Trask, Linda Stone, Renee Vaughn, Kevin Youngdale, Dan Hoekstra, Mario Van Heuckelom, Sandie Brown, Rebecca Bosna, Heather Hixson-Carver, Marilyn Stovall, Virginia Rogers, Lora Lee Patton, Tricia Ramer, Mike Foley, Al Brehm, Steve Basin, Jessica Mitchell, Kelly Swanson, Stephen Diephouse, Rebecca Diephouse, Jeanine Harris, and Tracy Quigley.

A lesson in ethics

In 2006, this new school learned a lesson in ethical behavior. One of the Antelope Hills parents won the Tour de France international bicycle race, a tremendous accomplishment. The entire school was ready to celebrate their home-town hero, until he was accused of using performance enhancing drugs, which he later confessed to doing.

Library

Cindy Lee was hired as the first Library Technician for this new school. The community was generous in donating books during that first year, with one parent donating $10,000 worth of books to the school library. Mrs. Lee was kept busy getting books ready for students to check out, in addition to reading stories to classes as they came into the library.

Distinguished School Award

Antelope Hills was named a California Distinguished School in 2008, just three years after it opened. This award is given by the California State Board of Education to public schools that best represent exemplary and quality educational programs. Approximately five percent of California schools receive this award each year following an extensive selection process.

School facilities

Antelope Hills Elementary School includes thirty regular education classrooms, three special day and one ABA classroom, a multipurpose room with a kitchen, computer lab, library, an outdoor lunch area, amphitheater, administrative offices, a health office, teacher workrooms, and two play areas, one for kindergarten students and one designated for students in grades one through five.

Lisa J. Mails Elementary School — 2007

On August 11, 2005, the Board of Education gave their approval to name the District's 11th elementary school after Lisa J. Mails (1953-2005), who had been an outstanding and popular teacher at E. Hale Curran Elementary School for ten years before succumbing to cancer.

The Architecture firm WLC designed this new elementary school, and the mascot is the Monarch butterfly.

Construction issues

Lisa J. Mails Elementary School's location provided challenges to getting it built. The school was located in a rural area with no paved roads, water, or sewage. To get the school plans approved, a paved road had to be built, sufficient to handle traffic in and out of the school. Parents would be expected to drive their students to this school, which would mean a large number of cars driving by twice a day. The city and county had not included a road in this area in their planning and were not going to pave a road there, especially under the tight timeline the school district needed.

Dr. Scheer and Bill Olien, Assistant Superintendent of Facilities and Operations, came up with a way to build a road, feeling it was better to be forgiven than to ask permission in this case. The plan was successful and a road was built and ready to go in time for the opening of school.

The city and county had not planned any water or sewage lines to this area, so again the District had to solve an impossible problem, and they did. The district spent $1.5 million to put in a water line and for the first year, the school had a large septic tank. It became, as Mr. Olien noted, a giant RV. This worked, and the school was ready for students on the first day.

Getting everything ready for the school opening involved the active support of many people, including Nick Newkirk from Purchasing, who spent a lot of time at the site. He handled accepting deliveries of furniture and equipment and getting these items safely stored until they could be put in classrooms.

The school opens

Lisa J. Mails Elementary School opened for students in August, 2007 with Principal Faythe Mutchnick and Assistant Principal Garrett Corduan. This was planned as a school of choice with a visual and performing arts (VPA) emphasis and attracted a staff of creative and dedicated teachers. This would be the district's first "school of choice," which meant students from anywhere in the district could attend this school, but parents were expected to provide transportation.

Students took classes using the regular district curriculum, so teachers learned how to integrate VPA into their class lessons. After-school programs were also available and regular performances were scheduled so students could demonstrate what they were learning.

Library

Patti Payne, with a technology background, was hired as the school's first library staff. The library was soon decorated with a mural painted on most of the walls depicting reading and books. The library grew rapidly, with books purchased before the school opened and a steady stream of donations. Mrs. Payne used her technology skills to create a library website for students and staff.

Staffing changes

When Mr. Corduan left to open Dorothy McElhinney Middle School, Mike Marble took his place as assistant principal. Mr. Marble left to become principal at Cole Canyon Elementary and Joe Shaw became the third assistant principal.

School facilities

The school has thirty-nine classrooms, a multipurpose room with a kitchen, computer lab, library, a lunch area, amphitheater, administrative offices, health office, teacher workrooms, and two play areas, one for kindergarten students and one for students in grades one through five.

Dorothy McElhinney Middle School--2009

WLC was also the architecture firm for this school, which was named for a former resident, Dorothy Dodge McElhinney, who was a local 4-H leader and owner of the Pinto Ranch. The mascot is appropriately a Colt and school colors are red, black and silver.

The school opening was delayed due to low enrollment. One thousand new homes were planned for community around the school, but the financial crisis that hit the country halted housing construction and families could not move into the school area. Until middle school student numbers increased, Lisa. J. Mails elementary school would teach students in kindergarten through eighth grades.

The move into McElhinney was gradual. Lisa J. Mails and Dorothy McElhinney schools are adjacent and students could easily walk from one school to the other. Some middle school classes were taught in classrooms at the permanent facility before the formal opening of the school. Experienced teachers from other schools transferred to McElhinney and provided continuity and experience, helping make the opening and first year smoother than it might otherwise have been. The school opened in August, 2009, with 750 students in grades six through eight.

According to Principal Gordon Corduan, "In my opinion, the school really came alive when we started building our staff. They work as a team and care about their students' success."

Dedication

At the dedication ceremonies on October 13, 2009, students, teachers, administrators and board members heard members of the McElhinney family share stories of the family, and each grade level did a presentation. Visitors also enjoyed tours of the new campus.

A highlight of the dedication was when Superintendent Stan Scheer joined the school band, playing the trombone.

Pinto Ranch history

In keeping with its location on the Pinto Ranch, the school has a western theme. Mrs. McElhinney (1900-1997) trained and sold horses on her 400-acre Pinto Ranch, where she raised pinto horses. She had a riding school in the mid 1940's and also had a riding group.

In 1951 her friend Doreen Foote wrote a book about Mrs. McElhinney, *Dude Girl.* This was a fictionalized account of driving a herd of horses from Laramie, Wyoming to the Pinto Ranch in California. Mrs. McElhinney had moved to California when she married Dr. Philip McElhinney. In Wyoming, she owned a herd of horses, and the best way to bring them to California was to herd them on horseback. Doreen Foote was one of the cowgirls on the two-month trip and one of Mrs. McElhinney's closest friends.

The McElhinney family still own and live on part of the Pinto Ranch nearby. Students and staff have taken field trips to the old homestead, where the family has shared stories of how things were in the early half of the last century.

Library

In planning the school library, the architect combined the number of shelves needed with the space available. This created a small library with many rows of very tall shelving. The result was canyons of shelving that provided hiding places for mischief and was too high for the smaller students to reach. The Facilities Department worked with the library coordinator to remedy this and remove some shelving, resulting in a more open, visible, and attractive library.

Corrie Cruise was hired to open this new library, with books that had already been purchased and donations. She also was given the task of handling textbooks, like the other middle school library personnel. When Mrs. Cruise became a guidance technician, Marie Hamilton was hired to oversee the library.

The entryway to the library was painted with a reproduction of the cover of *Dude Girl,* and the family donated two copies of the book to the school.

VPA emphasis

In addition to the district curriculum, Principal Garrett Corduan and the staff focused on continuing the visual and performing arts emphasis provided at Lisa J. Mails Elementary School. The school offered vocal and instrumental music, including strings, drama, dance and visual arts, ceramics and computer arts. In addition, the school has ASB, Yearbook, GATE, PLUS Forums, intramural sports, at-risk intervention programs and a wide variety of clubs and activities.

Facilities

McElhinney would be the second district middle school to have two-story classroom buildings. The buildings were constructed tall rather than wide because the area is home to federally protected fairy shrimp (*Brachinecta Lynchi*). Tall buildings occupy less land, leaving more shrimp habitat. The fairy shrimp live in freshwater pools that form during the rainy season.

The school has sixty-three classrooms, a multipurpose room, computer lab, covered lunch area, library, cafeteria, administrative offices, a gymnasium, athletic fields, and a track.

Murrieta Mesa High School — 2009

The architect for the dramatically different design of this school was NTD Stichler. The school name came from its geographical location, high on a mesa identified in an 1884 surveyor's map of the valley. Members of the community attended the school board meeting when the name would be selected and provided input. The mascot is the Ram, and colors are green and bronze.

The successful passage of a $120 million bond measure in June, 2006 allowed the district to begin construction of this third high school.

Finding a location was the first challenge, because there were not much empty land left within the city limits and the price of land had increased dramatically. The total cost of the school, $126 million, included $92.8 million for construction, $26 million for the land acquisition and $7.4 million for grading. Funding for the school was provided through the State School Facility Program, local bond measures and other sources, including developer fees.

Building this school coincided with the national financial crisis and presented new problems. Keeping construction going on schedule was especially challenging, since the State, also dealing with financial problems, delayed payment of promised construction funds. If the school was to be built, construction workers had to be paid. Creative financing was needed and Dr. Scheer, the Board, and Stacy Coleman, Assistant Superintendant of Business Services, found a way to provide money to keep the project going so the school could open in 2009 as planned, with ninth and tenth graders.

Dedication

The dedication ceremony on July 31, 2009 was open to the public and well attended. Featured speakers included Principal Mary Walters and tours of the campus. A few days earlier, on July 29, the school held a fundraising dinner, indicative of the financial issues facing the country. Speakers, including Mayor Gary Thomasian, Superintendent Stan Scheer, Board President Robin Crist and Mesa Principal Mary Walters, followed the luau dinner.

Administration

Mary Walters was appointed principal of this new high school on June 10, 2008, and began selecting staff and determining the school's overarching goals. District Superintendent Stan Scheer said, "We are excited about Mary's leadership at Murrieta Mesa High School and we look for her to establish a premier high school educational experience for the future students of Murrieta Mesa High School."

One of Mrs. Walter's early decisions was to offer a career track that would include culinary arts and expand the world languages program to include Chinese. Martina Beach-Hedges was the first assistant principal, working with counselors Erika Bennett and Adriana Alarcon to help organize the opening of school. This leadership team worked long hours to get everything ready for students on the first day of school.

Curriculum

In addition to the district-approved curriculum, students at Mesa have the option in their junior and senior year of several career pathways: Business/Culinary, Engineering, Liberal Studies/Education, Medical, and Visual/Performing Arts.

Extracurricular activities include ASL, AVID, Ballet Folklorico, band, creative writing, dance, debate, fashion, drama, robotics, Rotary, poetry, and paintball—a few of the many offerings.

A unique program at Mesa is the Digital Oasis technology center where students, teachers, and parents can create photo collages, posters, calendars, photo books, banners, and more. Funds raised through the Digital Oasis help support the Professional Sales class and Oasis Program. A partnership with Hewlett Packard provided the equipment for the Oasis.

Chamber of Commerce

The school district and Murrieta Mesa created a partnership with the Murrieta Chamber of Commerce, providing the Chamber with office space. In return, the chamber agreed to help Mesa students get internships, provide guest lecturers, and participate in other activities.

Library

Because of the financial issues faced by the school district, there was no money budgeted for library books for this new school. Other schools in the district sent books that were extra copies, but this was not enough. Jeanne Nelson, District Library/Media Services Coordinator, worked with Library Technician Lisa Rivera, setting a goal of 5,000 books by the end of the first year, with district-financed databases for research.

Thanks to an outpouring of community and district support and a newspaper article written by reporter and district teacher Carl Love, by the end of the year there were more than 10,000 library books on the shelves in the Mesa library.

Athletics

Like the other high schools, Mesa began with ninth and tenth graders, so the athletic program was built in stages. By the time the school had their first senior class, the athletic program was well underway.

First graduating class

Murrieta Mesa High School awarded diplomas to 348 students in the class of 2012, the first graduating class. Eighty-seven percent of the graduates planned to attend college.

"Not many people get to say that they're the first person to graduate from their high school," eighteen-year-old Josh Stark told Michelle Klampe of the Press Enterprise. "It was a chance for a new beginning."

Principal Mary Walters dedicated the ceremony to Britt Rees, the school district Director of Construction, who had died suddenly and unexpectedly only a month before at age 51. Mr. Rees had overseen the construction of Murrieta Mesa High School from start to finish and his efforts helped get it completed despite numerous obstacles.

The school's tower will be named for Mr. Rees, according to

Superintendent Stan Scheer.

The following year on June 5, the 565 members of the Class of 2013 graduated. These students were the first to complete all four years at the campus that opened in 2009. Superintendent Pat Kelley told the graduates they may experience failures along the way, and should use those experiences to their advantage.

Facilities

The sixty-two acre campus has eighty-two classrooms, a library, administration offices, and a 750-seat performing arts theater. Athletic facilities include a stadium, pool complex, varsity and junior varsity baseball and softball fields, tennis courts, basketball courts, sand volleyball court, and handball courts.

And the story is not over....

Sykes Elementary School is scheduled to open when issues regarding a bridge across Murrieta Creek are solved.

Superintendents

Despite being a school district since the late 1800's, as of 2014 Murrieta has had only five superintendents. The principals joked once in an Administrative Council meeting that to become superintendent in Murrieta, you had to have a one-syllable first name (or nickname), and so it seemed: Van, Tate, Chet, Stan, and Pat. Each one of them came into the position facing specific challenges and each had the leadership skills needed for that time.

Charles van de Wetering

The first superintendent, Charles van de Wetering ("Van"), was hired in 1971 as principal at the same time that the district hired a fifth teacher. A teaching staff of five allowed him to become principal/superintendent. During his tenure, the size of the teaching staff steadily increased as the district grew dramatically.

The district also faced a number of challenges: they fought off a takeover by the Elsinore School District, they unified as the Murrieta Valley Unified School District, and they started building schools. During this time Alta Murrieta, Avaxat, E. Hale Curran, and Rail Ranch elementary schools, Shivela Middle School, and Murrieta Valley High School were opened, though permanent buildings would come later for all of them.

To make all this happen, classrooms were leased or purchased or built, and recruiting trips brought newly hired teachers from across the country. Budget was a constant issue, since funding was determined by the number of students in attendance during the prior year. Technology was just starting to be used in schools, and both teachers and students learned together how to use the limited programs available at the time. There was no Internet, yet.

Van was not afraid to express his opinion, but checked facts before making decisions. Dave Hutt recalls that in 1989 the media reported an environmental scare story about Alar sprayed on apples, which were served to children in district schools. Van called the state department of agriculture for information and learned he was the only school person to call their office to check the facts, out of 1,056 school districts in California at that time. Apples stayed on the menu for student lunches.

Donna Brantly had served as Van's secretary and business manager for many years, but handling both jobs became too much. Chris Hanson was hired as the superintendent's secretary, and Mrs. Brantly became the Assistant Superintendent of Business Services..

The rapidly growing district-level staff needed room to work, so Van led the move to a district office building on the corner of Plum and Ivy (now Murrieta Day Spa). In addition to the superintendent's office, this building housed the growing Business Services, Human Resources, and Educational Services staffs, plus a team of consultants who would oversee the planning and construction of the new high school.

However, there was no room for the Maintenance, Grounds, Facilities, and Transportation departments, which occupied rental buildings elsewhere in the city. For a while, the buses parked in a lot near the corner of Jefferson and Ivy, where the Maintenance and Transportation staff shared a mobile home/office parked there. The Facilities staff occupied a house on Ivy Street, not too far away.

In 1991 Van retired, to pursue a dream of living on his boat. The school community held a large farewell part at the Town Hall, and it was packed with well-wishers who shared stories, poems, and pictures of the many years Van had led the Murrieta School District.

Tate Parker

In 1991 Dr. Tate Parker was hired to replace Van. For a while Chris Hanson continued to work as the superintendent's secretary, helped by Norma Cunnington. When Ms. Hanson left Patsy Wells replaced her. Mrs. Wells had a talent for gourmet cooking and decoration. She began preparing a small meal for the Board members, who arrived in the afternoon and worked until late evening, with no opportunity for an evening meal. Mrs. Wells was especially talented at preparing desserts and the board looked forward to those meals.

Dr. Parker came from Chula Vista, a large district, and began putting together the structure that Murrieta would need. One of his goals was to improve communication within the district and with the community. To make this happen, he formed a number of committees, many of which included community members. Two of the first committees formed were the Strategic Planning Committee and a Mission Statement Committee. These committees created documents that would guide the district for a long time. The mission statement that resulted was inclusive, but not easy to remember, so framed copies appeared in many offices. Dr. Parker also created the District Advisory Committee composed of members of the community, district administrators, and site staff, who would provide input into planning and programs.

As the workload increased, there was a need for more staff in the superintendent's office and one of Dr. Parker's decisions was to hire the first public relations officer, Ellen Larson, to provide information to the community. Dr. Parker also reached out to the PTAs at each school, working with Mrs. Larson to create the PTA Council. Under his leadership, site administrators began working more closely with their PTA or PTC groups and attended the PTA Council meetings.

During Dr. Parker's tenure, the Parent Center was created and staffed. Creekside Continuation High School (1993), Thompson Middle School

(1994), and Tovashal Elementary (1996) were opened, though again in portable buildings or sharing a site.

Dr. Parker left Murrieta in 1996 for a superintendent position in Simi Valley.

Chet Francisco

Dr. Parker was followed by Dr. Chet (Chester) Francisco in 1997, after an extensive search for a new superintendent. Mrs. Wells continued as his administrative assistant. Upper level administrative meetings were changed to Cabinet and Senior Cabinet, the latter composed only of the assistant superintendents and the superintendent. Directors were included in Cabinet meetings, along with any invited guests.

Under Dr. Francisco's leadership, more changes happened in the school district. When he became superintendent, there were ten schools in the district and new students were still arriving. Additional portable buildings were added at most schools and the north parking lot at MVHS was turned into additional classroom space with portables classrooms. Two-story portable classrooms were added on the south side of the school to house the 4,000 plus students now in attendance.

Dr. Francisco oversaw the construction of new schools to help mitigate the crowding. These schools opened in permanent buildings: Cole Canyon (2000), Buchanan (2001), Warm Springs Middle School (2002), Monte Vista Elementary (2003), Vista Murrieta High School (2003), and Antelope Hills Elementary School (2005). Tenaja Canyon Academy was opened on the Creekside campus in 2005.

Mrs. Larson left the public relations position and was replaced with Delores Badillo, but the need to cut funding at the time led to the loss of this position. When the budget improved, Karen Parris took over public relations duties, which now included overseeing the district website and publishing regular newsletters to the community.

Dr. Francisco participated in the grant application that led to funding

100

and construction of the Murrieta Public Library on Town Square.

During his eight-and-a-half years in the district, the number of students increased from 9,680 to approximately 20,000. When he was hired, there were ten schools and when he left there were 17. Dr. Francisco left for a superintendent's position in Chico in 2005.

Stan Scheer

After an intensive search for a new superintendent, Dr. Stan Scheer accepted the position in 2006. For a while Mrs. Wells continued as the superintendent's administrative assistant, but when she left, Dr. Scheer hired Laura Gonzales as Executive Assistant to the Superintendent and Board.

One of Dr. Scheer's first tasks was to revise the Strategic Plan, which included the district mission statement. After eight months of planning and discussion, on March 22, 2007 the Board adopted a new Strategic Plan that clearly defined the district's beliefs and strategic directions. They also adopted a new mission statement: "To Inspire Every Student To Think, To Learn, To Achieve, To Care," and a district focus: "Service And Commitment To Every Student, Every Day."

The rapid growth in the district had abated and the focus turned to programming and state-mandated standards. During Dr. Scheer's tenure, the district Academic Performance Index (API) score increased from 805 in 2006 to 843 in 2011.

However, the school district was not finished building schools. Three more schools, Lisa J. Mails Elementary, Dorothy McIlhinney Middle School, and Murrieta Mesa High School, were completed. This was achieved despite a state freeze on school construction funding that delayed the building of this third high school.

This was also a time of nationwide financial crisis that was particularly acute in California. School district budgets across the state were cut, leading to teacher layoffs and program cuts. In Murrieta, budget cuts meant the loss of $139 million.

Dr. Scheer was firm that the Murrieta district would maintain staffing levels if at all possible. This was achieved through the use of budget reserves, cost-cutting measures, staffing adjustments, leaving some positions unfilled, and salary reductions of 9.66% for all employees.

During his tenure, Dr. Scheer was very involved with the community, attending as many school and community functions as possible. Thanks to his collaboration with the Murrieta Chamber of Commerce, MVUSD was the first school district to have a Chamber of Commerce located at a school site.

In 2012, Dr. Scheer left for a superintendent's position in his home state of Colorado.

Pat Kelley

On October 1, 2012, Pat Kelley became the district's fifth superintendent. Mr. Kelley had a long history with the district. He started working in the district as a teacher at Shivela Middle School and moved on to become the district's first Coordinator of Child Welfare and Attendance. He held a number of different positions in the district, becoming assistant principal at Rail Ranch Elementary School and then principal. His next position was principal of Daniel N. Buchanan Elementary School. Promoted to Director of Human Resources (HR), he returned to the District Office, by then called the District Support Center, or DSC.

Before long, he was promoted to Assistant Superintendent of Human Resources. Briefly he held the position of Deputy Superintendent and then was appointed Superintendent by the Board of Education.

The adventure continues....

Board of Education

Over the years, many members of the community have given their time to serve on the Board of Education. For many years, Murrieta had a three-person Board, which increased to five members in 1982. Their job which has become more challenging as the district has grown in size. Even with dramatic growth, the Board has continued to be a five-person entity.

Board Responsibilities

One of the Board's responsibilities is making sure that the district follows Education Code (Ed Code). Ed Code is a collection of laws that regulate what school districts can and cannot do. It has become increasingly more complex over the years, and filled twelve thick print volumes before becoming an online digital document.

Based on Ed Code, the Board of Education develops local Board Policy and Administrative Regulations. Board Policy is a collection of policies that the district uses to guide how it does business, and Administrative Regulations provide more detail on how those policies are implemented. Whenever Ed Code is revised, which is often, Board Policies and Administrative Regulations must be updated. Since every Board Policy effects student education, they must be carefully considered. Usually the superintendent recommends a new or revised policy to the school board, after it has been reviewed and recommended by the appropriate staff.

Better-known Board member responsibilities include hiring and firing staff, issues with student misbehavior, and student transfers into and out of the district (more in than out, since Murrieta is a respected school district). A darker aspect of overseeing a school district is illustrated by newspaper headlines about school shootings. These have raised concerns about student safety, so measures to protect students have to be in place. In recent years, access to strangers through technology and the issue of on-line bullying have been added to the list of threats to students.

As curriculum changes, new textbooks and instructional materials are adopted following a lengthy review process. New programs and courses are added in response to student needs. All of this requires Board review and approval. The Board must approve all purchases, and the Board also must approve getting rid of obsolete materials.

The Board also oversees a complicated budget involving categories of funding that can only be spent according to legal guidelines. The district budget changes annually because the amount of funding from the State is determined by the legislature and by the number of students in the district. Often money must come from other sources, which includes grants, donations, and school bonds. The Board has always taken a leadership role in getting school bonds on the ballot and encouraging the community to support them.

To help new trustees understand their complex role, the California School Boards Association (CSBA) provides training and holds conferences with information about current issues, laws, and programs. In addition to their official duties, Board members are expected to attend school events and represent the school district in the community. Board members generally enjoy this, seeing how their work has supported students and the community. Most Board meetings include student presentations, employee recognition, and opportunities for community members to address the Board.

Murrieta Board members have had the unique opportunity to participate in the creation of a new school district, overseeing the design, construction, and opening of new schools, as well as creating new programs. For some schools they even selected the mascot and school colors.

Murrieta has a proud history of building excellent schools, hiring capable and talented staff, and providing a quality education for all their students and Board members have contributed immeasurably in making this happen. Over the years, many individuals have served on the Murrieta School Board. While the following is not a complete list, it gives an idea of who these people were and the challenges they faced.

Board members through the years

1898 Oliver W. Miller, Charles Hadsall and William Brown oversaw the addition of a room to the first school, due to an increase in the number of students.

Mr. Miller was station agent at the Murrieta Depot for many years, Mr. Brown was a rancher and dairyman, and Mr. Hadsall was a farmer in the primarily agricultural area that was Murrieta.

1920 T.R. Wickerd, Amos Sykes, and Walter Thompson served on the Board during the construction of Murrieta Grammar School on 2nd Street. They also approved the implementation of different grade levels, a change from the one-room, one-teacher model, and introduced indoor plumbing in the design of this new school.

1956 George Blake, Charles Yoder and George Contrera faced a serious problem: the aging Murrieta Grammar School was declared unsafe and needed to be replaced. They needed money, and thanks to hard work and community support, the first Murrieta school bond was passed for $60,000. These funds, combined with $200,000 from the state, allowed the community to build a larger school.

1958 George Blake, Charles Yoder and George Contreras stayed on the Board and enjoyed the opening of the new Murrieta Elementary School, the first new school in 36 years.

For many years, the small Murrieta School dealt with limited budget, to the extent that the purchase of a new mop for the custodian would be a Board decision.

1965   Charles Yoder, Ann Miller, and Marvin Curran brought their knowledge of business management to the Board.

Charles Yoder owned the farmland Murrieta's third high school would be built on, 44 years later.   Ann Miller was co-owner of the Murrieta Country Market, one of the few Murrieta businesses still around in the 21st century.

Marvin Curran also served as Chief of the volunteer fire department and ran a gas station. Years later he would share his family photos for a book about Murrieta.

1966 Ann Miller, Marvin Curran and Carroll Anderson saw the need for a full-time custodian position. When they voted to create the position, Mr. Curran abstained from voting, and when it passed he immediately resigned his place on the Board to take the job.   Local farmer Curtis Thompson filled his open Board position.

1967 Ann Miller, Charles Yoder, and Curtis Thompson tried to pass a school bond to build a larger auditorium that could be cordoned off into separate classrooms, but the measure failed.

1970   Mike Devitt joined Charles Yoder and Curtis Thompson on the Board. Mr. Devitt worked for Highland Labs at what was then called "the goat farm." In 1982 this became International Immunology Corporation (IIC) producing high quality goat polyclonal antisera.

By this time, there were a dozen major horse breeding farms and track and training centers in Murrieta. These thoroughbred race horse facilities brought affluence to the community and an increase in tax base that made the Murrieta School District much more interesting to neighboring

Elsinore School District.

1971 Curtis Thompson, Mike Devitt, and Kennadine Turner were challenged with preventing the Elsinore School District from unifying and taking over Murrieta Elementary School. The school and community rallied and their determination paid off. Thanks to a massive effort, Murrieta did not get swallowed up by Elsinore.

This was also the year that the Board hired Charles van de Wetering, who became principal/superintendent—the first superintendent-- and provided exemplary leadership during this tumultuous time.

1973 Curtis Thompson, Mike Devitt, and Kennadine Turner continued to serve as trustees on the Board.

In the years prior to Proposition 13 in 1978, according to David Hutt, "the local school district set the tax rate to fund the school. Murrieta School District was the largest district geographically in Riverside County, but one of the smallest in student enrollment."

1978 David Hutt was appointed to the school board, joining Curt Thompson, and Anita "Chick" Williamson.

Mr. Hutt would stay on the Board for the next thirteen years and was instrumental in introducing new programs to the school district and helping plan the K-12 Murrieta district.

1982 The Board increased from three to five members:: Peter Lemke, David Hutt, Andrew Craig, Karen Payne, and John Sullivan.

With this increase from three to five members, the Board was allowed, for the first time, to receive "pay" for their work, up to $120 a month. They voted not to do this.

1984 New trustees Andrew Craig and Gary Whisenand joined David Hutt, Peter Lemke, and George Parrott.

A highlight of this Board's actions was bringing in technology. George

Parrott, Donna Brantly, and David Hutt went shopping and purchased the district's first computer.

1987 Patty Julian, David Hutt, Austin Linsley, Peter Lemke, and Evelyn Henning wanted to expand the subjects taught and one of their priorities was providing music, Spanish, and art lessons at every elementary school.

This board consisted of sixty percent foreign-born naturalized citizens. Mr. Lemke came from Germany, Mrs. Henning from the Philippines and Mr. Hutt from England.

Board meetings at this time were long, often lasting into the following morning, but everyone who wanted to provide input had the opportunity to speak, and every item on the agenda was addressed.

1988 Patty Julian, David Hutt, Austin Linsley, Peter Lemke, and Evelyn Henning were Re-elected, and faced a big challenge: Temecula Union School District wanted to unify, which meant Murrieta would become part of Elsinore or Temecula. This was an unpopular idea, given Murrieta's many years as its own K-8 school district. Mr. Van and the Board came up with a third alternative, creation of the K-12 Murrieta Valley Unified School District. The ballot included this option, along with a $38 million bond to build a Murrieta high school. Both measures passed

1990 Patty Julian, David Hutt, Austin Linsley, Evelyn Henning, and Jim Keown immediately faced the district's net challenge. Dramatic growth had begun, with new students arriving daily. The Board struggled with facilities issues, applying to the state for emergency portable classrooms, and purchasing land for new schools with existing developer fees. Funding was needed to build permanent schools for Avaxat, Alta Murrieta, Rail Ranch, E. Hale Curran, Tovashal and Shivela.

The state was broke, and dependent on passage of an upcoming statewide facilities bond to provide its share of the money. Statewide,

California added 230,000 new students, and classrooms were desperately needed.

If that wasn't enough to worry about, Eastern Municipal Water District (EMWD) had built a large water storage tank behind and above the Avaxat school site. The Board was concerned about student safety if this water tank broke open due to an earthquake or other disaster. So the entire board went to inspect this water tank. Board member Jim Keown, a contractor, discovered that the earthen berm around the tank had not been compacted properly. The Board threatened to sue EMWD if they did not fix this—and they did.

The Board also began planning year-round schooling, to be implemented first at Avaxat and E. Hale Curran schools, and then other schools. Year-round scheduling was a state requirement if the district was to remain eligible for state matching funds for new school facilities.

1991 Austin Linsley was joined by new Board members Judy Rosen, Shauna Briggs, Margi Wray, and Alan Christenson.

These Board members brought a wealth of experience in real estate, budgeting, and knowledge of the school district and community. The community trusted their judgment, and they were re-elected for many years.

Margi Wray would continue as a member of the school board for twenty years, which may be the longest term for any Murrieta trustee.

After twenty years with the district, Superintendent van de Wetering retired, and the Board conducted a search to find a replacement. Dr. Tate Parker was hired and tasked with providing the structure needed for a soon-to-be large school district.

1997 Kenneth Dickson was elected to the Board, joining Austin Linsley, Judy Rosen, Margi Wray, and Alan Christenson.

Mr. Dickson, a lawyer, provided a perspective on the legal aspects of Board business. Superintendent Tate Parker left the district for another position, and the Board completed the search for a new superintendent,

109

hiring Dr. Chet Francisco.

At that time, all district support services were housed in rented or leased facilities, and the Board saw a need for a permanent District Office. In 1999 they planned to build two facilities: a Transportation/Support facility for Maintenance, Grounds, Operations, and Facilities/Planning, and a separate Administrative Office building that would house Business Services, Educational Service, Human Resources, and the Superintendent's office.

Plans to build the Administrative Office building in the new City of Murrieta Civic Center fell through, so the district decided to build a 40,000 square foot tilt-up building on the property intended for Transportation/Support. This building would house all district departments and provide a place to park the school buses.

Mr. Christenson moved away from the Murrieta area, and was replaced on the Board by Scott Attebery.

Mr. Attebery had an identical twin brother who worked for the police department, causing confusion in those who didn't realize there were two Attebery brothers.

2001 Austin Linsley, Judy Rosen, Kenneth Dickson and Margi Wray, and new Board member Kris Thomasian faced issues with school funding. Grading for VMHS was completed and construction would begin the following year, but the $32,900,000 in state funds was on hold. The Murrieta voters had passed a bond in 1998, and $21,673,000 from that was earmarked for this school.

This year the first California High School Exit exam was administered, and 85% of the students taking the language arts portion of the test past, while 65% passed the math portion.

Mrs. Thomasian was very active in the PTA, in addition to owning her own business. Her husband served on the city council, which helped increase communication between the school district and the city.

2002 Austin Linsley, Judy Rosen, Kenneth Dickson, Margi Wray, and

Scott Attebery saw the completion of the long-awaited District Support Center. The Board, which had always met in Murrieta Elementary's multipurpose room or the city hall board room finally had its own room for meetings. With a kitchen nearby, the superintendent's secretary, Patsy Wells, created delicious food to help the board members stay energized throughout their meeting.

Warm Springs Middle School opened with 675 sixth and seventh graders. At MVHS, 4,200 students enrolled, packed into a school intended for less than half as many.

To provide more classrooms on available space, the district added two-story 12-plex buildings at Murrieta Valley High School and Thompson Middle School.

The district put Measure K on the ballot, for $40.4 million to purchase land and build two schools: a third high school and a fourth middle school. It would also build a pool and stadium for VMHS, and was passed by the voters.

2003 New member Paul Diffley joined Austin Linsley, Kris Thomasian, Kenneth Dickson, and Margi Wray. Mr. Diffley, a former art teacher, focused on visual and performing arts, keeping this as a priority during his tenure on the Board.

Vista Murrieta High School and Monte Vista Elementary School opened.

2005 Kris Thomasian, Ken Dickson, Margi Wray, and Paul Diffley welcomed Robin Crist to the Board.

Mrs. Crist, a business owner, brought her business experience and years of serving on the PTA board to help guide Board decisions.

Dr. Chet Francisco left the district for another superintendent position, and the Board began a search for new district leadership. The following year, they hired Dr. Stan Scheer from Colorado.

For seven years, there were no changes to the membership of the

Board.

In 2006 the district passed Measure E, a $120 million bond measure, to fully fund Murrieta Mesa High School and provide funding for numerous other major school improvement projects throughout the district over the next 10 years.

They also weathered the economic crisis, working with administrators, teachers and classified unions to implement budget cuts that would not result in a loss of staffing.

2012 Membership in the Board changed, with new member Barbara Muir joining Paul Diffley, Kris Thomasian, Ken Dickson, and Robin Crist.

Mrs. Muir, a former teacher in the Murrieta district, brought her years of teaching experience to help in the decision-making process.

These board members enjoyed a long-awaited upturn in the economy and some increased educational funding. At the same time, the nation and California adopted new Common Core Standards that mandated new ways of teaching and assessing student learning. Among other impacts, digital testing required that many more computers be available for student use.

What dramatic changes have taken place in 128 years! The district grew from a small one-room school serving fourteen students to a district of 20,000-plus students in twenty different schools. The many people who served on the Board of Education during these years worked hard and faced many challenges. Through their commitment, expertise, and genuine caring, they helped create the great school district that now exists.

Business Services

For many years, Business Services could hardly be called by such a formal title, since one person handled it all: purchasing, receiving, accounting, clerical tasks, and anything else that needed doing.

In 1965, that person was Carolyn Donaho, who was handling these duties on a part-time basis. When she learned she had cancer she recommended Donna Brantly, a friend who was a bookkeeper, as her replacement. So begins the story of the Business Services Department.

Donna Brantly, from ledgers to computers

That year, 1965, Teacher/Principal Gordon Harmon hired Donna Brantly as a part-time bookkeeper. She also worked at other bookkeeping jobs in the community.

At the time Mrs. Brantly was hired, the School Board handled the creation of the annual district budget. After learning what goes into a school district budget, Mrs. Brantly submitted a proposed budget and the Board members were delighted. They put her in charge of creating the budget and she became the business manager. Later her title was expanded to "Business Manager/Administrative Secretary," in lieu of a raise.

According to Board member Dave Hutt, Mrs. Brantly broke down extremely complex budget numbers into a format that parents, reporters, and board members could understand. This was not easy, because a school district budget is composed of entitlements, education code funds, federal grants, and other sources of money, each with its own budget code and different rules for how each can be spent. Mrs. Brantly would continue to provide budget numbers for the school district until she retired 25 years later.

In the early 1970's Marie Curran and Jackie Shield were hired as office workers to help with the steadily increasing paperwork. Mrs. Curran also did playground supervision and if a teacher was out, she served as their substitute. Cindy Crismon was hired as a part-time secretary in 1981. In 1988 Mrs. Brantley was named Assistant Superintendent of Business Services, the first person in the district with that title. The increasing workload meant that more people were needed to handle the work, so the district hired Vickie Henry as a personnel clerk and accountants Ron Peace and Barbara Carver.

The Riverside County Office of Education (RCOE) oversaw the finances of schools in the county, providing support and training as needed. One of the changes they made was to begin using computers to manage financial records, replacing the ledger books previously used. RCOE hosted a server and provided the Nexus accounting program to each school district and each district used computer terminals to access RCOE.

There were problems with this early technology, which depended on phone lines: distance and weather. When it rained or there were heavy winds, the computer terminals were likely to go down and work stopped. This was very frustrating to the people using this system, because there was always a huge stack of paperwork to be input and when the connection was down, there was nothing anyone could do but wait for it to come back up again. This was a frequent problem.

Roland Werner is hired

When Mrs. Brantly retired in 1990, her replacement was Dr. Roland Werner. He came into the district with a vision for Business Services that included much more than was currently in place and set about implementing it. One of his ideas was a central warehouse, allowing bulk purchasing and rapid in-district delivery for school and custodial supplies.

Dr. Werner hired JoAnn Dailey as his secretary. She would continue as secretary for the four assistant superintendents who succeeded Dr. Werner.

Dr. Werner needed a purchasing agent to implement his plans and for a while Ron Peace performed double duties, accounting and purchasing, without any support staff. As a result, his office soon filled with stacks of purchase orders. He was delighted when Julie April was hired in 1990 as the first full-time purchasing agent so he could return to doing one job again.

Ms. April's introduction to the rapidly growing district began when she went to see her new office. Warehouse facilities occupied several small commercial buildings on Hobie Circle, south of Murrieta. To get to Hobie Circle, Ms. April was given directions at the District Office: go to Jefferson Street, turn right and then turn left on Date Street. It seemed simple, but the sign for Date Street had been knocked down and in this pre-GPS/cell phone world, Ms. April spent several frustrating hours finding the building where she would be working.

Linda Diaz was hired as the purchasing clerk and she and Ms. April worked to get purchase orders out and create some order to the stacks of paperwork representing orders submitted and received. Before they could start, their first task was getting rid of the many spiders who had found a home in that warehouse building!

Ms. April was able to bring a system to ordering materials for new schools, creating a 'laundry list' of what most teachers needed in their classroom at each grade. This included the size of chairs and tables needed at each grade level, and furniture for the library, teacher workroom, and offices.

Over the years there were changes in the purchasing staff. Mrs. Diaz left the purchasing department for a school secretary position and was replaced by bus driver Debbie Venegas. When Mrs. Venegas took another Business Services job, she was replaced by Taryn Orellana. As the workload increased, the purchasing staff increased with the addition of Martha Reina and Joanyn Pearce-Miller.

After many years and many new schools, in 2006 Ms. April opted for retirement. When Ms. April retired, Mrs. Orellana left and was replaced by Nick Newkirk. The next Purchasing Agent was Rebecca Abeyta, who had worked at Riverside County Office of Education. Mrs. Abeyta did not stay long and in 2008 Robin Haigh, formerly of Food Services, assumed the duties of this position. Mrs. Haigh retired two years later and former principal Chuck Jones, who was serving as Director of Facilities Planning, took on the additional duties of Purchasing Agent.

By this time, the workload in purchasing had reduced dramatically, since the district was no longer growing or opening new schools.

Reprographics

Dr. Werner's other dream was a reprographics center, providing low-cost, quick turnaround printing for the entire district. In the 1990's, options for getting printing done in the Murrieta area were limited, expensive, and often slow. When the District Office moved to new facilities on Beckman Court, the building included a warehouse area and a large reprographics room. Long-time employee Marie Curran was hired as the reprographics clerk, running several large copy machines and filling printing requests. She also delivered mail when needed. As Marie said, she "did a little bit of everything."

Handling heavy boxes of paper became too much for Mrs. Curran, a smallish woman who was close to retirement. She was moved to the receptionist position at the district office and Dorothy Flores was hired to take over the printing duties. The number and size of machines in the reprographics area increased. One machine put covers on workbooks, another machine folded and stapled consumable readers for younger students, and other machines printed, collated and stapled high speed copies.

Mrs. Flores could not do all of this by herself and got part-time help. For a while the workload was so big that Mrs. Flores had full-time helpers. Reprographics printed order forms, board agendas (which were delivered to the board members by warehouse staff), student handbooks, worksheets, letters to parents, and many other documents that were used in a large district before the Internet.

Warehouse and mail delivery

When Ms. April was hired, she was given the additional duty of overseeing district mail delivery to the school sites. At that time, Marie Curran was delivering mail to the schools and Bill Racz had been hired to work in the warehouse. When Mrs. Curran went to Reprographics, Mr. Racz handled the warehouse, mail delivery, and took over the inventory of fixed assets (large expensive equipment). The district soon got too large for one person to receive deliveries, maintain stocks of materials, and deliver daily in-district mail, so Ben Holmes was hired to work with Mr. Racz. After many years, Mr. Racz retired and Glenn Noorigian was hired to replace him.

Mr. Racz told of one (of many) memorable experiences. He had been sent to one of the schools to pick up textbooks the district no longer used, and expected to find them neatly boxed. Instead, they were stacked in the multipurpose room and had to be moved before lunch. He was driving a "stake-bed" truck, with a short wood fence around the truck bed. After a heated discussion with the principal, Mr. Racz loaded his truck with stacks of loose books and drove down Jefferson Avenue approximately five miles to the District Office. In his wake he left a trail of textbooks lining the road behind him.

The warehouse soon expanded from being temporary storage of materials for the school sites and became a supply warehouse. Ms. April set up stocks of school supplies, which were less expensive when purchased in bulk. She found out what materials most teachers needed at each grade, how many were likely to be used, created a catalog of these items, and ordered enough so there would be some on hand after the school year began. Getting the orders sorted, boxed, and delivered to the school sites was a challenging task!

CAL Cards and phones

As the district continued to grow, technology changed and other duties were added to the Purchasing Department. Ms. April worked with the administrators and cabinet to implement credit cards (CAL Cards) to expedite purchasing small items and take advantage of time-sensitive pricing.

Another change in technology was cell phones, which soon replaced radios as the communication tool of choice for administrators. Someone had to keep track of the phones, plans, and billing, and these duties also fell to the Purchasing Department.

Not the least of problems was the increasing amount of paper records that had to be kept on hand for many years, according to law. Initially these were stored in the warehouse, but they soon outgrew available space, even with the construction of a small upstairs storage area. The district found a company that would store these materials and provide them as needed.

Food Services grows

When Ms. Beaulieu left the district in 1998, Robin Haigh took over as Supervisor of Food Services. She was promoted to Director when another reorganization of departments took place and Food Services was moved back to the Business Services division. Having worked in the program since 1992, Mrs. Haigh knew all the people and understood the regulations and bookkeeping, all of which had increased in complexity. She had no idea how complicated the job would become!

Trying to keep up with student growth was a challenge district-wide, and Food Services was no exception. At E. Hale Curran, the fastest growing school in the district during the first year, a classroom was used as a lunchroom. However, by spring break they needed the room for another class of students, so lunches for the rest of the year were served under the hallway cover, outside, and on rainy days the food carts were moved into the staff lounge.

Everyone in the district was involved with Food Services in one way or another. People had to eat, someone had to prepare and serve food, and things didn't always happen as they were supposed to. One of the stories from those early days comes from Avaxat Elementary School when Tovashal Elementary School was sharing the same campus. When it rained, there was soon a small river running through campus between the permanent school and the old portable buildings, where the Tovashal students' classrooms were located. Lynn Farmer was the Tovashal school secretary when the school opened and recalls those rainy days. One day when it was pouring rain she, the principal, and the custodian served lunches from the teacher workroom. Mr. Jones, the principal, went back and forth between the two sides of the campus with lunch carts, fording the "river" and getting soaked in the process, but the students all got lunch.

The food service staff at each school was small, so whenever there were absences this caused problems and district and site personnel would be called to help out. Everyone, including principals, handed out food to hungry youngsters whenever they were needed.

Ron Peace recalls when there was a shortage of staff at Murrieta Elementary School to set up and serve lunch. The Business Services staff answered the call for help, and Mr. Peace, Barbara Carver, and Assistant Superintendent Roland Werner went to the school where they "probably broke a multitude of food health safety rules that day." Canned peaches were on the menu and Mr. Peace began opening the large cans with the high speed can opener, with disastrous results, slinging peach syrup all over the kitchen. Then he and Mrs. Carver started serving food to students and Dr. Werner, a large bearded man, began talking to the youngsters waiting in line, telling them what an excellent meal they were getting that day. "The most delicious tater tots and chicken nuggets they'd ever have," he said dramatically. Mr. Peace says the baffled looks on the faces of the students were priceless.

Food preparation is more dangerous than it looks. Cheryl Dufresne remembers being called as an emergency substitute when Suzie Cooke, fixing lunch at Murrieta Elementary School, cut off the end of her finger with a food processor. Mrs. Cooke had been making pickle relish for tuna salad, and the relish was a gory mess. The kids got tuna salad with no pickles that day. According to Mrs. Dufresne, Mrs. Cooke made "the best Mac and Cheese back in the day..."

Issues with how money was handled at the sites continued to be a problem, and not only in Food Services. Throughout the district schools had different methods of handling any money that was collected and sometimes their record-keeping was pretty casual. Dr. Werner worked hard to implement standard procedures and Mrs. Haigh created ways of ensuring accurate record-keeping from the site Food Services staff.

Originally food was purchased locally, but the size of the district meant that this was no longer possible, which brought complications of a different type. One memorable Friday afternoon, late, a large load of government commodity frozen food was delivered to the District Office on Beckman Court. This was too late to get it delivered to MVHS, where it could be kept frozen. Mrs. Haigh was able to get Smart and Final, located close by at that time, to store the food over the weekend in their freezers.

When Mrs. Haigh took over the Food Services operation, she began making many changes, implementing healthier menus and salad bars at all the schools in addition to removing soda sales before it was mandated by the government. Food service and nutrition laws changed, mandating a district-wide nutrition plan and precise monitoring of the nutrients served to students. The new government regulations were intended to reduce childhood obesity. The new laws regulated the type of snacks that could be sold in vending machines. Soda machines, which had generated a lot of money for each school, were banned from all schools.

These changes resulted in a big decline in sales at the middle and high schools. A district-wide computerized food service program was implemented at all the school sites which tracked each student's funds and meals served. This information was transferred to the central Food Service Office for monitoring. In addition, the program also provided nutrition analysis for the foods served to ensure the menus were in compliance with the new regulations.

PTA parents could no longer sell cookies or cake to raise funds during school hours. This was not a popular change with many people and one of the unexpected consequences was that children began carrying the snacks they liked, including canned soda, to school in their backpacks.

Mrs. Haigh decided to retire in 2008, only to be offered the job of Purchasing Agent. She put off retirement for a while to take this job, and Jill Lancaster was hired to replace her as Director of Food Services.

Transportation

For many years the district did not provide bus service, though there were many requests. State funding did not cover the expense of operating and maintaining buses, and the Board would not take funds intended for the classroom to pay for buses.

Bus transportation was finally provided in 1970, supported by bus pass fees, but managed by the district. Marvin Curran was the first bus driver and handled all the maintenance himself. This included changing tires and oil, cleaning and repairs. He even hand-lettered "Murrieta School District" on the sides of the first district bus. Mr. Curran was also the Murrieta Fire Protection District's Fire Chief, so if there was a fire, the school bus might not be picking up students because Mr. Curran would be out with the firemen. He served as the district bus driver for fourteen years.

Providing bus transportation to school was a challenge, because the school district is geographically large, 167.5 square miles, extending west to the San Juan Capistrano School District, north to Elsinore and Perris, east to Hemet, and south to Temecula.

Other challenges to providing bus transportation included the annual rainy season with flooded roads; seasonal fog; and fires that also resulted in road closures. Patty Norcutt, the Director of Transportation when the district began growing, personally drove the bus routes early in the morning to make sure that the buses could get through.

As the district grew, the number of school buses increased, especially during the days of dramatic growth. The district also began providing free bus transportation for students. Transportation became part of Maintenance, Operations, Transportation and Construction (MOTC), supervised by Assistant Superintendent Chuck Depreker.

When Mrs. Norcutt left, there were some changes in staffing and Dave Kempf became the Director of Transportation. Jack Martin worked with him as Supervisor until retiring. When Mr. Kempf left, Mr. Martin came back out of retirement and served again as the transportation director. Barbara Ortiz-Munson became Supervisor.

Reorganization of the district moved transportation under Business Services. One of the reasons for this change was the decision to again charge for student transportation. State funding had never covered the cost of purchasing and maintaining school buses or paying and training drivers. Finally, the Board felt the district had to charge students to ride the bus, to make up the increasing difference between transportation income and expenses. One expected consequence of this decision was an increased number of family members who drove students to school, resulting in more traffic around each school twice a day. However, the increasing number of students in the district helped keep the number of students riding the buses at about the same level.

Risk Management and Safe Schools

A desire to provide a safe workplace resulted in the creation of the Risk Management department, and John Preston was hired to manage this program. Over the years, this program has expanded to include district insurance programs (workers' compensation, property and liability and employee insurance benefits). Other functions include coordination of employee safety training programs and coordinating property/liability control activities. Additional staff included Christina Hill and Felice Quisol, Risk Management Specialists.

Another program targeting safety was the Safe Schools Unit under the direction of Wayne Sakamoto.. This program later included oversight of Safe Schools Plans, Emergency Preparedness and the Home to School Safety Patrols.

Payroll and attendance

The Payroll Department was originally part of Personnel, with Cheryl Glasser and Vickie Henry as the only payroll staff. Mrs. Glasser left the district and Mrs. Henry began working with Dr. Toukonen as an administrative assistant. Cindy Baldwin was hired as Payroll Supervisor, working in that position for many years. Payroll added technicians AnnMarie Lopez, Alyssa Breckon, and Susan Corby. Nick Newkirk was hired to replace Mrs. Corby when she left.

School district payroll is very complicated. Employees work different hours on different pay schedules, with different benefits provided, depending on their hours. Some are salaried, some are hourly, and for some overtime and weekends are paid differently. The district employs many substitutes in both support and teaching positions, and these are paid different rates. There are also employees who are on paid leaves, such as maternity leave, and there is also pay when an employee is sick.

When salaries and benefits changes are negotiated by the unions, these changes need to be made in the records, so that employees get a correct paycheck. There are also "step and column" increases in pay for experience and/or additional education, which also mean changes in payroll records..

If that isn't complicated enough, there are stipends for teachers who perform extra duties, and there is extra pay for coaches, with different levels of coaching pay for different sports.

Perhaps the most frustrating business services job is keeping track of how many students are in school at any given time. This is critically important for a school district, because the amount of money the state provides for the district depends on attendance numbers. Teachers need to provide accurate counts of students in class each period of the day, this information has to get to the site attendance technician, who in turn has to get accurate numbers to the District Office. Any inefficiency means that the district loses money, and in education, every dollar is important.

Additional staffing

During the district's peak growth years, all departments added personnel to handle the workload. When Stacy Coleman was hired as Assistant Superintendent of Business Services, one of his first hires was Stacy Fisher (Matusek) who became Director of Fiscal Services. Other staff included Jan Baltikauski, Accountant/Budget Analyst; and Dawn Cherry, Accounting Supervisor.

As growth slowed, there were some reductions in support positions in Business Services, but the size of the district meant that there was still plenty of work to do.

Facilities and Construction

In the early years of the district, the Board of Education and the superintendent managed facilities, maintenance, and transportation, none of which was too complicated in a one-school district. There had been no school construction since building the new multipurpose room and remodeling the old multipurpose room into two kindergarten classrooms in 1985. And transportation? The district began providing bus transportation for students in 1970, with one bus and one driver. But things were changing......

Planning for growth

In the early 1980s the Board had no experience in dealing with what would be a tsunami of students—no one did. When the first wave of students began arriving in 1986, it was clear that they needed another school.

There was a complication: school districts did not receive funds for new students until after those students had arrived. The district had to provide classrooms, teachers, and teaching materials for students who had not moved into the community yet, and the question was how to pay for those things? And nobody could provide accurate information on how many students might be moving into the area, or when they would arrive.

The only option was to create a school with portable classroom buildings, on land the district purchased. As additional students arrived, more portable buildings could be leased or purchased.

To keep up with the steadily increasing workload and rapid changes, the Board began meeting weekly, holding long marathon meetings that sometimes lasted into the morning hours. They needed to do this because they were doing the work that would normally be done by full-time assistant superintendents and their staffs. They had no assistant superintendents, or staffs, but they did the best they could.

Tom Tooker is hired

The Board needed advice, so in 1988 they hired Tom Tooker as a consultant and retained Marshall Krupp, of Community Systems Associates. The following year the Board hired Mr. Tooker as the district's first Assistant Superintendent of Facilities Services.

Mr. Tooker and Mr. Krupp helped solve their two biggest problems, predicting enrollment and paying for facilities for incoming students. They developed a method of finding out how many new students would be arriving, when they would arrive, and where, using aerial photographs of the district. With these photographs, Mr. Tooker was able to provide weekly enrollment projections that were very accurate.

In addition to state school funds, the district received developer fees. This was money paid by contractors building new housing, and intended to help mitigate the impact of new residents on the school district. The fees were a minimal amount and did not begin to meet the needs. It was Mr. Krupp's idea to sue Riverside County for increased developer fees, which were desperately needed to build temporary schools.

Temporary schools were all that the district could provide, partly because they needed classrooms immediately for incoming students and partly because building that many permanent schools, all at once, would be impossibly expensive. Added to their problems, there was a building boom in Murrieta and the price of land had soared. The district had to purchase land for each new school and this meant at least ten acres for an

126

elementary school, 25 for a middle school, and 35-40 for a high school.

Thankfully, after a complicated legal battle, the district lawsuit for increased developer fees was successful. With these additional funds, the district could provide portable classrooms and instructional materials for the students who were arriving daily.

They still needed money for permanent schools because those portable classrooms would not last forever. Again Mr. Tooker led the way. He lobbied in Sacramento for Murrieta's share of limited state school building funds and was successful, getting $26,000,000.00 for the district.

Mr. Tooker had a quirky sense of humor. One of his pranks was putting a department store mannequin under a desk in the Facilities offices after everyone had left for the day, with the trouser-clad legs sticking out. The first person arriving at work the next morning discovered the mannequin and was terrified, believing it was a dead man. Some explaining was in order!

Chuck Depreker joins the staff

In 1989 Chuck Depreker was hired as Director of Maintenance, Operations, and Transportation. Mr. Depreker was a hard-working, get-it-done retired Marine, and learned by doing. He was one of many newly hired people that year and finding office space for all the new staff was a problem. The District Office at the corner of Nutmeg and Ivy (later Murrieta Day Spa) was not large enough, so other space had to be rented. Construction and planning found a house on Ivy Street for their offices, while purchasing and the warehouse rented commercial units on Hobie Circle.

Mr. Depreker's office was in a mobile home parked on a lot on Jefferson, near the intersection with Los Alamos Road. The buses parked in a dirt area behind this building and bus maintenance was done under a shade structure. Some of the bus drivers were young mothers and they brought their preschool children who stayed there while mom drove her route, so sometimes it seemed pretty chaotic.

127

They needed someplace to store the various construction plans, which were thick rolls of maps, and the shower stall in the mobile home was perfect for this purpose. Lori Noorigian worked as the secretary and Denise Umphress served as receptionist, greeting the steady stream of people who came there daily, including the bus drivers.

When Mr. Tooker left the district, Mr. Depreker was promoted to Assistant Superintendent of Maintenance, Operations, Transportation and Construction (MOTC). By then, the District Office had been established on Beckman Court, but Mr. Depreker preferred his original office, citing the increase in interruptions if they moved in with the other departments. When the District Office on McAlby Court was planned, he made sure that the Facilities Department had a separate entrance.

More schools means more staffing, facilities use

Charlene Stone (Boone), formerly a clerk at Avaxat, was added to the facilities staff to keep track of community growth. Her job was predicting where new students would live and estimating how many students this would be. She even drove around Murrieta to the new housing tracts, counting how many houses were being built, what size they were, and how many were occupied. The district needed this information to provide classrooms, supplies and teachers, and Mrs. Stone was incredibly accurate in predicting the number of students who would arrive for the first day of school each year.

The department expanded as the district kept building schools. Jeff Boone was hired as Director of Construction and Randy White came on board to keep track of the many plans and maps and changes that the ongoing school construction necessitated. Ron Peace moved into the department to handle contracts and budget. Brett Rees was added as Director of Planning and Construction and later Principal Chuck Jones would join the department, helping ensure that new schools would support the needs of teachers and staff.

The school district buildings and athletic fields provided attractive

128

facilities for local organizations and athletic teams. State law-- the "Civic Center Act"—and Board Policy supported sharing school facilities with community groups. As the community and district grew, scheduling and overseeing this became such a big job that someone needed to do it full time, and Judy Gould became that person.

The community continued to grow, facility use increased, and anyone wanting to use a particular facility needed to get it booked almost a year in advance! For the drama teachers, this was especially challenging, because they needed the heavily-booked performing arts centers for both rehearsals and performances. They had to leave their sets up, often around other group's use of the stage.

Year-round scheduling and maintenance

When the district went to year-round schools, this presented a new problem to the Maintenance staff. They used to be able to clean rooms, shampoo carpets, and make repairs during the summer when students were gone. With students in school all the time—and sometimes only a weekend between tracks—they could no longer do this. Don Burkes, Maintenance Supervisor, and Chuck Ekstrom, Director, Maintenance, Operations and Grounds, came up with a solution: the night crew was created. This team went to schools after school hours, cleaning and doing maintenance.

The maintenance crew also worked during the Christmas break, but ran into a problem with the library staff. During the summer, the middle school and high school libraries were stacked with textbooks, so it was impossible to clean the carpet, and during Christmas break, the library staff was often doing catch-up work, including inventory and book repair. Mr. Burkes worked with each library individually on scheduling cleaning and repairs.

By 2001, Maintenance was taking care of more than a million square feet of facilities, including ongoing repairs, cleaning, painting, and upgrading.

Grounds

The Grounds Department was created as new schools and playing fields were built, requiring regular maintenance that included pest control, weed abatement, and irrigation over miles of PVC pipe. The department grew dramatically as the district expanded and by 2001, school district buildings occupied 207 acres of land, each with landscaping, lawns, trees, and many with playing fields.

A highlight of those earlier years was striping the football field in red, white and blue for Murrieta Valley High School's Homecoming game.

There are sometimes unpleasant surprises to this work. Beautiful bushes used for landscaping at Shivela Middle School turned out to be popular habitat for rats and had to be removed. The grounds along Los Alamos Road by Rail Ranch Elementary School kept the irrigation staff stumped for a long time on how to keep the water from running off onto the road. Food wrappers tossed during school lunch, even into trash cans, attracted bees and seagulls, adding to the maintenance problem.

Technology expands to meet growth needs

Technology was undergoing dramatic changes by the end of the 20th century. Superintendent Chet Francisco decided that to provide students and staff with current computers, the district needed someone with expertise in both educational and business technology. Thanks to his efforts, in 1998 Bill Olien was hired as Director of Technology, with a small staff of techs, including Tom Paulsen, Jimmy Catamas, John Richardson, and Ron Derrick.

Alda Christy was hired as the department secretary and became sort of a "mother hen" to the crew of young men. When more computer techs were needed, Scott Culbertson and Robert "Zimm" Zimmerlee were hired. The technology crew soon became well-known in the district, providing support that ranged from plugging in a printer to replacing the entire computer.

Technology continued to get more complicated and as new schools were opened, more technology positions were added. Erin English was hired as the Technology Coordinator; focusing on the educational uses of technology. To provide more direct technology support for teachers, tech assistants were hired for each school.

When Chuck Depreker retired in 2004, Bill Olien was promoted to Assistant Superintendent of Facilities and Operations and Ken Balliger was hired to replace him as Director of Technology. Mrs. Christy moved to Facilities as Mr. Olien's secretary and Cathy Diyorio was hired as the Technology secretary.

The District kept building schools

The Facilities and Construction staff was kept incredibly busy, building a new school almost every year for fifteen years. This meant finding and purchasing land for each new school, finding an architect, drawing up plans—or re-using existing plans—getting the plans approved by the State architects office, and finding a contractor to build the school. Sometimes there was a lag between the opening of a school and the completion of the school site, so some schools opened in portable buildings, or shared the classrooms at an existing school.

While schools were under construction, there were "change orders." Things cost more than expected, took longer than planned, or changes had to be made in the plans because there would be a different program, or someone noticed that a needed component had not been included, had been forgotten, or was no longer available.

With the addition of each new school, the bus routes had to be changed, sometimes requiring a new bus or additional bus drivers. Custodians were needed and each new school had to be added to the maintenance schedule. The district mail courier had to change the mail route to include each new school.

Each school presented unique challenges for facilities planners, architects, and the construction team, as described elsewhere. With a wealth of hands-on experience, the Facilities and Operations staff knows how to build and maintain schools.

Personnel/Human Resources

When the school district began growing rapidly, they needed teachers for the wave after wave of incoming students. For a while at E. Hale Curran Elementary School, a new class of students and a new teacher were added weekly. Dr. Arvo Toukonen, the first Assistant Superintendent of Personnel (later Human Resources, or HR), was the person whose job it was to find and hire those additional teachers.

It could be said that the overall success of the Murrieta Valley Unified School District was due to hiring the right people for each position, people who cared about children, people with skills, imagination, courage, and a willingness to work very, very hard. Mr. van de Wetering had been instrumental in finding those people and Dr. Toukonen continued the practice.

Hiring many teachers rapidly

Dr. Toukonen was fondly referred to as "Dr. Frugal," because he tried to cut costs wherever he could. This was true for hiring new employees: he tried to hire the best people for the least money. The district needed a lot of teachers and they needed them rapidly. All of California was experiencing growth and it wasn't easy to find unemployed high-quality teachers locally. To solve this problem, Dr. Toukonen went on recruiting trips to Ohio and Minnesota. California teachers have a five-year degree, but teachers from elsewhere have a four-year degree, and so new teachers from out-of-state were less expensive to hire than more experienced teachers.

The recruiting trips were memorable. A small team of administrators went to college career fairs across Ohio and Minnesota and interviewed recent graduates with teaching credentials, almost nonstop. If there was an opportunity to interview in between these career fairs, that happened. Dr. Toukonen's staff found inexpensive (cheap!) hotel rooms for the recruiting team in each town. Everyone piled into a rental suburban, with suitcases and people wedged in together, to drive long distances between the cities they would visit. Dr. Toukonen drove and after hours on the road, there were piteous cries from the back seat: "Are we there yet, Dad?"

To select the best teachers, the District used Teacher Perceiver Interview questions for each candidate. These interview questions were created by the Gallup organization, based on research on what the best teachers would answer to each question. This process was successful-- the district was able to hire the teachers they needed and many of those teachers stayed with the district until they retired.

When Dr. Karen Lynch left the district, she was not replaced and Dr. Toukonen assumed her duties, overseeing both Personnel and Curriculum and Instruction. Kimberly Bowman had worked with Dr. Lynch as her secretary and would continue to work with Dr. Toukonen until cancer ended her life. Georgia Calkins was hired as her replacement.

Staffing increases

The influx of teachers created huge amounts of paperwork for staff in the District Office, and additional people were hired to manage this workload. Vickie Henry had been hired in the mid-1980's as a personnel clerk, but increased numbers of district employees meant more paperwork and recordkeeping than one person could handle. Technicians to check teaching credentials, experience, and details like TB testing were needed, and Linda Diaz and Keri Baldridge were hired. Angie Scholz, Susan Carlson, Maggie Estep, and Andi Emde soon joined the staff, helping keep track of the myriad personnel records.

As the number of teachers and classified personnel increased, the need for substitutes also increased. For a while Keri Baldridge was in charge of getting teacher substitutes, working long hours until she had someone for every classroom that needed a sub. When the district was still small, if she could not find a substitute teacher, she got one of the district administrators with a teaching certificate to sub for a day.

When the automated sub-caller system was implemented, Michelle Elder became the Substitute Services Clerk and arranged for substitute staffing. Mrs. Baldridge's duties shifted and she became the Certificated Analyst, while Linda Diaz became the Coordinator of Certificated Personnel. Keeping track of what teachers are qualified to teach, how long they have been teaching, and what additional courses or degrees they have requires lots of record keeping. In 1999, there were 596 teachers in the district and by 2011 this number had increased to 1,015.

Brenda Brandley, and later Susan Carlson, Coordinator of Personnel and Maggie Estep, Senior Personnel Technician, handled paperwork on classified personnel. When an employee got promoted or transferred or changed positions, someone had to make sure they got the correct salary, per their union contract—and this contract changed whenever it was renegotiated. In 1999, this meant record keeping for 421 classified personnel and by 2011, this number had doubled, to 843.

Part of the duties of both the certificated and classified management was finding candidates for job openings, scheduling interviews, and checking references and qualifications. During the district's peak growth years, this was a formidable task!

Negotiations, MTA and CSEA

Contract negotiations with the teachers union, Murrieta Teachers Association (MTA), were sometime contentious and always time-consuming, as the teachers worked for improved working conditions while the district tried to keep costs down and still support teachers. Bargaining issues usually included salary increases, sometimes step-and-column changes, extra-duty pay, the district calendar, and vacation days. When the California economy got bad, the district and teachers negotiated furlough days to help reduce costs.

Contract negotiations with the California School Employees Association (CSEA) were much more complicated, since the union represented almost all the classified employees. This included custodians, secretaries, food service workers, instructional aides, mechanics, bus drivers, and campus security, among others. The members worked many different hours, their duties varied widely, and their issues were different. There was no tenure for classified employees, so their union contract was their job security and negotiations were often contentious.

In the mid 1990's, in an effort to improve the negotiations process, CSEA and the district tried a new negotiating strategy, interest-based bargaining. The intent was to focus on the interests of both sides, and work toward mutually beneficial solutions. In some ways this worked, but the process was more time-consuming than traditional negotiations, and was abandoned after a few years.

When Dr. Toukonen left the district, Dr. Ruth Lander was hired as Assistant Superintendent of Educational Services and Personnel. Both departments had become larger and increasingly complex over the years. The help manage the workload, which included attendance at many committee meetings and serving on negotiations teams, in 1997 Principal Buck DeWeese was promoted to Personnel Director.

Educational Services and Human Resources departments separate

Dr. Lander soon realized that overseeing two large departments was a difficult, perhaps impossible task. Her heart was in curriculum and instruction, so the decision was made to again have two separate departments, Curriculum and Instruction, and Personnel. Mr. DeWeese was doing a great job as personnel director, and was promoted to Assistant Superintendent of Personnel. He rapidly realized that he still needed a personnel director, or as he put it, "I need a Buck." However, it would be a while before another personnel director was hired.

Pat Kelley, a principal in the district, was hired as Director of Human Resources in 2003. In 2005 when Dr. DeWeese was promoted to Deputy Superintendent, Mr. Kelley was promoted to the now-open Assistant Superintendent's position. Pamela Wilson, an assistant principal at Vista Murrieta High School, was brought in as the next Personnel Director. In 2012, after six years with the district, Dr. Scheer left and the Board was comfortable appointing Mr. Kelley as Superintendent and Mrs. Wilson as Assistant Superintendent of Human Resources.

Curriculum and Instruction/Educational Services

When the district hired its first assistant superintendents in 1988, Dr. Karen Lynch became the first assistant superintendent of Curriculum and Instruction, with Secretary Kimberly Bowman. It was a small department and would stay small for many years. The staff that Dr. Lynch worked with included Carol Gurulé, Coordinator of Categorical Projects, Karen Robertson, Technology Coordinator, Jeanne Nelson, Library Coordinator, and Cathy Boisvert, District Nurse. Their offices were in the back part of that first District Office on the corner of Plum Avenue and Ivy Street. District psychologists shared a space in the building where they wrote reports. The speech therapist, Joanne Abrassart, had an office at Murrieta Elementary School.

Dr. Lynch leaves, Mr. Romero promoted

When Dr. Lynch left in 1990, she was not replaced as a cost-saving measure. Dr. Arvo Toukonen, Assistant Superintendent of Personnel, took over Dr. Lynch's duties and hired a new Director of Curriculum and Instruction, Guy Romero. Mr. Romero, who had been the principal at Avaxat Elementary School, brought his secretary Lorna Benson with him, and she became the department clerk, working with Mrs. Bowman.

Mr. Romero had served in a leadership role when the district was being planned and continued to provide leadership in many district committees. When he became principal of Avaxat he was the youngest

138

principal in the district, an appointment due in no small part to his leadership abilities. When he was promoted to director, his youth was duly noted by the seasoned staff he would be supervising, who had between them decades of experience.

Mr. Romero envisioned making the Curriculum and Instruction Department the backbone of the district, focused on teaching students what they would need to know, and supporting parents in helping prepare their children for future careers. Mr. van de Wetering served as his mentor in helping to make this vision a reality.

Creating curriculum, selecting textbooks

One of Mr. Romero's immediate tasks was creating curriculum for all the courses that would be taught at the new high school. In California at that time, each district created their own curriculum and course descriptions, which had to be approved by the California Department of Education (CDE) if they were to be offered as college preparatory courses.

CDE approved a list of state-adopted textbooks in each subject for grades K-8 and provided funding to purchase them. There was some funding allocated for high school texts (not enough!), but no approved list. Each district selected their own high school textbooks and there were some guidelines in California Education Code on a process to follow. Mr. Romero would be kept very busy helping the new high school teachers write course descriptions, get those course descriptions approved by CDE, and select instructional materials.

To help with this process, he formed a district committee, the Curriculum, Instruction and Assessment Committee (CIA), with representatives from all schools. They would recommend textbooks for district adoption, help create curriculum, help implement the various assessments the district used, and provide a two-way conduit for communication with the school sites.

However, they did not handle the logistics of ordering and distributing instructional materials. Jeanne Nelson, the library coordinator, had come from a district where she oversaw the libraries and also ordered and distributed textbooks. Mr. Romero was happy to delegate purchasing newly selected textbooks for the new high school to her. He soon realized that centralization of all textbook ordering could save the district money and expanded Mrs. Nelson's responsibility to include overseeing K-12 textbook ordering and distribution. She also served on textbook selection committees, gaining content information that helped when selecting library materials that supported the curriculum.

Special Education

The district special education program was also part of Curriculum and Instruction. As the student numbers increased, so did the number of students needing special services. It soon became evident that a special education coordinator was needed. Dr. Jerry Bergmans was hired and the position was upgraded to a director before long. When Dr. Bergmans left, Barbara Moore-Brown was hired to replace him. Barbara Jo Hughes was her secretary, and two Barbaras was much too confusing! Mrs. Hughes started going by "BJ Hughes," which solved the problem.

Thanks to hard work and dedication by a knowledgeable staff, the district gained a reputation for having a strong special education program. As a result, families from other school districts moved to Murrieta so their children could receive this support, further increasing the workload of the staff and the need for more personnel.

As the district grew, there were changes in the Special Education Department. In 1999, Zhanna Preston was hired as Director of Special Education, replacing Dr. Moore-Brown. Additional support staff included Lisa Cratsenberg, secretary. The three Program Specialists moved their offices to the department, freeing up needed space at the school sites.

Alan Young was hired as Director of Student Support Services. Mr. Young oversaw expulsions, suspensions, and readmissions, discipline, health services, transfers, and home schooling, among other duties. The school district by now had a distinctly urban feel, with many urban issues.

When Mr. Young retired in 2006, Principal Butch Owens took his place, working with Secretary Gabrielle Tingley. Mr. Owens retired in 2013 and was replaced by Principal Mary Walters, working with Secretary Tracey Cooper.

The district nursing staff

After Cathy Boisvert left the district, Cathy Owens was hired in 1991 and assigned to the new high school as the school nurse, also serving as Lead Nurse for the district. Working as a school nurse is more complex than scraped knees and aspirin. According to Cathy, "It is a job where everyday I am an ER nurse, a resource, a teacher and a friend." Over the years, the school nurses have given medications, insulin, catheterization, epinephrine, and even CPR, and the school district, the community and the nurses' association have recognized Mrs. Owens for her nursing skills.

Teaching the teachers

In a district growing as rapidly as Murrieta, the steady hiring of new teachers presented a problem. Each teacher arrived with their own ideas on organization, teaching practices, and expectations, based on their previous school. In 1992, the district decided to train all teachers in "the Murrieta way" of instructing students, which became known as Elements of Effective Instruction.

Initially, an outside agency was hired to present the four-day training. In 1995, Karen Robertson became the district Staff Developer and took over teaching the Elements course. Until 2002, all new teachers, including teachers with many years of experience, were required to take this training. Some of the more experienced teachers grumbled about this, but usually said after the training that they had found it helpful.

141

Mrs. Robertson also developed a training program for substitutes, classified employees, and DARE officers from the Police Department.

In 1988, state law on the process California teachers would follow to get teaching certificates changed and a new program, Beginning Teacher Support and Assessment (BTSA) was implemented. BTSA was a state-funded teacher induction program co-sponsored by the California Department of Education and the Commission on Teacher Credentialing. Elizabeth Ellsworth was hired to develop and coordinate the district BTSA program.

Initially this program required enormous amounts of paperwork, including writing the district BTSA plan, and Erica Franklin was hired to help with this. Mrs. Ellsworth supervised a team of BTSA providers, experienced teachers who worked directly with new teachers providing in-classroom support.

MVHS gets a swimming pool

One of Mr. Romero's contributions to the district was helping plan the construction of the swimming pool at MVHS. The pool was not part of the original plans, but there was support for building one and Mr. Romero clearly saw the need. He attended stakeholder meetings, persuading people of the importance of a pool. The final decision rested on finding money to pay for pool maintenance. The high school had not budgeted for this expense, and Mr. Romero was able to allocate funds from the Educational Services budget to make the pool a reality.

Dr. Lander becomes full-time in Curriculum and Instruction

After Dr. Toukonen left the district, Dr. Ruth Lander became the full-time Assistant Superintendent of Curriculum and Instruction. Dr. Lander selected Norma Cunnington as her secretary. Mrs. Cunnington had been working in the superintendent's office. In addition to having secretarial skills, Mrs. Cunnington knew the community, which was very helpful for

Dr. Lander, who had come from another district. When Mrs. Cunnington retired, Karen Parris was hired to replace her.

In 1998, when Bill Olien was hired as Director of Technology, he and his staff were included as part of the Educational Services Department (formerly Curriculum and Instruction). Mr. Olien attended most district meetings, to ensure that there was constant communication on technology issues.

Dr. Lander saw a need for additional staff to support the needs of the ever-growing district. In 1999, principal Shari Fox was promoted to Director of Educational Services and Mr. Romero became Director of Assessment and Categorical Projects. Mrs. Fox hired a secretary, Gale Hill, while Lorna Benson served as Mr. Romero's secretary.

Another change in 2000 was the addition of Erin English as Educational Technology Coordinator, working with Mr. Olien. Among Mrs. English's contributions to the district was the creation of a district technology night, where students from every school and every grade level could show off their skills using various technology resources. This proved so successful that providing enough electricity to power all the devices and gadgets posed a serious problem! Even kindergarten students participated, proudly showing their PowerPoint creations.

In 2000 Bonnie Cringan was promoted to a district coordinator position. Sadly, Mrs. Cringan succumbed to cancer the following year. She had worked in the school district as a teacher, counselor, and assistant principal, and was instrumental in creating the technology focus at Alta Murrieta Elementary School.

Dr. Lander leaves, Mrs. Fox is promoted, and more changes

In 2005, when a position opened up closer to her home, Dr. Lander left and Mrs. Fox was promoted to assistant superintendent, taking her secretary, Gale Hill, with her. Karen Parris, who had served as Dr. Lander's secretary, was given the responsibility of handling public relations and communications.

Mrs. Fox made more changes in the department, adding two Curriculum Coordinators, Sean McCarthy and Debbie Wall. Mr. McCarthy's background was high school, while Mrs. Wall's experience had been primarily elementary. They provided in-service training and instructional materials to teachers district-wide.

To help coordinate programs from K to 12, the district schools were divided into two instructional units, a Red Team and a Blue Team, using the colors of the high school in each team. All the schools that sent students eventually to MVHS were Red Team members and Blue Team schools were those that sent students to VMHS. Activities to encourage collegiality and promote articulation between the schools in each team were added to Administrative Council meetings and Mrs. Wall and Mr. McCarthy became "Articulation Coordinators."

Mr. Romero becomes assistant superintendent

When Dr. Francisco left the district in 2005, Dr. Fox was promoted to interim superintendent, but left almost immediately for a superintendent position in another district. Mr. Romero was promoted to Assistant Superintendent, and he hired Jeanette LaBella as his secretary.

The department needed a Director of Curriculum and Instruction and Mr. Romero hired Char Gollogly, who brought her secretary, Joanne Seedborg, with her from Murrieta Elementary School. Two additional coordinators were also hired at this time: Dean Lesicko, working with the district counselors, and John Vandenburgh, overseeing the Peer Leaders Uniting Students (PLUS) program.

To fully implement the many programs and provide needed teacher training, Mrs. Gollogly needed a larger staff and hired Teachers on Special Assignment (TOSA) to help with this workload. Some of the first group of TOSAs included Michelle McCarthy, Mary Sousounis, Sue Hall, and Tammy Koeppen.

Mr. McCarthy continued as coordinator, taking on the additional responsibilities of BTSA after Mrs. Ellsworth left. He also began developing the district online instruction program, creating or finding digital curriculum and often teaching courses himself.

Another of Mr. McCarthy's duties was oversight of course outlines. Creating new course outlines, getting them approved by CDE, and revising or updating existing course outlines is a massive job. When he took over these duties Mr. McCarthy was given a three-inch thick notebook with printed copies of all course outlines, some of which were for courses no longer taught, some sadly outdated, and some missing. Not all of it was in digital format and all of the course outlines had to be reformatted for consistency. The course outlines now available on the District website represent untold hours of work.

The Family Services Program again became part of Educational Services at this time. It had moved physically around the district, had been part of Business Services for a while, and finally returned to Educational Services. Kate Hamaker started this program as the Parent Center, which expanded to include the district child care program. The childcare program was re-named the Student Enrichment and Extended Day (SEED) program. More recently, a State Preschool Program and a Kindergarten Readiness Program were added to the Family Services offerings. Coni Stevens, Family Services Coordinator, Patti Talamantes, Secretary, and Audrey Russell, School Readiness Supervisor have ably assisted Mrs. Hamaker.

Still more changes coming

The district continues to evolve. In 2013, there were some dramatic personnel changes, as the principals of two of the high schools moved into district office positions. Executive Director Darren Daniels, formerly principal at VMHS, was added to the Educational Services Department, overseeing secondary education, while Director Char Gollogly would focus on elementary programming. Mary Walters, principal at MMHS, succeeded Mr. Owens as Director of Student Support Services. Recently developed Common Core Standards necessitated changes in what is taught and how it is taught. That meant more teacher training and new instructional materials.

There will continue to be changes, especially in the area of how technology is used in teaching and learning. Future district leaders will need to step in and support Mr. Romero's vision of Educational Services as the "backbone of the district

The Students

Since the late 1800's, thousands of students have attended Murrieta Schools, and a tribute to how they feel about the district is reflected in a Facebook page where they are sharing memories. Those memories center on the people who lived in Murrieta, teachers and friends, and the feeling of being part of the community, of belonging. That is the culture and climate that district administrators have attempted to keep in place, even as the district grew and of necessity changed.

As the district added programs, the benefit to students was always foremost in planning. Providing that small community feeling was the reason for "wing" and "village" scheduling, with students placed in small "school within a school" groupings, seeing the same teachers and students each day.

When each new school opened, students experienced the excitement of being the first, of creating "the way we do things here." At some schools, students selected the colors and mascot. At many schools, they left their handprints in tiles that decorated the school walls.

Students help others

Reaching out to help others was part of the Murrieta culture. Students collected food and clothing for the poor, or money to send to disaster victims. They wrote letters to people in the armed forces serving in distant wars. They helped new students get oriented to their school. They annually held a "senior prom" for senior citizens in the community.

Students were inclusive, too, electing a young lady with Downs Syndrome as homecoming queen one year, and another time electing an openly gay young man as homecoming king. The PLUS program, Peer Leaders Uniting Students, allowed students to help other students and was popular with students. Student PLUS leaders not only provided leadership on their own campus, but went to other schools to help students work out problems and serve as role models.

Students enjoy many school activities

In the elementary schools, activities were provided to include students with varying interests, ranging from athletics to clubs and after-school programs. There were fifth grade camp, trips to the Santa Rosa Plateau, Odyssey of the Mind, musical theater, dance team, running, "Rockstar" band, choir, and drama productions. There were reading events, when the principals made rash promises if students would read a certain number of books—which they always did. Principals Charlie Riendeau and Guy Romero each spent a day sitting on the roof of the school honoring those promises, to the students' delight.

Principal Randy Rogers was "slimed" by the students—buckets of green slime were poured over him—and hr was a great sport about it. Principal Karen Michaud was pelted with marshmallows, which immediately melted on the hot concrete walkways. The gooey mess was walked on by hundreds of kids and tracked into the classrooms, a first and last run at that activity!

The reading events included guest readers from the community or the school district, often taking place on Dr. Seuss' birthday in the spring. By the time they left elementary school, all students had listened to and read Dr. Seuss's books. Christmas (later "holiday") reading events also meant guest readers, with a focus on favorite holiday stories.

Kathy Linsley, School Board member Austin Linsley's wife, started the Murrieta Young Writers' Project in 1988, a program that has continued ever since. District elementary school students were encouraged to write a book, which was bound into a "real book" by volunteers, and then judged and given awards during a Young Writers' Conference in the spring. Some of these books were given to the school library, and the young authors were proud to see their books on the shelf for other students to read.

Activities available to middle school students varied from year to year, depending on student interests and teacher expertise. At different times, this has included peer tutoring, Running Club, band, choir, drama, Associated Student Body (ASB), Cheer Club, Community Services Club, dance, movie, Junior Honor Society, robotics, science, soccer, Star Wars Club, Student Venture Club, Odyssey of the Mind, community service, writing, yearbook, PLUS forum, chess, basketball, Shakespeare Club, Book Club, astronomy, volleyball, cheer and pep squad, drumline, color guard, and greeters.

During the time the district operated with four-track scheduling, Mrs. Karen Robertson implemented the Student Assistants Kindling Education (S.A.K.E) program. Off-track middle school students served as aides in the elementary schools, and were paid by their parents. Students got work experience and their parents knew caring adults were supervising their youngsters.

The high schools offered a spectrum of sports for student involvement. Over the years, at the three high schools, this included football, softball, baseball, basketball, swimming, water polo, tennis, golf, soccer, track and field, volleyball, cross country, dance team, cheer, wrestling, and sports medicine. For a short period of time there was even fencing! From a small, one school district, Murrieta grew to be as strong in athletics as in

149

academics. The coaches emphasized the importance of grades and positive behavior, and students responded.

High school activities also ranged widely and included National Honor Society, Ballet Folklorico, Chess Club, Interact Club, Mock Trial, Computer Tech, Chess Club, photography, Equestrian Club, marching band, Latino Union, science, robotics, Student Venture Club, student newspaper, Gay/Straight Alliance Club, yearbook, PLUS, digital video, Virtual Enterprise, Student Council, bikes, mock trial, Model United Nations, and more. Students worked hard and did well, so many of the teams went on to compete at the county, state, and national level.

Additional opportunities to succeed

Students participated in programs initiated by the county office of education, including the County Spelling Bee, History Day, Mock Trial, and the Science Fair.

After computers became integrated into the schools, the Technology department began holding an annual Technology Day for students in grades K-12, where students could show their computer-based creations. Even kindergarten students proudly presented their PowerPoint slide shows!

Students in grades K-8 are eligible to compete in the District Spelling Bee. This is a popular activity for some students with an interest in language and words, and can become a family activity. Sometimes siblings have won the District Bee in successive years. In 2012 Shruti Amin, an eighth-grader at Thompson Middle School, won the District and County spelling bees, going on to compete in the National Spelling bee.

The PTAs provided an additional opportunity for student creativity through the Reflections program. K-12 students were encouraged to submit original work in six areas: Literature, musical composition, photography, visual arts, dance choreography, and film/video production.

Alternative education programs

Programs were added to help students who struggled in a traditional school setting. Independent study let students like Olympic tennis player Lindsay Davenport juggle classes and a grueling tennis schedule. The alternative program at Creekside High School helped students who dealt with other issues in their lives and needed the focus provided in a small school. Some students still struggled, and online instruction programs were created to help them attend school from home.

For students needing more challenge, there were Advanced Placement (AP) courses in English, calculus, world languages, statistics, chemistry, physics, biology, government/politics, European history, and psychology.

But that still wasn't enough, students wanted—and could handle--more. The district began offering college courses, for college credit, in partnership with Mt. San Jacinto College. They also began offering International Baccalaureate (IB) courses at MVHS, for students interested in this internationally known program.

For students interested in vocational/technical careers, some options had been available since MVHS opened, such as auto shop, drafting, business, and construction. Over the years more courses were added, including health careers, food preparation, clothing construction, photojournalism, multimedia, and graphic design. When VMHS opened, there was an emphasis at this new school on career track programs. Students could transfer for these courses, and many did.

Each school, including elementary schools, originally had a full-time counselor to help students who needed extra support. Psychologists, speech therapists, and program specialists were shared between the schools. As the district grew, elementary counselors were also shared. Dean Lesicko, Student Support Coordinator, developed the RAIN elementary school counseling program to ensure that counselors were available as needed, and to provide guidance lessons for 4th and 5th grade students.

To provide more opportunities for students to get help if they needed it, several methods were used. Class schedules at MVHS were adjusted to provide a home room period (LAB) before regular classes began, but as the school grew there were too many conflicts in scheduling and this program had to be abandoned. Later, tutoring was offered after school in the high school library and was popular with students.

The Breakthrough student assistance program was implemented to provide "last chance" support for students who had not been successful in any regular programs or interventions. Students and their parents enrolled in this program together.

The district looked for additional tools to help struggling students, including Read 180, Fast Math, Math 180, and Accelerated Reader, providing teacher training and materials. For some students, these programs were the difference between success and failure.

As is true in many California school districts, some students arrive speaking another language. Some speak no English while others are fluent in both English and their home language; some read and write English fluently, while others have had no prior school experience. Spanish is the most common home language, but students have arrived speaking Italian, Russian, Hmong, Japanese, Chinese, Farsi and many others.

The district had tried to support this group of students through English as a Second Language (ESL) classes, Spanish for Spanish Speakers, and a Structured English Language Immersion Program. For a while, Alta Murrieta Elementary School offered bilingual classes, taught in Spanish and English. The number of English Language Learners in the district has increased, from just under 500 in 1998 to almost 1,000 in 2009.

Student success stories

The Murrieta Schools scholarship foundation began giving out scholarships in 1994 and since then has given out over $2 million in scholarships. Renamed the Murrieta Dollars for Scholars (MDFS) to reflect a district focus, the foundation gave out $176,600 in scholarships to 284 seniors in 2014. The scholarships are funded by donations, and awarded to students based on their career goals, academic and athletic accomplishments, community service and for overcoming challenging circumstances.

MDFS President Robin Crist said, "This is our opportunity to come together as a community and recognize our young people and help their dreams come true."

Many students went on to successful careers, like Ms. Davenport in tennis, or Ricky Fowler, golf, and Alan Long, mayor of Murrieta. Students came back to work as teachers for the district, and there was general excitement when the first "home grown" teacher was hired. Other students returned after graduation to work for the school district as support personnel and sometimes an entire family--mom, dad, and their grown children—all became district employees.

Murrieta was, and remains, a good place to attend school, to live and to work.

PART TWO
The People Who Helped Make It Happen

It took a lot of dedicated and hardworking people to create this district. Here are some of their memories, in their own words, of how it all came about.

1. Memories of the Second Street School

By John Hunneman, May 21, 2006

"More than two decades after it burned, Murrieta Grammar may have to be leveled," by John Hunneman for *The Californian*. Reprinted with permission of Mr. Hunneman.

Some were classmates, others brothers, sisters or just old friends. Many remembered the names of different teachers and principals; some didn't.

A few attended class in the 1930s when the school was almost new. Others were students in the 1950s, when state officials declared the building unsafe and a new school ---- present day Murrieta Elementary School ---- was built to replace it.

Whether they graduated with the class of 1932, as Leonard Michaels did, or were in the class of 1956 with Bruce Erdel, those who gathered at the site of Murrieta's second school all smiled about one collective memory ---- ringing the school's bell.

On a recent Friday morning, 10 graduates of Murrieta Grammar School gathered at their former school site ---- much of which was gutted by fire in 1984 ---- to remember what was and ponder what might be.

157

The residents speak

The scorched stucco walls, all that remains of the former school on Second Street, sit on a 10-acre site purchased by the city in October 2003.

Measure H on the November ballot that same year ---- championed by a group called Citizens for Historic Murrieta ---- had called on the city to buy the land and also change the zoning designation to preserve the site. Several years before, a developer had proposed building homes at the location. The residents group wanted a park built there instead, one that might also include a history museum.

Measure H passed by a wide margin, even though the city had already bought the land.

Last month, the city hired a consultant to design and develop plans for a park on the site that was also once the location of the Murrieta train depot.

However, city officials, citing safety concerns, said it was likely that what remains of the old schoolhouse would have to be taken down if and when a park is built.

My old school

It wasn't the first school in Murrieta. Children of settlers who came to the community in the early 1880s first learned their lessons in Marcus Hedges' barn near the corner of Washington Avenue and Ivy Street.

Daniel Buchanan built the first schoolhouse in 1885. It was enlarged in 1900 and served the community until 1918 when a new building was needed.

The first school was torn down and the Murrieta Grammar School was built on the same site. The stucco building was U-shaped with three classrooms and an auditorium. A lush lawn covered the middle of the "U" and palm trees were planted at each end near the street.

From 1920 until 1956, first- through eighth-grade students were taught there.

An auditorium held a stage and a piano. One of the classrooms was used primarily as a "shop" class for boys.

"From the shop class, we could look out the window and see the train go by," Leonard Michaels said.

Well, not everyone.

"The girls weren't allowed to go in the shop class," said Pauline Michaels, class of 1936 and Leonard's wife.

The school also had a library, a small kitchen and an office.

"This place used to be huge," said Mary Dunham Kean, class of 1952. "Now, it seems so small."

Leonard Michaels pointed toward the northeast corner of the building where students used to tie up their horses.

Not far away, there once was a tall flagpole.

"We used to stand outside every morning and say the Pledge of Allegiance," said Loretta Erdel Barnett, class of 1952.

Each grade had six to eight students and two or three grades were taught in each class.

"Whoever you started school with, that's who you graduated with," said Barnett.

Alice Sotello Vose, class of 1943, came to the impromptu reunion with pictures, books and programs from her school days.

"This was our music book," she said, holding up a copy of "The Music Hour." "I used to love to sing. There was a piano in the auditorium and we sang all the time."

The Sotello family came to Murrieta in 1900, and many family members, including one of her own children, attended the school.

Once a month, a teacher ---- for many, it was a Mrs. Prouty ---- would come down from Riverside to teach a music lesson. An art teacher also visited once a month.

For most of its existence, Murrieta Grammar School did not have nicknames, such as the Cougars, Panthers and Jaguars, that are attached to schools these days.

"We were just kids going to school in Murrieta," said Kay Curran Hudson, class of 1948.

However, sometime in the 1950s, the nickname "Indians" was adopted, several students said

"We probably should have been called the Murrieta Ruffians," joked Marv Curran, class of 1943 and a former Murrieta fire chief.

The school did have a motto, however.

160

It was "climb though the rocks be rugged," Curran said.

Upon graduation, most students of Murrieta Grammar School went on to Elsinore High School.

Down by the schoolyard

As with any school, many of the fondest memories happened outside the classroom.

Murrieta Grammar, with its large adjacent field, was often home to "play days," athletic competitions pitting the local kids against schools from Temecula, Wildomar and the Alberhill area.

Running races, softball tosses, high jumping and other competitions were held and winners were awarded ribbons.

"Annie-Over" ---- a game involving tossing a ball whose rules seem to differ depending on which former student was doing the telling ---- was very popular and several of the graduates recalled fondly the time "we beat Wildomar" in an "Annie-Over" tournament.

And, of course, there were pranks

Marv Curran recalled one Halloween evening when the boys took four of the school's picnic tables and put them on the building's roof, one on top of each chimney.

"We just finished when all of a sudden a spotlight came on," Curran said. "It was the sheriff. He told us, 'You boys are going to bring those tables back down just as carefully as you put them up there.'"

But above all, there was the school bell.

Classes began promptly at 9 a.m. but the bell was rung at 8:30 each morning, its sound pealing across the rural valley calling children to class.

Some graduates said it was an honor to be selected by the teacher to ring the bell. Others claimed there was a lot of favoritism involved. One former student said that only boys were allowed to ring the bell.

"That's not true," said Pauline Michaels. "I remember ringing that bell."

Time marches on

In 1956, Murrieta Grammar School was declared "unsafe to occupy" by state officials. In July that year, residents approved a $60,000 bond to help build a new school to be located at Adams Avenue and B Street. Students were taught at the Murrieta Methodist Church while the school was built.

The new school, built for $148,000, was finished in May 1958. The old school bell, which had been used at both the community's first school and at Murrieta Grammar, was brought to the new campus and rung every school day at 8:30 a.m., just as it had been for more than 70 years.

The old school was purchased by Ray Van Zyl, an artist who made the building both his studio and his home.

Up in flames

Just before 2 a.m. on a warm October night in 1984, the alarm sounded at the Murrieta Volunteer Fire Department.

From all corners of the still mostly rural community, firefighters rushed to the site of the former schoolhouse, some arriving within minutes.

There was little to be done.

Flames fanned by Santa Ana winds jumped a hundred feet into the sky as the building, which was stuffed from floor to ceiling with old furniture, magazines, cardboard and other flammables, consumed the structure.

"Every room had things stored in it," Marv Curran, then Murrieta's fire chief, told a reporter for The Californian. "There were little trails through the stored items and little ladders to get up on things. You can't believe how bad it was."

At that time, the building had no electricity, water, gas or phone. The closest water to fight the fire was blocks away, Curran recalled.

Van Zyl "was sleeping at the time and narrowly escaped the fast-moving blaze," the newspaper reported.

"He was really an eccentric and a recluse," Curran remembered.

Peggy Thompson Goffman, class of 1951, recalled Van Zyl used to ride around town on his bike, collecting everything he could find and bring it back to his home.

"He picked up everyone's junk," Goffman said.

The blaze was finally put out around sunrise, but firefighters remained at the scene for three more days, pouring water on the ashes to make sure it didn't rekindle.

An idea with promise

Arlene Garrison is on a mission.

Murrieta's resident historian had finished her school days in her native

163

South Dakota before she moved to the community in 1939 to marry her husband, Victor. However, the couple's children attended the grammar school on Second Street.

Last month, Garrison brought a small model of the Murrieta Grammar School building, made for her by local resident Peter Ruhe, to the annual Murrieta Firefighter's Barbecue.

Garrison hopes what's left of the building can be restored and eventually be made part of the museum she hopes will be built at the proposed park.

"Everyone I talked with at the barbecue said it was a good idea," she said.

Even if it's not possible to save any of current structure, Garrison hopes the museum will be built as a replica of the old school to help preserve the community's history.

"I'm going to try and convince them over at City Hall," Garrison said.

The former students who gathered recently at the school site were each doubtful the remaining walls could be saved, but embraced Garrison's idea of modeling a museum after the school.

"This was such a beautiful building," said Curran.

Everything old is new again

They don't ring the old bell at Murrieta Elementary School every school day at 8:30 a.m. anymore.

However, each Friday morning, a student is still selected to pull the rope and clang the old bell, as it has been rung since 1885 ---- in a community that now has 17 schools and more than 20,000 students ---- continuing a

164

tradition and helping to keeping Murrieta's history alive.

2. Kay Curran Hudson and Elaine Rail Gagnon
Graduates of the Murrieta School on Second Street
March 31, 2006

Kay Curran (Hudson) is E. Hale Curran's daughter and one of the Murrieta elementary schools is named for her mother. She graduated from the old Murrieta Grammar School on Second Street in 1947, in a class of six eighth grade students. At the time there was one teacher for grades 1-4 and another teacher for grades 5-8, and Mr. Blake was the principal.

The school building

There were three classrooms, but only two were being used, and were referred to as the Little Room and the Big Room. The Little Room was where the lower grades met, and the Big Room was the upper grades. Oh, how the little ones looked forward to going to the Big Room!

The Little Room was smaller because one end of the room had been walled off for boys' and girls' bathrooms. There was a third room which was used briefly for woodshop, and later on became a classroom. During the time when Mr. Hunt taught woodshop, the boys took woodshop while the girls did handwork. The girls' teacher said, it's "better to learn how to sew by hand before you learn to sew on a machine."

The school also had an auditorium, an office, and a "book room" with shelves. The floors were hardwood and very beautiful. There was a big clock with Roman numerals, and many students learned their Roman numerals from that clock. Desks still had inkwells, though no one used them by the 1940's. The desks were old and all marked up from the many students who had used them.

There was no kindergarten until 1960. When Kay Curran attended the Murrieta Grammar School, there were about 20 students in first through fourth grades and perhaps 15 in fifth through eighth grades.

The school bell, the same bell that is now located at Murrieta Elementary School, rang at 8:30 and again at 9:00. Kay called it the "get ready" bell. "If you did something real special, you got to ring the bell at recess time," she recalls.

Community and family

In a small town, many people are related by marriage or birth. Elaine's Uncle Ross Rail's wife was a Thompson. The Currans are related to the Sykes, since Amos Sykes was Hale Curran's uncle. There were twelve Sykes kids, not uncommon for a family in those days. The Sykes Ranch was a gathering place for the community, and usually everyone ended up in the house singing. There was a reservoir on the ranch where kids learned to swim, a "round house" which is still left on the property, and a windmill.

Area schools

Elaine Rail (Gagnon) grew up on the Rail Ranch property where the current elementary school is named for her family. She attended the Alamos School on Benton Road, which was part of the Perris District until Hemet took it over. Miss Field was the teacher for the Alamos School, where grades one through eight learned their lessons in the same room.

At the time, Murrieta students had a choice of going to either school, and the Alamos School was a little closer to the Rail property (the Alamos School building is now at Lake Skinner). When Elaine was in the third grade, she got a bicycle for Christmas and was able to ride it to school, five miles each way, over dirt roads.

Elaine went to Murrieta Grammar School for the seventh and eighth grade, because her parents didn't want her attending the more isolated

166

Alamos School. She graduated from the Murrieta Grammar School in 1944. The Rail home was five miles away, and sometimes she rode her horse to school, and left it with family members who lived in town while she was in school.

All Murrieta students in those days went to high school in Elsinore, which was not Lake Elsinore at that time. According to Kay, Murrieta kids were looked down on by the Elsinore kids as being "country."

Cora Stollar was the custodian at the Murrieta Grammar School, and was always there through Kay's school years. She did everything: maintenance, grounds, and cleaning.

The Murrieta School had a kitchen, but there was no hot lunch---students brought their lunches. Priscilla Burnett tried to have a cafeteria when Kay was in seventh or eighth grade, but it failed.

Memorable teachers

In those days, art and music teachers came from the County. The music teacher, Mrs. Prouty, came every six weeks. She was a "city lady, and very well dressed."

Mrs. Bennett, the first grade teacher at Murrieta Grammar School, taught Kay how to carry a chair properly, by picking it up by the sides of the seat, not the back. Miss Margaret Dunworth was her teacher in second grade, and married Bill Rice, the third/fourth grade teacher. One Christmas Mrs. Rice gave every student little Santas made of pipe cleaners, and the children were thrilled. There was a Christmas program every year at the Second Street school.

Mr. Hunt, the fifth grade and wood shop teacher, was very short-tempered. When a student misbehaved, he took the offender into the cloakroom and "gave them a whack." He was followed by Miss Neff, who stayed only a year. Miss Neff was a red-headed teacher and had a voice that carried and could be heard lecturing from out on the street. Miss Neff told Linda Olivera and Kay that if they stayed after school for an hour and studied, they would be promoted to the sixth grade. They agreed to do this, but Miss Neff failed them anyhow. Miss Neff didn't stay long, and was followed by a Quaker teacher who wore a bonnet.

Miss Domenigoni, who taught Kay in sixth grade, was a firm teacher and very strict, but the students learned and loved her. The courtyard of the school at the time was packed dirt, but Miss Domenigoni said it was a lawn, an imaginary lawn, and no one was to step on it. So the students were careful not to, and it did turn into a lawn, with roses planted by Mrs. Stollar.

In the seventh and eighth grades, Kay's teacher was Arthur Blake who lived in Wildomar and commuted to Murrieta.

Early testing

In those days, students had to pass "the Constitution test" to go to high school. Uncle Mike would quiz the kids on government, and helped them to pass this test.

Transportation

Before bus transportation, many students rode horses to school. Elaine's father bought her first horse, Beauty, from Dorothy McElhinney, for whom another Murrieta School is named. "Mrs. Mac" was a small woman, 5'3" or so and trained and sold horses on her Pinto Ranch, where she raised pinto horses. She had a riding school in the mid 1940's, and also had a riding group.

Murrieta students rode the train to Elsinore High School and back home in the evening during the 1910-1920's. Hale Curran went to Elsinore High School for two years, around 1913. The Fountain House Hotel, where Hale Curran lived, burned in 1936. Elaine was five at the time, and Kay was three. There was a train depot by the Fountain house and the railroad tracks ran along New Clay Street. The depot was torn down in the mid 1930's.

In the 1940's there was a bus stop on Washington, right next to Ray's

Café, and Elsinore High School would send a school bus to pick up students. There was only one bus and it started in Temecula and worked north to Elsinore.

3. Donna Brantly

Assistant Superintendent, Business Services, Retired
March 11, 2006

I applaud Jeanne Nelson for wanting to preserve memories of our school district. I am currently writing my autobiography, which includes three chapters and 40 pages of my 25-year career with the district. That's a bit much to include here, but after Jeanne called me a "legend," I figure I've got to give it a try. She requested stories from the time we were a small district. So on my 73rd birthday, hopefully with memory still intact, here goes.

There is no written record of when I first worked for the Murrieta School District, or how little I was paid, but in 1965 my dear friend, Carolyn Donoho, who was part-time bookkeeper and clerk, came to my house to tell me she was dying of a fast-moving cancer. She knew I was an accountant and she asked me to go to the school and see Gordon Harmon, the teaching principal. He was thrilled to have me walk in. He hadn't opened anything but paychecks in months. He was closing out his career. This was an era when he took the board minutes and the board did the budget themselves at their meeting, using an old ten-key adding machine.

In addition to Mr. Harmon, who taught seventh and eighth grades, George Contreras taught fifth and sixth, and Edith Lambert and Ethel Holl shared the primary grades. We had 79 students. There were two classroom pods with two classrooms each, and a multipurpose room with a small kitchen and a small stage. The 9' x 9' office next to Mr. Harman's classroom contained one wall of storage cabinets and a sink, on which sat a mimeograph machine, and there was barely room for a wooden desk, one file cabinet, and a typewriter stand. No Xerox, no computer, only carbon paper and an old manual typewriter. The unisex adult toilet cubicle shared a wall with the classroom. At the first board meeting I attended, I was hired. There was also no Affirmative Action. Board members included Charles Yoder, on whose farmland Murrieta's third high school will be built. The other board members were Ann Miller, co-owner of the Murrieta Country Market and Marvin D. Curran, gas station owner and local volunteer fire department chief.

Making my own hours, since I also worked at Rancho Los Cerritos, I began my on-the-job training. Carolyn had taught me to pay a bill and generate a pay warrant only. I soon learned that public accounting is much different than school accounting. There is no profit or loss, and with our tiny, financially--strapped district, budgeting was a challenge. One year they debated whether they could afford a mop bucket on rollers for Bonnie Swain, the part-time custodian.

In 1966, I prepared a sample budget, and the board was so thrilled not to have to do it themselves, they adopted it immediately and I slid into the position of business manager. Mr. Harman had retired, and Ethel Holl had become teaching principal. Her credential would only allow her to supervise four teachers. She took care of the student affairs and I did all the rest. She was 5' tall and I am 6' tall. We made quite a visual pair. Umpiring a baseball game one day, the ball hit her nose and broke it. It was my first Worker's Comp case. Incidentally, Ethel's husband, Ellis Holl, had served as a principal in our district when the school was on Second Avenue.

We invited the Dept. of Forestry to present their fire safety program with Smokey Bear in 1967. Three burly firemen arrived and asked for our dressing room. Well, they all had to cram into our tiny office/toilet to prepare. After Smokey got his furry suit on, he stood between my desk and the toilet wall, which held the heater, and I noticed smoke curling up behind him. Smokey Bear caught on fire at the Murrieta Elementary School.

In 1966-67, Mrs. Goodhope taught 6/7/8, Rod McQuillan 4/5, Ethel 2/3,

170

and Edith Lambert K/1. Rod McQuillan's wife, Sandy, was the daughter of then Riverside County Superintendent Leonard Grindstaff. Carroll Anderson replaced Charles Yoder on the board. During our budget meeting, the board decided we could actually afford to hire a full-time custodian. Carroll and Ann voted "yes" and Marvin abstained. When the vote carried, Marvin resigned and asked to be hired as the custodian. Curtis Thompson, a bachelor farmer who didn't relate well to kids, replaced Marvin on the board.

When you are a little school in a friendly community, you can do some fun things. Christmas was special. I bought a Santa suit and we invented ways for him to arrive with a bag of candy canes, provided by a very active Parent Teacher Club. One year Santa came in a sleigh pulled by horses, driven by Walter Cooper. One year I convinced my boss at Los Cerritos, William Pascoe, owner of Pascoe Steel in Pomona (who had 3 boys in our school) and commuted to work by helicopter, to be our Santa. Just as the copter was circling for a landing on the playground, with all the students, parents and staff circled around, it began to snow. This was my favorite memory. You had to be there. We did close the school once for a deep snow in 1968. We had a parent calling tree to notify all the parents.

We had our own "Papertowelgate." Edith Lambert, trying to be frugal, told her little students to use only one paper towel in the restroom. Parents created quite a stir over this rule, and it was rescinded. Another debacle was when Rod McQuillan volunteered to be in charge of milk money. At the end of the year I asked him for an accounting and he handed me a mayonnaise jar full of change. Needless to say, that also became one of my duties.

In 1967-68 the face of Murrieta School changed with the arrival of Verdell Adair LaValley, commonly known as Satch. His college friends, noticing how fat and dumpy he was getting and how he tried to cover it up with a big overcoat, said he looked like an old satchel. He loved his nickname. He took over English, history, and social studies in grades 7 and 8, Rod took over math and science in 7th and 8th grades, Eunice Cain

171

came out of retirement from our district to teach 4th and 5th, Edith taught first and Ethel had the kindergarten class in our multi-purpose room in the mornings. I always thought it odd we had three women teachers whose names all began with an "E."

Satch was what one might call a creative type. He first taught a ballet class. Then he went on to full Broadway-type productions. His first original show in 1968 was titled "Spring Song." No one dared to enter the multipurpose room when he was in rehearsals. Ethel was cowed by him. After his first production, students' moms were lined up to sew sequins on costumes for him. The board began work with Wendell Harbach, our architect, to build a larger auditorium, which could be cordoned off into classrooms, but Curt Thompson, labeled it the "Taj Mahal," and the bond issue failed. This was one of many bond issues to fail during my tenure, I fear.

We used to end our school years with an all-school picnic in Live Oak Park, in Fallbrook. Whole families would come. One year everyone brought baked beans but one family. We would also end our year with lovely graduation ceremonies, outside on the center lawn, with the girls wearing formal gowns. Our graduating classes were around 15 students. In 1969, everything went wrong. It poured rain on the outdoor chairs and the lights went out in town. The pianist showed up drunk, the speaker was awful, and I forgot to letter the diplomas. Ethel gave out blanks which I quickly grabbed from the office, and during the reception I took them all back, calligraphied in names, and got the board members to sign them. That was probably my most embarrassing moment.

I picked up a third job, at Hyland Labs on Adams, working for Mike Devitt and recording the 'plasmaphorising' of animals. My background with thoroughbred horses didn't help much. Mike Devitt replaced Ann Miller on the board in 1970. Dorothea Tiss, our first aide, was hired soon after Mike came on the board. Dorothea spent over 25 years working in the school library, and her picture is rightly over the door of the new library. Cancer ended her career.

Marie Curran and Jackie Sheld came on board as office workers that year and the office was a mite crowded. Satch put on "Showtime," starring Susan Brantly (my daughter) and Jerry Renon. Thereafter, they were the stars of every extravaganza until they graduated in 1973. Satch went to the MGM auctions and came back to Murrieta with a lot of famous costumes. Marsha Kempf, still working in the Murrieta Elementary office since the 70s, was one of his favorite models. Marsha, a very lovely and classy lady, was the only person I ever knew to do playground duty in high heels.

Satch would cook snails every year while teaching about French history and the kids were supposed to eat them. Eunice Cain served up kelp with her Japanese history lesson. Rod McQuillan kept twin horse fetuses frozen in our school refrigerator for science. We had no cafeteria.

During the summer of 1971, the board hired Charles van de Wetering as principal. He immediately hired one more teacher, and this qualified him to become our superintendent. He hired Greg Lockett to replace Rod, who took a principalship job in Northern California. There was a rumor that Van and Mike hired Karen Fountain because not only was she qualified, but she also had great legs. Karen, who later married Barry Robertson, was a 4-H leader for me in the Murrieta Livewires and my mentor in writing. More importantly, she was an outstanding educator in our district. Edith, Ethel and Satch remained. The board now consisted of Curt Thompson, Mike Devitt, and Kennadine Turner.

As leader of the Murrieta Livewires 4-H Club for five years, I had spearheaded, along with Everett Greer, the planting of the triangle by the parking lot at Murrieta Elementary (which no longer exists), and putting up the bell from the old Second Avenue school.

Van and I got along great for nearly twenty years, even though we worked in a storage closet, a trailer, a portable classroom and a day spa. In order to actually get a decent office, we formed a non-profit corporation that built the Murrieta School Administration Building and a 4-classroom pod.

Another thing we were responsible for was getting HUD to build the Town Hall. We were promised that the school could use the building for indoor sports and programs. After putting all the paperwork together for the building, we were not allowed to use the Town Hall without paying a fee. They carpeted the walls and played Bingo. When I had to pay a very large fee to rent the Town Hall for Van's retirement dinner in June 1992, I felt this was very unfair, since it was due to his efforts that the building was even there.

Shortly after Van came on board, we were faced with a greedy Elsinore School District who coveted Murrieta's and Temecula's tax base at the time. They set out to try and unify our three districts. Van has written about the campaign, which we won with 27 votes. Obtaining the voter list for Elsinore, I would drive to Wildomar to use David Turner's phone at his real estate office, on my off hours. It was long distance then from Murrieta to Elsinore. I made hundreds of phone calls, on a rotary phone, politely asking the voters to allow our little district to remain in control of its school. After we found out we were victorious, Eunice Cain asked to ring the old school bell, and when she yanked, her feet flew into the air.

Van told me that he was giving me the title of Business Manager/Administrative Secretary in lieu of a raise. The salary I was paid was so small over the years, until the last three, that I can't even remember what I got. I do know that overtime was not in the board's vocabulary, but in 1980 they saved my overworked life by hiring the wonderful, task-oriented Cindy Crismon as an accounts clerk.

It was at this time that Susan Reynolds came on board as principal, and Van, Cindy and I moved to a mobile home. The back room was the English as a Second Language (ESL) classroom. Wayne Jones, custodian, when told to turn the old office into an archival storage room, brought the old unisex toilet into the mobile home and asked me if for old times' sake I would like it as a flower planter. Kathleen Quinlan, Sharon Gunrud, Carl and Sally Lyons, Mary Godfrey, Carmen Stratemeyer, Charlie Riendeau, and Constance Gray are teachers who have been in the district a long time, or recently retired.

In my opinion, and this comes from spending 25 years taking board minutes until the wee hours of the morning, we have had some

174

outstanding board members who really cared about educating our students above all else. The first was Kennadine Turner. In 1973-74, the board welcomed David Hutt and Peter Lemke, and they served for a long time. The board increased to five members in the 1980s. Peter Lemke was a telephone installer and prone to putting out his orange cones and stopping by the school office, now in a portable classroom.

In the mid-80s, we finally hired Chris Hanson as Van's secretary and Vicki Henry as personnel clerk. George Parrott, also a board member at this time, went shopping with Van and me and we bought the first school computer not connected to the Riverside County Office of Education. Van's office had the only window and Vicki was claustrophobic in her windowless cubicle. Peter Lemke picked a bad day to walk into our office. Cheery as usual, he said, "Hi, Donna, how's it going?" I said, "My mother is going to die of ovarian cancer and I want a window right there!" as I pointed to Vicki's cubicle. We got a window.

The camaraderie that had always existed in our one-school district, with secret pals and diet/weight races, went away when unions appeared. I took minutes for the board of union negotiations, and used "expletive deleted" a lot. This gave new meaning to my classification of confidential employee.

As we began to grow, my job got overwhelming. I was working one Saturday on the budget in the mobile home when nature called. Being important, I took my master keys and walked to the administration building. I spotted four young boys using the handicapped ramp of our new cafetorium for their skateboards. I politely asked them to leave, saying I would not report them. I was risk management at this time, also. When I tried to exit the ladies restroom, I found they had carried a heavy picnic table from the playground and barricaded me inside. To be honest, I could have gone out four other doors, but I pushed my way out. The next Monday, Susan Reynolds caught the culprits and they wrote me apology letters.

I intended to name some outstanding board members. The most intelligent member was David Hutt, who wrote the Plan for Excellence for our district. In his wake came Austin Lindsey, who with his caring for students and knowledge of real estate was a wonderful resource when we became the fastest-growing school district in California. I loved going to Sacramento to lobby for more money for our situation, but we were not successful. Other board members I remember fondly were John Sullivan, Patty Julian, Andy Craig, Gary Whisenand, Kenny Turner, and Peter Lemke.

Perhaps now my favorite board story is appropriate. In my final four years we had a once-a-year board retreat at a very inexpensive place. Austin selected Rosarita Beach and my husband, a retired border patrolman, predicted dire consequences if I went. It would be really tough to plan a budget without the chief financial officer, so I drove down with Austin, his wife Kathy, and Elizabeth Ellsworth, the MTA representative.

On the return trip home we stopped so that Austin could push a stalled car across the border to help someone, so it took a long time. When we got to Elizabeth's parent's home in Escondido, we all needed a potty stop. Elizabeth said, as we walked up the hill with her, that there were two pit bulls behind glass by the front door. She felt that if we walked slowly behind her to the door, they would not break the glass and attack us. That worked, but as I was waiting in her mother's bedroom while Kathy used the bathroom, the pit bulls showed up at the glass sliding door to the bedroom. I told my husband that the scariest thing about our board retreat was the "pit stop" on the way home.

I have many fond memories of Charles van de Wetering. If I had not worked for someone I liked and respected. I would have not stayed for twenty-five years. I put my two daughters through college with my paltry salary, so it was worth it. Van was taller than I was, which was a relief, and very handsome. He had an extremely quick temper. His face would get all red and then a minute after the incident, he forgot it completely. Parents would ask me if they thought he would forgive them, and I would reply that he wouldn't remember he was ever angry at them. We had angry words only once in twenty years, and he apologized to me. He pretty much kept out of my way in the business field, and showed great trust for my financial management. During my tenure we never had a budget without an appropriate reserve, managed to build schools with portables when bonds failed, and never had a bad audit report.

Van loved to play Devil's Advocate at board meetings. Sometimes when in the office when presented with a problem, I would say, "Oh God," and Van would answer, "What do you want?" His punishment of students was fun to watch. One day he gave a small boy who had called a classmate a maggot the choice of a swat or writing an essay on a maggot. He took the swat. One day he got fed up with dogs on our unfenced campus and he told Marie to call Animal Control. They came and picked up Van's dog. He was a magnet for speeding tickets, and so it was good that he only lived a couple blocks from the school and could ride his bike to work. He started an outstanding wrestling program and the wrestling room at MVHS bears his name.

In 1979, my daughter Cheryl got married to an Englishman and we were entertaining his family, who had never been to America. I begged for vacation time after the August wedding so we could show our guests scenic areas of our country. Van said "No," he was going backpacking in the Sierras with his son, Stan, and his friends at that time. He was the boss, so that was that, or was it?

After he left and after the wedding, my husband Jim and I took our new English in-laws up Highway 395 to Reno, where my brother worked at the MGM Grand, returning home through Yosemite and Sequoia National Parks. As we got out in the parking lot at the General Sherman Tree in Sequoia, I thought I recognized Van's RV and his sister-in-law, Alice. Couldn't be. As we got to the foot of this magnificent tree, from around it came a sunburned, hairy, dirty, stripped-to-the waist Van. His group had just arrived to meet his wife Barbara and Alice in the parking lot. I was embarrassed to even introduce him. He said, "Who is minding the school?" I said, "Marie." And he said, "OK." How could you not love a boss like that? For all he has done far our district, especially his efforts at keeping it our district and not Lake Elsinore's, I sincerely hope some day they will name a school after him.

If you are a classified person at the District Support Center or in a school office, and are not a bus driver or custodian, then you know the scope of my job because I did all of yours. Riverside County Office gave me it's first ever Classified Person of the Year Award, and I felt like I was getting an Oscar, with the spotlight and the speech.

At a board retreat in Bathos Park in 1988, the board made me the first Assistant. Superintendent of Business Services, with an appropriate salary to increase my pension, as they knew I would be retiring in 1990. I spent my last six months in an attic over the Murrieta Day Spa, which served as the District Office at that time, culling down 25 years of boxes of records for our archives, while Roland Werner took over my job.

It is an honor to be part of the written history of the now-called Murrieta Valley Unified School District, and to be remembered as time passes. Thanks for the career of a lifetime.

4. Marie Curran

District Office Receptionist
March 20, 2006

Marie Curran first started working for the school district in 1968 and stayed for 31 years in various jobs. Her first job in the district was playground supervisor, in the late 1960's. In those days, there were no substitute teachers to call, so if a teacher was out, Marie would take over the class. Ethel Holl was kindergarten teacher/principal at the time, and Gordon Harmon was the principal before Ethel.

For a while, Marie served as registrar of voters, and was the only registrar who would go out where the goats were pastured and register voters. To become qualified for this responsibility, she attended an all-day class. Later on, she worked on the election for school district unification, the only election the school district won until the bond election that funded Murrieta Valley High School.

One afternoon in the 1970's Marie, Donna Brantly and Carroll Anderson, Board Member, drove out to the bar at the Hot Springs on the dirt road because yet another bond election had failed, after a lot of hard work. Donna, who never drinks, was the driver. On this occasion, she bent her rules and enjoyed a drink with Carroll and Marie. When she drove everyone back to Murrieta Elementary School, it was after dark and there were no streetlights in those days. When they pulled up to the school, they saw someone through kitchen window with a flashlight. They parked, and in the darkness a man came toward them with a flashlight. One of them rolled down the car window…the man turned out to be Marie's ex-husband, Marvin, who was custodian at the time. Whew! There were no cell phones in those days, and even if there had been, there were no local police.

During the summer, Marie "held down the fort" at school while everyone was on vacation and Donna told her, "Think messy!" Summer was when supplies were delivered and mail stacked up. Marie got to where she could sign Principal van de Wetering's name as well as he could.

A new science teacher was hired for Murrieta Elementary School, Mike Napolitano, and promised to do great things for students. Shortly after Mike was hired, the UPS delivery man came in the back door of the school and yelled, "Anybody home?!" scaring Marie, who hadn't heard him drive up. He had a load of large boxes, all science materials, and he left them in a stack. Marie's job was to check them in and make sure that what was ordered was what they got. Marie opened the boxes, and discovered a dead cat! She came unglued and couldn't believe anybody had ordered a dead cat! Marie told Mike when he returned to school that he could at least have let her know what to expect.

In Edith Lambert's class (first and second grade) a student brought in a snake for show and tell, and wrapped it all around himself. Edith, who didn't like snakes at all, jumped completely over her desk in her hurry to get as far from it as she could. Van (later Superintendent Wetering) made

179

Edith nervous and she wouldn't even go into the office with him. She'd stand outside the door nervously playing with her collar. When Edith retired, she traveled and visited, going from one daughter's house to another daughter's house. When she was in her 80's, visiting one of her daughters in Michigan, they decided to go across Lake Michigan on the car ferry. Edith had gone downstairs in the ferry to take a nap, and later when her daughter went down to check on her, she found the top bunk had collapsed on her, killing her.

One memorable year the entire staff went on a diet and everyone took losing weight seriously. They made a deal, that they would each put a dollar in the "pot" if they didn't lose some weight each week. At the end of each month, the one who lost the most weight got the money. One morning Marie came in early to meet a parent who had to be at work at 6:30 in the morning and was having trouble getting her children registered in school. Marie agreed to meet her at the office and register her children. Not realizing Marie would come in early, Van showed up, riding a bike in a torn t-shirt and shorts to weigh himself. He was not going to step on the scales with people watching if he had gained any weight. Edith Lambert had the "official" scales in her classroom, and one day after the students had left, Marie discovered her in a half slip and bra, weighing herself! Edith was totally embarrassed.

Marie was the first librarian. One year, the County of Riverside gave away library books from a library in Perris that was closing, and at the time there were no books at Murrieta Elementary School for children to check out. There was also no place to put them. Ethel and Marie went to Perris and brought boxes and boxes of books back. The library was set up on stage, and Ethel Holl's husband, Ellis (who had been a principal at the old Murrieta School) built the shelves. This was the first library ever in the district.

After the library opened, Marie decided to take classes on how to run a library and got Dorothea Tiss, who at the time was the custodian, to go along with her to UCR. Marie decided library work was not for her, but Dorothea enjoyed it and worked in the library for many years.

Before Murrieta Elementary School was built at its current location, students went to the old Murrieta School on Second Avenue. The big bell at Murrieta Elementary School came from this old school. One of the reasons for building the new school was a problem with the roof and earthquake safety. The walls of the old school are still there (March 2006), though the roof is gone.

A Dutchman bought the old school when the new school was built, and moved into it. He was a packrat, keeping everything and taking anything. Finally the city sent dumpsters to clean out some of the junk. They burned his stacks of old newspapers and it took days to get them all burned, there were so many.

Marie's husband, Marvin, became the first full-time custodian at Murrieta Elementary School, going directly from serving as a member of the school board that approved the full time position to taking the job (he abstained from voting to approve the position). Marvin was also the first school bus driver.

One year when Lake Elsinore flooded, a trailer park that was in a low area flooded. Some of the people who had lived there moved to Cottonwood Trailer Park in Murrieta. When they came to Murrieta Elementary to register their children for school, one of the women in the group had a magnificent tattoo on her breast, most of which was visible. She bent over to pick up something, exposing a portion of her backside, which also featured a tattoo. She registered her children in school, and one of them ended up in Mary Godfrey's class. This little boy ended up spending much of his time in the office with Marie, since he was a behavior problem. He called Marie an obscene name, but when Valentine's Day came around, this little boy had made a beautiful valentine with lace doilies for her.

When there was an epidemic of lice in the district, everyone was assigned to inspect and remove lice from the children. But not Marie. She said, "I will not pick lice out of anybody's hair." Van replied, "I am the boss and you will do what you're told." Marie stood her ground. "I'm not a nurse or a lice-picker and I won't do it! " Van got so mad he said he would take Marie to the Board, and she told him to go ahead and do it. She won that one!

Marie brought the classified union to the school district in 1974, because she felt that the classified staff needed union representation. She served as CSEA president from 1975 to 1983. She said, "We needed to bring the union in or go underground." In those days, whenever the teachers got a raise, the Board threatened to cut costs by getting rid of the aides. One year when the teachers got a raise, Marie went to Van and negotiated a raise for the classified staff by herself.

Marie was president of the Parent Teacher Club for a couple of years. "Dime-a-dip" dinners were a popular fund raising strategy. Everybody brought a pot, a salad, a hot dish, or a dessert. People did their very best in bringing home-cooked food. After everything was set up on a long table, each person asked for a dip or two of whatever they wanted, and then Donna, at the cash register, would count the dips and charge accordingly. The PTC also sponsored mother-daughter teas, and one year the entertainment didn't show up. Marie, Karen Robertson, and Carl Lyons decided they had to have entertainment, so they put on bathing suits (Mr. Lyon's was a 1920's bathing suit, and had moth holes) and sang "By the sea, by the sea, by the beautiful sea...." This was held at the Hot Springs.

Teacher Satch Lavalley put on elaborate plays and musicals, most of which he wrote. Costumes came from his collection, and were added to as needed. Everybody took part in the plays, some of which were community theater and some of which were student performances.

Board member Charlie Yoder wore satin shirts when he was out working with his tractor, and Mrs. Brantley had to run in front of the tractor to stop him and ask him to sign the papers when they hired Satch.

As the district grew and more opportunities opened, Marie moved to Reprographics, which was in the bus barn on Jefferson at the time. She ran a large Xerox copier, printing workbooks and paperwork for the entire district. Later Reprographics moved to a storefront on Date Street. When the District Office moved to Beckman Court, Marie continued to work in this department, running high tech copiers. "I had the biggest office of everybody," she says.

Marie left Reprographics and became the district office receptionist. Those boxes of paper were getting too heavy. She finally said goodbye to the district on December 2nd, 1998, retiring after 31 years.

5. Dorothea Tiss

Library Technician
May 18, 2001.

Dorothea Tiss was the only librarian in Murrieta for many years, and spent thirty-one years working for the Murrieta School District. Dorothea came to Murrieta because her grandmother lived here and as the single mother of four children, she wanted to be near family and provide a quality life for her kids. Providing this quality life wasn't easy. She bought a mobile home and had to put in her own water and sewer lines. Yes, that means moving a lot of dirt with an old-fashioned shovel, and she did the work herself.

The district had no bus in those days. Dorothea soon decided that hauling four kids to school and then going to work somewhere else was too much, so in 1970 she applied for and got a job with the school district as a custodian. Ironically, this was the same year that the school district purchased a school bus.

Later Dorothea became the school's only instructional aide and playground supervisor. As the first Chapter 1 aide for the school, she was able to use Chapter 1 money to buy the district's first computers. For a long time she worked half time as a Chapter 1 aide and half time in the library.

Marie Curran opened the first tiny library at the school with books discarded from other libraries, because budgets were slim then, too. However, her heart wasn't in the library and when Dorothea wanted to take it over, that was fine.

When Marie started that first library, it was in a small room near the office, and she worked in it half time. The library was moved into a trailer, and then to a classroom. The classroom was needed for students so the library was moved to the auditorium. When that didn't work, it was moved back to a classroom, and then into two classrooms with the wall removed between them. Dorothea remembered those moves clearly--moving a library is no easy job.

When Dorothea finally started working full-time in the library, Superintendent/Principal van de Wetering ordered new furniture for it. Before that they had used odds and ends of shelving which served the purpose, but the students knew that it wasn't a "real" library. Part of the new furniture order was a real librarian's desk--quite a step up and very exciting!

Over the years Dorothea took classes and went to workshops to improve her library skills. She actively sought donated books and by the late 1980's had added almost 10,000 books to the library. By this time there were almost 500 students at the school.

Everyone in Murrieta knew Dorothea. She happily enlisted student library helpers, teaching them to check out books, shelve books, and perform repairs as needed. During breaks, small groups of students headed for the library to "he'p Mrs. Tiss."

When the school district started growing in the late 1980's, Avaxat Elementary was the next school to open. Dorothea sent some of the Murrieta School Library books to Avaxat to help get a library started there. The district soon grew to five elementary schools in a very short period of time, and Dorothea was deeply involved in preparing orders for the first library collections.

For many years the Murrieta Elementary School Library was the only library in the area. Parents checked out books for themselves in addition to the books their children read. Dorothea purchased some high interest mysteries and westerns for both older students (the school was a K-8 school then) and their parents. She hoped that a public library could be

184

opened, and helped when one of the banks gave space for a volunteer lending library. The city would not get a public library until many years later, however.

When Murrieta cityhood became a reality, Dorothea decorated the entire library with red-white-and-blue streamers and articles about the hard-fought cityhood battle. She kept clippings of current events on the bulletin board so that students would know what was happening in their city.

Dorothea celebrated her retirement with friends at Murrieta Elementary School on June 16, 2001. Sadly, she had been diagnosed with cancer and did not live to see the new Murrieta Elementary School library being built.

6. Charles van de Wetering

Superintendent, 1971-1991

When I was hired, the official interview committee was composed of Ethel Holl (teaching principal) a County Schools Office representative, Curt Thompson, Kennadine Turner, and Mike Devitt (board members). The real committee was Donna Brantly, Marie Curran, and Dorothy Renon, who met me in the school office. I took over as principal of Murrieta School and began my tutelage under Donna Brantly, whose title was "whatever needs doing," from bandaging "owies" for students to typing board agendas, minutes, all documents and forms required by the county schools office and state, formulating budgets, paying the bills and keeping the books. She wasn't real good at the "owies" because she can't stand the sight of blood, but everything else she did was excellent. Any success I eventually had as superintendent was due to Donna's polishing.

When I was hired, there were five teachers and about 144 students, as I recall, K-8. Teachers were:

K   Ethel Holl
1-2   Edith Lambert
3-4   Karen (Fountain) Robertson
5-6   Russell Love (first half of the year)
5-6   Greg Lockett (second half of the year)
7-8   Satch LaValley (Social Studies and Language Arts)
Special Education—Joan Watson

In rapidly-growing districts in San Ysidro and Walnut, California, where I had worked previously, I had participated in and led my staff to contribute to the successful passage of bond issues, but I had never dealt with unification. In California, the education code requires that a non-unified district or separate K-8 district whose high school students were educated in a joint or union high school district must present a plan every four years to the local School District Organization (SDO) Committee and then, if the state approves, present the plan to the voters, It was then the popular philosophy in California that unified districts were the way that districts big or small, town or country could best function, and therefore was the way that all districts should be "nudged," not necessarily softly, to move toward.

It appeared that this "Giant" of unification was about to defeat the armies of God (Murrieta School District, if you will permit a religious analogy). The opposing army was our neighboring school district of Elsinore (not then named Lake Elsinore) who had read the state plan and decided very likely that the wealth of the tax base down in Murrieta and Temecula area school districts was attractive and an attempt should be made to add their tax base to the less moneyed base of the Elsinore school district area.

Elsinore would therefore quite soon initiate an attempt to unify all three existing districts into one. I thought I was ill prepared to lead the troops, although I had assured the interview committee that I believed districts should not be consolidated against their wishes and that I could produce a cogent argument to support this position.

186

When I inventoried all the local David's I was impressed, and became convinced that we could do it. It was a desperate long shot (so was David's sling shot at Goliath) but doable. The giants we had to fight included:

- A serious majority of the voters in the Elsinore High School district (which at the time included all three of our elementary districts—Elsinore, Murrieta and Temecula) with at least a 5:1 registration edge over those in Murrieta and Temecula. The high school students of these three districts attended the high school in Elsinore.
- An attempt made by the rapidly developing Temecula K-8 district to pull their high school students away from Elsinore in the form of an ill-conceived plan presented to the Riverside County SDO Committee. This attempt evoked a rapid and negative response from the Elsinore Board in the form of a plan to unify along EUHS boundary lines, thus eliminating two elementary districts. That started the big battle that would turn out to very nearly obliterate both the Murrieta and Temecula school districts—to the point where the current status of these two school districts could very well have turned out differently.
- A county and state reorganization committee and education code that favored unifying districts along joint high school district lines.
- And a well-liked and very competitive new superintendent in Elsinore named Jim Sheridan.

Our team would be led by a "David," Dave Turner, Realtor and Developer, and later Elsinore Union High School District Board Chairman. David wasn't any better trained than I for the battle, but we both believed in local control. Armed with our slingshots we stood before Goliath. The army behind us included some stalwarts who did the grunt work:

> Board members Curt Thompson, Kennadine Turner and Mike Devitt
>
> Chick Williamson, wife of Willie, the manager of Bill Pascoe's Los Cerritos Rancho,
>
> E. Hale Curran and Nellie Thompson, scions of old Murrieta Families
>
> Dorothy Renon, Postmistress and Town Hall leader
>
> Audrey Cilurzo, Temecula board member
>
> Sam Hicks, right–hand man of Earl Stanley Gardner, author of the Ellery Queen mysteries
>
> Tom Hudson, Elsinore publisher
>
> Warner Stuart and Kenny Lee, Market owners with strong ties in Elsinore
>
> The Reverend Dr.Bert All, Methodist minister in Murrieta
>
> The Murrieta school staff
>
> Herman and Jean Baertschiger
>
> Dorothea Tiss
>
> Marsha Kempf
>
> Butch and Judy Gonzales, service station operators
>
> Arlene Garrison, Murrieta Machine Shop owner and Murrieta historian
>
> Joe and Connie Roe, store owners
>
> Gordon and Virginia House, retired engineer, college professor and school volunteers.

There were so many I have not named, I have to plead my age and beg their pardon.

Dave and I put together a team that took the battle into Lake Elsinore to every publication, club and event and we kicked their butt, as the kids would say today. "Their" refers to those we dubbed "The Unificators." I don't remember who coined the word, probably Dave Turner, but it packed a wallop in cartoons, in ads, and on posters. It referred to the undefined group of legislative bureaucrats who required a unification or consolidation (as it was known in other states) plan be considered by voters every four years in California. Those who think that big is always better and cheaper for the taxpayer due to economies of size give little or no thought to the loss of local control of school districts in small communities and rural areas that we felt was so very important.

Dave Turner and I ate so many meals at Elsinore clubs and special occasions that we gained weight. The team's editorials and cartoons were works of art and worthy of note by accomplished pamphleteers. Warner Stuart's rather unorthodox way of handling Elsinore thugs who were out tearing down our "No on Unification" posters from telephone poles was something to behold! Warner could make a pretty persuasive nonverbal argument.

After the war was over and we had won, by an extremely skinny margin of some 27 votes in our favor, my honeymoon with the district lasted a few years. With the lowest tax rate in Riverside County (less that $1.00 per hundred assessed valuation) made possible by virtue of the vast tracts of undeveloped land on the mesa, we could add a teacher to provide special education and we lease-purchased portable rooms to house the kindergarten, first grade and special education children, and a locker room for physical education classes.

Things went smoothly and we enjoyed good community support, so the board decided to resurrect a set of plans for the "Taj Mahal," as those who previously opposed approving bonds to build it had dubbed it. This was a plan for a multipurpose room, cafeteria and performance stage. It really didn't do justice to the talents of Satch LaValley and his musicals, but we hoped it would get the support of the previous opposition. As I remember it, we lost this bond vote by a close margin. At this time, Dave Hutt and Peter Lemke joined the board.

Enrollment continued to grow slowly. One day a development map appeared on my desk. I looked at it and rolled it back up. Before the next monthly board meeting, I unrolled it and spent some time studying it. It was one with large parcels subdivided up on the mesa. I took it to the board and shared it and we decided it was a good thing to file and got back to school district business. Every month after that there were several more development maps. I had to build a rack in which to file them.

Then gradually those parcels started selling and houses got built on them. Kids started living in those houses and our enrollment crept up. The first impact was the need for a teacher, then a bus, and then another classroom. Other isolated tract maps began to appear but we were still not alarmed. Kids were coming slowly enough to plan for. But the board decided we had better try to get an application for the state building funds and/or a bond passed to build classrooms ahead of the curve and state of the art, instead of just second-hand portables.

The battle was joined to pass a bond to build two classroom pods with four classrooms in each and demountable walls (this was at the height of the team-teaching craze), a new school office and workroom with rooms for a nurse and psychologist, and the redesigned multipurpose room/cafetorium previously rejected. As I remember it, this bond failed twice. We met with the major protagonists in an attempt to bring them on board but they wanted to buy portable units being built in Los Angeles by a government-supported program to train the unemployed. The program was commendable but the product did not impress our board members who traveled to inspect them. The bonds finally passed by a slim margin (66 and 2/3% required for approval).

Those who opposed bonding to build schools were delighted when Proposition 13 passed. Now a school district could not ask its voters to bond themselves to build needed classrooms. The only way a district could build was with cash or the State School Building Program. The state program was designed to look back three years at a district's enrollment and then project the growth increase ahead three years. It was not designed to handle rapid development.

The legislature ducked the issue for two years and finally came up with a builder or impact fee to be levied on builders to mitigate the impact of rapid development on schools. Instead of changing the state school building process, they dumped the responsibility on the developer. To many this made sense because it used the developer's profits to pay for new schools. But the developer passed the cost on to the homebuyer. In many people's opinion that was worse than bonding and spreading the cost of new schools out to everyone in the community. Builder's fees became a fact of life, but were not enough to build new classrooms, only to lease portables until the state building program recognized a district's growth and supplied the funds to build permanent structures. This is usually a three to five year process from design to occupation by students. Negotiations were initiated with the county and developers to increase the amount of the fees to cover permanent structures.

Water from the east and a superhighway from the west arrived at the same time as Proposition 13 passed (1978). It was time to get serious with the developers. We could see the future just by looking east to Temecula or west to Lake Elsinore school districts where there was a sea of red tile roofs. We had to identify school sites and boundaries and begin negotiations for them. It became evident that most developers preferred to sell us what they considered unusable land, acreage which required more work to develop into home sites. Lots of interesting canyons and potential ponds in the event of a hundred year flood were located at the edge of developments, and available.

The small developers said, "We aren't large enough to be required to set aside a site in our tract, so you can just use our ninety-seven cents per square foot fees to buy someone else's land for school sites!" Some of the shortsighted developers of large tracts did not want preferred sites taken which would serve children from other tracts. It was time to take off the gloves and get tough. We did and we had the support of the people because they were pretty much anti-development. The board members and I were not anti-development, but we weren't about to see a good school system destroyed in the development process.

We took the fight to the County Board of Supervisors and the Building Industry Association (BIA) as well as the state legislature. We joined with other districts and cajoled them and the County Superintendent of Schools to take a stand and allow us to levy higher builder fees or place a moratorium on building until we got voluntary compliance from developers or a change in the state building fund application process to meet our emergency.

It became obvious that Elsinore Union High School District (which served our 9-12 students as well as those of Temecula) would not be able to build us a high school within the boundary of Murrieta School District, even though developer map projections documented the need for one or more high schools to serve the projected 9-12 population of Murrieta. First Temecula received a high school built with EUHS funding (combined with bonds, builder fees and state funding). The next high school was slated to be built northwest of Elsinore towards Corona. In all likelihood the fourth high school would have been built in Murrieta but we decided not to wait and hope, in case Elsinore was still smarting from their earlier defeat by us.

We began to think and whisper that maybe it was time to pull our kids out of the Elsinore Union High School District (our students were allowed to attend either Elsinore or Temecula high schools). This was risky thinking for those who wanted to retain control of their children's education. We had not forgotten the unification wars. Elsinore had used their state school building fund eligibility, some builder fees (from the EUHS boundary) and bonding capacity to build Temecula High, and we figured any talk of pulling out of EUHS might tweak the giant's beard. We did not want to repeat the error Temecula had made years before. We owed it to Temecula to consult them before taking any public steps because they could lose their district, as Murrieta also might, in a successful unification along EUHS boundaries.

The most likely scenario based on the purpose of the state unification legislation would be the formation of one unified valley district. This would mean the dissolution of both Temecula and Murrieta school districts into one district. A reasonable alternative, based on the numbers derived from developer maps, would be the unification of three districts

192

and dissolution of the union high school district. Quiet discussions ensued with Dave Turner, president of the EUHS board, playing a key role. The decision was made by the three elementary districts to present the latter plan to the Riverside SDO Committee, and with their blessing, to the state.

By this time Dave Hutt and Austin Linsley were asserting themselves as leaders of the school board. Sometimes this was in opposition to each other but more often in support. Austin brought his background as a realtor to the board and really helped us understand what drove developers and how to deal with them in the most positive way possible. He kept us focused on the value of a good school system to the developer, and they listened to him as a fellow developer. Dave Hutt's focus was constantly on the fact that a whole new district was going to metamorphose out of the old Murrieta School and we were in a position to overcome inertia and status quo and create an excellent state of the art curriculum and buildings in which to deliver such a program.

At first Dave Hutt's focus was on improving the curriculum and improving standardized test results. This led him to the hiring process to obtain the best teachers possible and to push for improved staff training. Then it was exploring the role computers might play in the learning process (this was still prior to the Internet, at the time when mainframes were giving way to Personal Computers (PC's). The board was ready to contract for the Plato mainframe system from the University of Chicago, via the University of California. Karen Robertson led the fight against this and convinced the board that students were not ready to trade a warm teacher's touch for cold plastic. Karen definitely had a way with words! As testimony to her flexibility, she became the Technology Coordinator for the district in subsequent years—go figure!

As soon as PCs replaced mainframes at affordable prices, Dave Hutt pushed for an outcome- based math program that regrouped every student and teacher as each objective was achieved, usually at least once per week. Board members and volunteer teachers came in after school and helped regroup for the following day, but this turned into a logistical

193

nightmare and we had to drop it within six months.

Dave also pushed in the direction of merit pay contracts for teachers. This was negotiated and lasted one year. Other board and staff members and I were obviously contributors to the successes and I will take the blame for the failures.

When approval to hold a unification election was given by the state, it became obvious we would need to pass a bond election to build a new high school. Dave and Austin focused the district office staff and board and anyone else who wanted to participate on the development of a Murrieta School District Manifesto for future education. We brought in futurist speakers for community and staff meetings, and held administrative staff retreats for discussion and development of concepts.

Our assistant superintendents and our principals contributed a great deal to the discussion and mulling over of ideas. We were all stimulated by the rich discussion, though at times we wondered where Dave was going with all this. The outcome was the "Plan for Excellence" which was used in the campaign to pass bonds to build a high school, should the unification election be successful. We were certain the unification election would pass, but we didn't have a very good track record on bond issues. Without the funds to build the high school, the dream could turn into a nightmare! Both issues passed and as they say, "The rest is history!"

We started our high school by keeping our ninth graders when they graduated from eighth grade. We then added a class each year. The high school students were first housed at Shivela Middle School with the seventh and eighth graders who had left our K-8 schools to start the first middle school. The first elements of the high school staff were hired and contributed to the design of the plant.

Then the state hit us with another zinger. In order to get our elementary and middle school building applications approved for funding we had to go to year-round scheduling. This was the last straw for me. I stayed until we worked out the plan and dealt with the barrage of parent complaints, but by this time I was tired and either had to trade

194

Dave Hutt and Austin to another team or retire. I retired and went sailing in the Northwest.

7. Karen Robertson

Coordinator of Instructional Support
June 28, 2006

In the summer of 1971, I was desperate for a job and it was getting late in the year. Some friends drove me to Blythe, where I'd heard there were openings. The Superintendent offered me a job on the spot and wanted me to sign the contract before leaving. I told him if I couldn't find a job in a week, I'd be back.

On the way back to San Luis Obispo, I stopped by the Riverside County Office of Education and asked if they knew of any jobs. "If you're willing to go to a little country town with only 150 kids, teach two grades, and coach girls P.E (5-8th grade), we might have something," was the answer. I was a small town girl and loved the idea. Ethel Holl interviewed me over the phone and practically gave me the job. They were desperate also. Van was coming on the scene for the first time on the following weekend, so she invited me to come down and interview with him.

A week later, I went to the goat farm in Murrieta (now owned by International Immunology Corporation) where the three board members came together for the interview. Mike Devitt managed the goat farm, Curt Thompson was a farmer with a perpetually bent hat and a raggedy cigar, and Kenny (Kennadine) Turner was a realtor.

I was hired on the spot, signed the contract and went home to gather my things. It was about the first week in August. Van rented one of the only two houses in town for me at $100/month. 42036 D. Street.

When people ask me how I ended up in a little town like Murrieta, I tell them, "Blythe was my other choice. What would you have done?" And the pay was great!!! I had 2 -3 years of experience that I got credit for (even though my years in private school didn't count), so I got $7,200 the first year.

In 1976, I planned an event that included every child in the school and

196

almost every adult in town. The idea was to relay a Bicentennial flag from Murrieta Elementary to Machado Elementary at the north end of Lake Elsinore. My idea was to have K-8 students spaced along the route by having two buses shuttle, drop, and pick up students so that every student (with an adult partner) would run and relay the flag. Ultimately everyone and the flag was to end up at Machado School. It was 16.5 miles.

Marvin Curran (bus driver) and I worked out a plan and I measured the distance and location for every student. Van told me to make sure I had clearance from the Highway Patrol. When I called them, they said, "Absolutely NO!" We would be dropping 155 students and 155 adults along the road to run in the wrong direction (with traffic) and endanger runners as well as drivers. I reported back to Van. He replied, "If you and Marv think you can pull this off, go for it!"

Every student had a number on their back and an adult partner . . . well, there may have been a few older kids on their own. The results were magnificent. We all ended up at Machado for a wonderful welcome ceremony and Bicentennial Celebration. It made four newspapers and it was the wildest event I ever pulled off. We didn't lose a single child or adult! And nobody got hurt. Charlie Riendeau followed in his car and filmed the event with a Super 8 movie camera. I still have a copy of the film.

Van gave me a plaque that year for doing it. The teachers thought I was nuts and some of them didn't even participate.

There is a law that a school district with less than 250 students is not required to give teachers tenure. It still exists today. Because of that, tenure wasn't even available until about 1978. I taught for eight years before I finally got tenure. Mrs. Holl and Mr. LaValley were the very first and they asked for tenure at a board meeting one night when they realized the student population was finally over 250. They didn't tell the rest of us until after they were granted tenure.

Carl Lyons and I served as the negotiating team for the teachers, before the teachers union was organized in the early 1980's. After the union

197

came on scene, negotiations became ugly, drawn out, and were harmful to school morale. At one meeting, John Jacobsen took his shoe off and pounded it on the table, making the point that he had a hole in his shoe! I think that was mostly for effect, more than anything. Nikita Khrushchev, President of the Soviet Union, had just done that in front of the United Nations, and we'd all read about it in the newspapers. Van loved to argue. He was a great boss to work for because you could disagree, even disagree disagreeably, and know that it had nothing to do with job security or the weakening of your friendship.

After the district started growing, there was a need for lots of teachers. Arvo Toukenon, Assistant Superintendent of Personnel, got to hire young teachers from Ohio and Minnesota. They were four-year graduates, so they were lowest on the pay scale. Several trips were made to those states to recruit. I went on a trip with five others for a whole week. We went to every college in Ohio, and we made at least 50 offers. I was the technician who shot a video of each candidate so we could remember who each person was and take the film home to show all the hiring principals. I think we hired about 25 of the 50 on that one trip.

The new recruits were surprised when they arrived in Murrieta. Their schools didn't overlook the Pacific Ocean (as they may have dreamed), it was 45 miles to a college where they would need to take another whole year of course work plus three more classes, no night life, no family, and sometimes their assignments were in schools that were barely built.

8. Carmen Stratemeyer

Retired Teacher, Murrieta Elementary School
January 4, 2006

When I arrived in seventy-four
The campus was so small
Donna worked in a cubbyhole
And Marie by a toilet stall

198

I was hired by Van in 1974 to teach a Temecula/Murrieta Special Education class. The classroom was a small portable building with the library on one end. Brenda Williams was my aide. That year the other teachers were Mrs. Holl (Kindergarten), Mrs. Lambert, Mr. Jacobsen, Mrs. Fountain (Robertson), Mr. Lyons, Mrs. Wagner, Mr. Lockett, and Mr. LaValley.

In 75/76 our special education program was a joint program with Menifee. The Menifee children came by bus. Charlie Riendeau was my aide that year. He was taking classes to get his teaching credential, and was hired as a teacher a year or two later.

Marie Curran was the school secretary. Her office and the one-stall unisex toilet were in a tiny room later used by psychologists. A Special Day Class was added in 1980, with Mary Godfrey as a teacher.

John Jacobsen organized the Murrieta Teachers' Association, I am not sure of the year.

In the 1970's I believe Van knew every student by name. He was a truly caring administrator. My special education students were eager to share their reports and writing projects with him. These would be returned to the students with personal comments praising their work.

In those days, corporal punishment was still allowed—and expected. There were a number of students who had to bend over and receive their swats. One way Van handled fighting was to get out the wrestling mats and let the combatants battle following rules.

9. Charlie Riendeau
Teacher, Creekside High School
June 5, 2006

Charlie Riendeau first came to the Murrieta School district in the fall of '75. He had just finished working for the Hemet School District as a groundsman. The morale of that particular group was extremely low and

199

he responded to an instructional aide position that was advertised in Murrieta. Dorothea Tiss saw him coming into the grounds in the late afternoon and strode over to say hello and welcome him. He didn't think she was the official greeter, but she sure acted like it. "She talked as if she had known me for many years and made it seem like I was coming home. "

Then Charlie met Marie Curran, the very, very formidable Irish woman who was the school secretary. She did not make him feel like he was just coming home. She was straightforward, polite and professional. She didn't seem to have the same magic as Mrs. Tiss. What she had was a very good eye for people. She looked you over and if she thought you were all right you got a sort of a "he'll do" and then you were accepted.

The interview went well. Charlie explained that he had just completed The Old Globe Educational Tour. In 1974 and 1975 he was the assistant director, the stage manager, and one of the actors on a theatrical tour that covered San Diego and Imperial Counties and about 150 of its schools, parks and other public places. The tour performed one hour Shakespeare productions. For some of the schools the actors went into the classroom and helped the students prepare for Shakespeare and for watching our show. During these two tours Charlie saw a lot of school districts and a lot of schools. Most of these, with the exceptions of some of the magnet schools and one or two of the smaller districts, he would not wanted to have worked in for very long. But Charlie found out that working with the kids, regardless of the environment, was always uplifting and positive.

While they weren't as morale-deprived as the Hemet groundsmen, the lounge at way too many of the schools had a negative atmosphere. At the time Charlie didn't know why that was, but assumed it was the way things were. When he arrived at the interview in Murrieta, he saw immediately—and this was reinforced many times over--that it didn't have to be that way at all. He was hired as an instructional aide for Carmen Stratemeyer's Special Education class. At the time it was a structured "pull-out" program. Twenty-seven or so students came to see

Mrs. Stratemeyer at specific times during the day, at which time they were taught specific lessons that she had created for them for all grades 1-8.

Each day after the lessons were over, every student's Educational Plan was updated to the next lesson. Mrs. Stratemeyer was not only great with children but was also a master teacher from whom Charlie learned the most fundamental lessons of how to analyze tasks and prepare them for each student at just the right learning level for them. No class at UCR where Charlie later got his first teaching credentials was as thorough at teaching basic pedagogy as Mrs. Stratemeyer's practice.

During that year 1975-76 Charlie was also in charge of the G.A.T.E. program. It used a variety of subjects, principally Yearbook, Ceramics, and Film Making to achieve objectives for students who were able to learn very quickly and whose imaginations and intellect had plenty of room for a wider curriculum. During that year Mrs. Robertson held her famous relay race from Murrieta to Machado School in Elsinore. Charlie and the G.A.T.E. class filmed parts of it. They also made claymation titles, filmed class projects, dances, special events and even did a time lapse of the building of the new office and another classroom pod. The film still exists. It is 1600 feet of 8mm film or four reels. One of the reels had a black and white film within a film. That one has disappeared. But the other three still exist. It took more than 140 hours to edit the tiny 8mm film and was presented as one of the final projects of the G.A.T.E. class at several events at the end of the year.

This was a very special weather year. Charlie and his wife had moved out to the town of Sage just south of Hemet. Most people at that time couldn't find Hemet on the map so Sage would certainly be a wonder. Mrs. Riendeau dearly liked open spaces and the country, so they lived on a five-acre homestead, which belonged to a couple that visited the site only rarely and needed reliable tenants. This drive added about twenty miles to the commute, but it was worth it. To get to the main road there was a very steep dirt road that one had to climb. In fine weather, this was not a problem, but in bad weather the dirt turned to soft mud. The

Riendeaus had a Volkswagen, which they learned even floated over streams.

Then it snowed and Charlie had to call Murrieta and tell them that he couldn't make it to school because the snow was too deep and the car kept sliding down the hill. The hard part, of course, was making Marie believe that he REALLY was snowed in.

By the fall of 1976, Charlie knew that teaching was a career that he liked very much and decided to go to the University of California, Riverside to get his official teaching credentials. At the time, UCR had a book of teaching competencies that cataloged what a teacher had done during student teaching and each skill or task had to be signed off by the master teacher in charge. Interviews came next. He interviewed at several high schools in Riverside and one in Hemet. He also interviewed for a 6-7 social studies position at Murrieta.

The interview at Murrieta was scheduled for 10:30 P.M. The interview panel took their time to make sure that each candidate had adequate time to show the panel who they were and what they could do. Charlie brought two three-ring binders. In one there were photos and clippings of students he had worked with back several years and a complete daily lesson plan for an entire year for High School Speech. The other book held competencies and samples of other lessons in other subjects. He finally got into the interview just after 12:00 AM and it lasted until well after 1:30. The board members and panel staff didn't mind putting in the time necessary to screen to find new employees with whom they were compatible and who could accomplish what their goals for students were.

Charlie was offered a position at Ramona High School in Riverside as technical director of their extensive drama department. He was offered the job in Murrieta. It was a difficult choice. But, the ambience that Mr. van de Wetering and the staff created at Murrieta was so alluring, so prized by children and parents, such a wonderful place to work, that it won hands down.

Charlie began his formal teaching career just two rooms away from Carmen Stratemeyer in a semi-portable room with mystery leaks. When it rained, the water followed a course around the inside of the walls and came out of one or two metal door trims, wetting the floor. It would be some time before that mystery path was located. Fortunately, Murrieta only gets about nine inches of rain a year and it wasn't a major hindrance to health or education.

The six/seven combination class was no picnic as a first teaching assignment. Combination classes were created each year during summer staff meetings in order to accommodate the changes of student population and maximize resources. While combination classes pose certain difficulties, the reasons for creating them were always well known by all staff members who had input into the decision-making. Each staff member could see why the choice had to be made and barring other alternatives, they accepted it and dealt with any minor difficulties to the best of their creative and professional skills.

This style of leadership where each person had input was one of the hallmarks of Van's leadership. At first it seemed to a new teacher that the staff members had far too much freedom of speech. In fact, Charlie thought for sure after the first summer of preparatory meetings that at least two of the senior staff would be fired before school started, so heated and determined were their positions around the meeting tables. But, it seemed that Mr. van de Wetering had a tremendous tolerance for differing opinions and was not insulted by spirited presentations of them.

Although it was not ever directly mentioned, Charlie suspected that this was Van's choice of leadership style. There was never a time when a sacrifice had to be made in budgeting that a staff member didn't know why it had to be made and didn't have some input into making it. There existed a confidence and trust between them that allowed them to agree to another department's needs this time because they had already been assured that next time they would have the advantage if the situation called for it. Decisions were made not on the basis of the grade level or even how dramatically a presentation could be made for a grade levels needs, but rather on the basis of the student's needs.

The world of education enchanted him, as he worked alongside teachers who were making a difference in the lives of children. Seeing the light go on as a youngster "got" a concept was wonderful. As much fun were the philosophical arguments with the teaching staff, all of whom had opinions and were ready to "set the young fellow straight." Murrieta Elementary was an exciting place to be, with a creative and energetic staff. Charlie fit in well, and soon became friends with Karen Robertson and Carl Lyons, enjoying many long arguments over philosophical topics.

For several years, Charlie taught physical education for the middle school children of this K-8 school. Flag football, Basketball, Softball, Soccer and Track were the major sports. Charlie may have been the first soccer coach in Murrieta, certainly at the school, who had a co-ed soccer team. The girls were fearless. It may have been the clear well water or else just growing up around so many horse ranches. Whatever the cause, when a group of players surrounded the ball and a girl was fighting for it, it was usually the girl who came out with the ball in control.

While the classes were co-ed, the students competed with other schools in Flag-football on male or female teams, no co-ed sports there. Murrieta played against Anza, Temecula, and even Mt. San Jacinto Middle School. While the students had great heart, they seemed to be only half the size of the players in a 600-700 student middle school. Playing Mt. San Jacinto was a very difficult day for both coaches and students.

One of the line-boys was a fellow named Chris. He was very solidly built because he was training as a farrier and could practically lift horses off the ground without help. But as an 8th grader he didn't have much height. No amount of trashing could make him want to be taken out of the game. He was later to serve on the Volunteer Fire Department with Charlie for several years, and eventually became a professional fire fighter.

In 1978 there was a critical measure on the ballot called "Proposition 13" which changed the nature of school funding and who controlled it. Prior to its passage, school boards were able to raise the local tax for schools when they needed to. Although that was always a major battle at board meetings, nevertheless, it could be done. After the passage of this act, there was a limit on property tax and all money went to the state to be redistributed by them on the basis of a formula that they created.

Charlie and his wife bought a house built by the same local builder that built Van's house, and also built several of the classrooms as they were added to the school and many other homes around town. It was only 125 yards away from the Fire Station and 225 yards from the school. When the gas crisis came in the late 70s, this move proved to be very beneficial. Charlie could walk to work.

10. Patty Julian Powers
Health Technician, Rail Ranch
January 31, 2006

Patty Julian served as a Board member during the period of tremendous growth, with Evelyn Henning, Dave Hutt, Austin Linsley, and Peter Lemke.

I've been around so long it's hard to remember all that has happened in the last 30 years. I'm not sure what you would want to know. Both of my children went to Murrieta Elementary when it was the only school in Murrieta and it was K-8. Chuck van de Wetering was the principal and then superintendent. The road, Los Alamos was a dirt road and highway 215 was a two- lane road, and not called 215 then. Most of the homes that are here now were farms, oat fields or horse ranches. I may have a picture of the home site that was on the Rail property. There is so much I just don't know where to begin.

11. David Hutt

Board Member
January 15, 2007

I served on the school board for 13 years. I was appointed in 1978 and subsequently elected to three four-year terms before leaving the board (and Murrieta) in 1991. To understand the magnitude of the changes I witnessed, allow me a few comments as to how it was.

When my family moved to Murrieta in 1972, the town was just returning to its population of 100 years before, when the railroad ran south from Corona. We lived on Jefferson Avenue, which used to be the main road from Los Angeles to San Diego and still carries the main trunk lines for phone and natural gas. Interstate 15 did not exist at that time; the main road from Corona to Murrieta and Temecula was State Route 71, which regularly washed out any time there were heavy winter rains. 1982 was an El Nino doozie. There was no supermarket or theater in either Murrieta or Temecula. We went to Fallbrook to do our shopping. Murrieta Creek still had many cottonwoods and walnuts lining its banks and there were fish in the creek. One of the rainy season recreations was to charge the high water in the creek to see if you could make it across the rushing waters. If you got stuck, there was always someone with a tractor to pull you out. I understand that now there are iron gates that are closed during high water.

Unlike today when nearly everyone goes around with a cell phone, if you had business to conduct, you would go the local restaurant for breakfast or a cup of coffee. Sooner or later, the person you needed to talk to would come in. In Murrieta it was the Windmill Inn; in Temecula, it was the Swing Inn.

Talking of Temecula, in the old town, was The Long Branch Saloon. Nearly every Saturday night some Hell's Angels would ride into town and meet up with some of the local Indians from the Pechanga Reservation. Altercations would often break out, usually at the Long

206

Branch. In the late 70's, if I remember correctly, the Long Branch changed hands and was reborn as an Evangelical Christian Church. Some Hell's Angels rode into town and went directly to the Long Branch and one of them exclaimed when he discovered his favorite watering hole was now a church, "D---! Ain't nothing sacred?!"

Like most small towns, Murrieta had its eccentrics. One regular that I remember from my early years was "Indian Pete". The DMV had taken his driver's license away when he was in his 80's, but he could still drive his tractor (no license required). He was regularly seen on the streets in town driving his tractor to get a "cool one", usually at Ray's Cafe. He drove his tractor until he died at age 102. Another of my memories was seeing an old photo at Murrieta Country Market taken in 1902 showing a fisherman with his catch of steelhead. The photo was taken at Fish Camp in the hills just above Murrieta. Going back a little farther in history, the drilling log for our well showed pieces of Redwood from a depth of 300 feet. How things have changed.

The early years

Murrieta School District was a single school, K-8 district when I was first appointed to the board. Charles van de Wetering (affectionately known to everyone as Van, or Mr. Van if you were a student) was the principal/superintendent and Donna Brandy basically did everything else that needing to be done,, including secretary to the board. The school had an enrollment of a little less than 300 students and the ed code stipulated the size of the board at three members. Later on, when student enrollment increased, we went to a five-member board.

My fellow board members at that time were Chick Williamson and Curt Thompson. On warm summer evenings, when the details and the educationese would drag on and on, Curt would look at his watch and stand up announcing, "Got to change the irrigation water." He would return in about twenty minutes and ask if we had decided anything. He was a man of few words, but very intelligent and always voted to support what was best for "the kids". These were the days prior to Prop 13 and the local school board set the tax rate each year to fund the school. Murrieta School District was the largest district geographically in Riverside County, but one of the smallest in student enrollment so we never had any opposition on our tax rate decisions.

The district extended over the hills to the west of town and some students of the district actually attended San Juan Capistrano School District on an exchange agreement. We had no school bus service in those days even though we had repeated requests, especially from the developing La Cresta area. A full time paid lobbyist for the Los Angeles Unified School District had structured the state funding formula for school bus reimbursement to be very favorable to LA, but very detrimental to rural school districts. The board refused to take money out of the classroom to fund school bus transportation. When we finally initiated a bus program in 1970, the parents, not the district, paid for it although the district operated the program. Marv Curran, who also headed up the Murrieta Fire Protection District, was in charge of the buses.

In the early 80's, the board, under Van's direction, was systematically reviewing all existing board policies and comparing them to the model policies issued by the California School Boards Association. For the most part very boring, routine business. Boring, that is, until we got to the policy that could be best characterized as our educational philosophy. I wrote a revision and we put it out to the teachers for comments. The fireworks exploded!

We asserted that every child was gifted and unique and that it was the job of the school to discover each child's potential and make the child successful. That was too heavy a burden for the teachers. How could they be responsible for the success of each and every child when there was poverty, abusive parents, genetic afflictions, etc., etc., etc. Needless to say, there were good points on both sides and we ended up with a policy that was a compromise that no one liked. Hard feelings lingered on both sides of the table for many years. I still maintain that if you set mediocre goals, you will achieve less than mediocre performance.

Another example of the tension that existed between the board and the teachers who were now a local chapter of the union, California Teachers Association (CTA), was on the nature and structure of the pay schedule. Teachers usually work in a schedule of steps and grades. So many years of service translates into so much more money. So many credentials or course work, qualifies for so much more money. Critics derisively call this "warm body pay". The board wanted a performance based pay structure, or merit pay.

The negotiations were long and heated. We finally came to an agreement and signed a three-year contract with the teachers. A few details still had not been worked out, but were covered by a letter of understanding. The whole pay structure of steps and grades had been thrown out. It was replaced by three pay categories: beginning teacher, tenured teacher and master teacher. In addition, any teacher would be eligible for an annual bonus in addition to their salary based on a positive evaluation of a five point criteria.

The board felt that overall the pay schedule for teachers was wholly inadequate. The proposed contract raised the salary for a beginning teacher from $15,000 per year to $22,000 and nearly comparable increases for many of the other teachers. This was the carrot. The stick was merit pay. Talk about classic approach/avoidance behavior. The teachers finally signed the merit pay contract. The merit bonus was $2,000 or $3,000 per year. It was not competitively based where only a fixed percentage of the teachers could receive a bonus; every teacher measuring up to the criteria would receive a bonus.

As it turned out, the district did not pay one single bonus over the life of the contract. The sticking point was the details that were never finalized in the Letter of Understanding. Four of the five criteria were agreed upon including the observable phenomena relating to lesson plans, modeling specific behaviors in the classroom, etc. The hang-up was the fifth criteria having to do with student performance. The board expected that the students would learn one year's worth of curriculum as tested by standardized tests. (Students with IEPs were exempted from the pool. IEP's are Individual Education Plans and are written for those students who have demonstrated learning difficulties.) The teachers balked. The board fumed. Nothing happened. In retrospect, probably well over half the teachers would have received their merit pay if that last little bit of the contract had been finalized.

Interestingly, at the end of the three-year contract, the main office of the CTA sent their big guns down to the pipsqueak district of Murrieta to make sure this merit pay thing was done in once and for all. Back to warm body pay. Later on, the board, trying to establish a more collegial model, created the position on the board for a representative of the teacher's union. This representative did not have a vote, but did receive the full information package and participated in all board discussions. Exclusions included Executive sessions and matters covering the discipline of personnel.

One amusing side note about the merit pay contract negotiations played out in executive session. I had prepared a letter for other board members to consider addressed to the union and dealt with our frustration at their intransigence. It could be characterized as autocratic, high handed and venting our frustration and contempt. The other board members all jumped on it and said "Let's send it." My response was "No way. Here is the letter we need to send." I passed out a more reasoned and conciliatory letter. The first letter was to relieve the anger and frustration; the second letter was what needed to be said.

Van's leadership

To illustrate the nature of the main players in the board and administration of the 80s, Van's dual role as superintendent/principal was split as the enrollment at Murrieta Elementary School grew. He was mightily conflicted as to whether to take the superintendent's spot or to take the principal's spot. He has a real devotion and understanding of children and I'm sure his heart was saying principal while his head was saying superintendent. Fortunately, given the turmoil that lay ahead, he chose superintendent. I shudder to think what might have happened had he not been at the helm during the years when we were nearly overwhelmed by the onrush of growth and change.

Another small, but very telling example about Van happened when the press picked up and magnified the environmental scare story about Alar being sprayed on apples. Van called the state department of agriculture to obtain the real information. At the end of the conversation, the official told Van he had been the only school person to call his office to clarify the facts. At the time, there were 1056 school districts in the state of California. One out of 1056; that is a good mark of the man.

Van was never contemptuous of the board, and it can be taken as a measure of his self-confidence that he could work as an equal with the board members. We had what would be characterized as a pro-active board, rather than a reactive board that merely rubber-stamped the recommendations of the superintendent. At one point the composition of the board consisted of 60% foreign-born naturalized citizens. The three were Pete Lemke (Germany), Evelyn Henning (Philippines) and myself (England). I feel this diversity in perspective made a stronger board.

Kudos to Donna Brantly

A word about Donna. Intelligent, articulate, organized are all words that come to mind, but the quality that most endeared her to the board members was her handling and translation of the budget. The entire budget is expressed in entitlements, ed code sections, federal grants, and every other obfuscating verbiage that anyone can think of. She totally broke the budget down into basic units and reconstructed it so that parents, reporters and board members could understand it. If you do not recognize what a sheer work of genius this is, you are not familiar with public education. Later on this approach led us to zero based budgeting which enabled us to find money for special programs that could not have been funded if we did not have Donna.

As a small community, Murrieta had three focal points for town life: The Town Hall Association under Dottie Renon, the Murrieta Fire Protection District under Marv Curran and the Murrieta School District under Van. One of the extraordinary annual events put on at the school was the Christmas Program under the inspiration and direction of English teacher Satch La Valley. These were not fun little shows where parents cooed and reporters left half way through. These were productions. Many people in the community were involved on sets and costumes. The level of performance was such that, if it were a traveling troupe, you'd swear that the next stop would be Broadway. They were that good.

I'd like to add a few more observations about the board. In the early 80's, board members regularly started attending the annual conference put on by the California School Boards Association (CSBA). The main advantage of attending such conferences was the opportunity for board members to step outside of their local orientation and find out what else was happening in the world of education. Besides the presenters at the general sessions, the conference had a large assemblage of vendors. Spouses of board members usually attended as well. At one conference, my wife, Valorie, found the SWRL art program. Another program found at one of these conferences was the Junior Great Books Program. One consultant discovered at a conference was Marshall Krupp of Community Systems Associates. More about Marshall later.

Another board function that we initiated was an annual retreat for the board members. These retreats were held out of town and far enough away so that board members would not be tempted to cut their attendance short for personal reasons. We typically convened for Friday dinner and ran through the weekend with work sessions Friday night, Saturday morning and afternoon and then a summary session Sunday morning. At these retreats, board members hammered out a philosophical framework upon which we could all agree.

No action was taken at these meetings, but there were often intense discussions. I remember one retreat in San Diego where I lead off the retreat on Friday night by showing the video "Stand and Deliver." Olmas's brilliant performance as the protagonist who challenged his students to perform beyond anyone's expectations was inspirational. Dealing with expectations and setting the standard is at the heart of being a board member. I challenged my fellow board members as to whether we wanted to be champions of mediocrity or if we were going to take a stand for excellence.

Growth rate accelerates

By 1986, the district had grown to the point that we needed a second school. A 15-acre site was selected and the board settled on naming new schools after Indian words and pioneer families to reflect our local heritage. The new K-8 school was to be Avaxat, Indian for cottonwood. After Proposition 13 passed in 1978, funding of schools had become a state function. Locally we were only able to collect a fee for temporary housing of $200 per housing unit. An instant, temporary school was called for. It was to be built in the corner of the site so we would not impinge on the footprint of the permanent buildings.

One of the operative factors driving the timing was the state funding for a Special Day Class (SDC). This funding was $42,000, but the school had to be open and occupied by October 15" to qualify. Van had drawn up the contracts working with the architect and presented them at the board meeting for review before the board selected a contractor and awarded the construction contract. Van had included the standard $300 per day if the school was not ready for occupancy by the specified date. I was president of the board that year and I turned to my side and talked to fellow board member Jim Keown who was a contractor. After a brief discussion between the two of us, he introduced a motion to change the terms of the contract so that the one day late penalty was $42,000.

Van objected that this wasn't customary, but every member of the board saw the logic of the motion and it was approved unanimously. I turned to the five waiting contractors waiting and asked if any of them wished to withdraw their bid. You could see many of them gulp, but not one withdrew. We awarded the contract. When Avaxat did open on time, the district received its $42,000. There was not one utility in place. We had a generator for electricity; we had bottled water to drink, and the restroom facilities were port-a-potties, including a generously proportioned Taj Mahal for handicapped students. The students were in class by October 15th and education marched on.

Another note on Avaxat. Eastern Municipal Water District (EMWD) built a multi million-gallon storage tank behind Avaxat. The board adjourned one summer meeting and went out to inspect Avaxat. While we were there we checked out the water tank and its large, earthen containment berm designed to contain and deflect the water in case there was a catastrophic failure due to earthquake, etc. Jim Keown picked up a grading lath and was able to push it three feet into the ground that should have been compacted and hard.

The board hired a hydrologist to model a catastrophic failure and to give his professional opinion if students would be in danger if it happened during school hours. The hydrologist's response was in the affirmative. A governmental agency like EMWD does not have to have inspectors since they are supposed to be a responsible organization. We threatened to sue EM" if they did not correct the earthen berm. The final outcome was that EM" tore out the berm and rebuilt it with water, sheep's foot compaction and an inspector hired by us, but paid for by EMWD.

One difference of opinion that developed between the board and many new members of community was the grade configuration K-8 vs. K-6 and Middle School. What many newcomers never realized was that the state would fund a 15-acre site for a K-8 school, but only a 10-acre site for a K-6 school. There were many other arguments on both sides of the table, but the board rolled over and opted for the K-6, Middle School configuration.

As a K-8 district, we were a feeder district for the Elsinore Union School District where Murrieta students went for high school. At the time the growth really started, Temecula was running ahead of Murrieta and had applied to Riverside County to become a Unified school district. It made perfect sense for Temecula, but it left Murrieta as the only feeder district to Elsinore and the very real possibility that Murrieta would be absorbed into Elsinore. The community did not want to lose their identity and were adamantly opposed to amalgamating with Elsinore. The master plans for the Murrieta developments, Alta Murrieta and California Oaks, had already been approved, but the earth wasn't moving, waiting on the Eastern Municipal Water District to build the main water transmission line to Murrieta. We applied to Riverside County to Become a Unified School District.

This is where the community came together. Marv Curran should probably be considered "The Spiritual Father" of Murrieta. Under his inspiration and direction, The Murrieta Fire Protection District, with its gung-ho band of volunteer firefighters had become the top ranked district in Riverside County. This high level of accomplishment was funded over the years by a $30.00 parcel tax (the parcel tax was $30 whether you had a city lot or 100 acres). The social cohesion was the Murrieta Fireman's BBQ where the whole community came together to visit and inspect the new equipment. This was one of the main sources of community pride, and deservedly so.

The actual political process of school unification requires a petition. It is filed with the County Clerk and then forwarded to the Registrar of Voters for certification. If approved by the Registrar, the petition is then studied and recommendations are made as to disposition and then a process of public hearings is held before final action is taken. If everything is positive up to that point, the County Board of Supervisors will then order an election in the district.

Dottie Renon and I were the Chief Petitioners. A typical petition submitted to the county will have a 60% to 70% certification rate. Given the tight time we had to work in, we could not deal with that degree of uncertainty. We devised a very tightly controlled process to collect the signatures of registered voters. First of all, the signer had to be a registered voter, and secondly, the signature had to exactly match the way in which the voter had registered.

We obtained copies all the voter registration roles for the school district, and after intensive training of the volunteers, we went into the assigned streets and byways of the community to obtain the necessary signatures exactly as the voters had signed the voter registration roles. We counted signatures and struck out those that did not qualify. After only a few weeks we submitted our petition to the county. The signatures were certified at a 98% level. This feat had never been achieved before.

This was just the beginning of a very arduous process. The company that was hired by the county to study our unification petition made a negative finding. This negative finding, if sustained, would mean the end of the Murrieta School District. We were not only fighting for unification; we were fighting for our life. It came down to a question of demographic projections. If the projections showed enough student enrollment, we could become a unified school district. On the other hand, if the projections were flat to anemic, no unification was possible.

The public hearing, conducted at Murrieta Elementary School, was super charged and the room was filled to overflowing. I led the questioning. The lady who was the presenter for the contract company was evasive in her answers. I pressed and insisted that she be specific in her answers. I was never personal or insulting, but I was relentless and direct in my questioning. Finally, she broke down in tears and admitted that they had not done the demographic study, but had subcontracted it out to another firm in San Diego who was not aware of the explosive growth that lay ahead for Murrieta. The basis for the negative recommendation was destroyed on the spot.

After the meeting, which ran rather late into the night, the lady whose findings I had attacked so vigorously could not start her car. Fellow board member Pete Lemke and I were able to start her car and we assured her our objections were not personal. She said she understood.

The subsequent unification election was a resounding success. We were riding a groundswell of community support. We were a newly minted unified school district, and not having a clue what we were supposed to do. We had to learn very fast.

Cityhood, bond election and community organizations

The ground swell of community pride and identity spilled over to cityhood for Murrieta. Dottie Renon and I were again called upon to be the Chief Petitioners. It really had a little of the desperate expectations of "Once more into the breach rode the 600". Cityhood was not a slam-dunk because there were nagging questions whether the tax base was sufficient for the city to be financially viable. The petition circulators delivered the goods and the county certified 96% of the signatures valid. (We slipped a little bit from the 98% success rate on the unification petition.). An election was authorized and the voters overwhelmingly approved cityhood.

To be a unified school district, you need to have a high school. High schools cost big bucks. In 1978, the voters of California had approved Prop 13 that rolled back property taxes, limited their increases and stipulated that if a local district were to float a bond issue it had to be approved by a 2/3 vote rather than a simple majority. A 2/3 vote is virtually impossible to achieve in the world of politics. The state instituted a program for school construction. The downside of this was that the funding level did not keep pace with the needs. The board decided to try to buck the tide and hold a school bond election to build the new high school.

A bond committee was formed and beat the drum about the need for the high school. When the election rolled around, the voters turned out in large numbers and the high school bond was approved by 88%. We had not cleared the 2/3 hurdle; we sailed over it. If I remember correctly, this was the first school bond election in the State of California that had been approved by voters in 10 or 11 years. A truly remarkable feat. The size of the bond approved by the voters actually exceeded the bonding capacity of the district, but we were not concerned because the rapidly expanding tax base would make it viable by the following year.

The rate of growth in the whole of southwest Riverside County was

217

accelerating and causing friction in many separate areas. These rapid changes generated many community efforts to mitigate, modify or just plain stop initiatives that were proposed. Several of the efforts were aimed at developers; some efforts were directed at Riverside County. This generated a lot of interaction between developers, citizen groups, governmental agencies and Riverside County.

POP, the acronym for Preserve Our Plateau, was up and running to protect and expand The Nature Conservancy's Santa Rosa Plateau, one of the last pristine areas in Southern California and the home to vernal pools and Engelmann Oaks.

The county was revising the general plan for Southwest Riverside County. The meetings for SWAP lasted three years. Local realtor, Carmela Loelkes, headed the Murrieta subcommittee up. I served on that subcommittee and was the presenter of the Murrieta Plan. About 90% of our recommendations were accepted and incorporated into the new General Plan. Unfortunately, the subcommittee's recommendation on traffic and circulation was not adopted. We had recommended a bridge and road assessment district to fund access across 1-15 so the interstate did not cut the community in half.

Another effort was the CRWM, another acronym standing for Citizens for Responsible Watershed Management. We advocated the use of detention and retention basins to control flooding rather than put Murrieta Creek into an 11-mile concrete ditch. The group was not very large; it primarily consisted of Jim Marple and myself, but we made enough noise to garner the attention of the Army Corps of Engineers, the EPA, the US Fish and Wildlife and the National Park Service's Wild and Scenic River.

More than 10 years later, and after I had left the community, a compromise was reached leaving Murrieta Creek as a greenbelt and a 60 acre detention basin situated upstream from old town Temecula. The reality is if they had built the 11 mile concrete ditch, it would have accelerated the runoff and caused a much larger hydrological peak which they could never have moved through old town without tearing down all

218

development on one side of the creek or another.

Another group that was formed was MECCA, another acronym for Murrieta Educational Cultural and Care Association. The group is defunct now, but it was formed to provide social services in the community while Murrieta was still part of the county. The founders were primarily school and board personnel with Van, Evelyn Henning and myself as the major players. MECCA provided tutoring services for Murrieta students and served as the umbrella organization and insurance provider for many community sports activities. For a brief time, MECCA actually had paid personnel.

All of this activity drew the attention of one of the more aggressive local developers, Mr. Yoo of RANPAC. In discussions with him, he decided to help the district by sponsoring a benefit golf tournament at Bear Creek. He leaned heavily on all his business associates and we had a very successful First Annual Murrieta Golf Tournament. (As it turns out, it was also the last because Mr. Yoo declined to sponsor the district after we sued the county over development fees.) The First Annual did raise over S40,000 that went to MECCA to fund their programs. Also funded out of this $40,000 were all the costs associated with the publication of the board's vision statement, "Planning for Excellence" in October, 1989. These costs included mailing a copy to every family in the school district.

Growth goes into hyperdrive

Turning to the very contentious issue of funding school construction, we come to the heart of most of the controversies of the late 80's and early 90's. The state provides the operating funds for school districts under their ADA formula. (ADA stands for Average Daily Attendance.) It is crucial to understand the timing of the receipt of these funds because this basic fact drove many of the decisions the board made during these years. The bottom line reality is that the students arrive in the classroom before the money arrives.

The question then becomes how do you pay for the planning,

providing classrooms and hiring the necessary personnel before the new students arrive. Our only source of funds, without taking it out of the classroom of our existing students, is the nominal $200 per house that the builders pay before obtaining their building permits. Riverside County, the agency that issued the building permits at the time, could not even tell us how many of those permits were actually issued in the Murrieta School District. We needed to know what was coming down the road with our name on it.

We did several things, all of which drew criticism from one quarter or another. Since we had no staff to do the forward planning, the board switched from meeting every two weeks to meeting once a week. The board meetings became notorious for their marathon nature. We convened at 7:30 PM and ran until the business was finished, very often 2:00 or 3:00 A.M. After the opening Pledge of Allegiance and prayer, we always queried the audience if anyone wished to address the board, had business with the board that evening, etc. We then reordered the agenda to place all these people first. Everyone was welcome to stay, but usually no one did after 10 PM or so. We took breaks; we sent out for pizza; we did whatever it took to make the necessary decisions on a timely basis. Basically, the board did the work at these meetings that would normally be done by various assistant superintendents.

The board did hire Tom Tooker as a full time consultant and we did retain the services of Marshall Krupp and his company Community Systems Associates. I had found Marshall at one of the CSBA conferences and personally invited him to the district. The following year, the board created four assistant superintendents positions and staffed them as follows: Donna Brandy was promoted to Assistant Superintendent for Business; Tom Tooker was switched from consultant to Assistant Superintendent of Facilities Services; Dr. Karen Lynch was hired as Assistant Superintendent of Instructional Services; Dr. Arvo Toukonen was hired as Assistant Superintendent of Personnel. We were starting to look and function more like a regular district.

We addressed the issue of how many new students and when they

220

would arrive by a novel process devised by Tom and Marshall. We took aerial photographs of the district, all on a particular day. This date became our benchmark. We counted graded pads, foundations, and houses in the framing stage, etc. from the aerial photos and then started counting permits issued on a day-by-day basis after the benchmark date. It took a merchant builder about 90 days to build a house. With our pupil generation factor in hand based on the demographics of the community, Tom gave us weekly enrollment projections which were incredibly accurate, usually better than 97%.

The board's most controversial action was undoubtedly filing the lawsuit against Riverside County regarding school construction fees. The county maintained that the State of California had preempted the field of school construction financing after Prop. 13 and the county had no standing to authorize builder fees other than the nominal amount authorized for temporary classrooms. (This temporary classroom fee was about $200 per house if I recall the number correctly. Do the math. A 600-pupil elementary school would generate about $120,000 in fees, but the cost of an elementary school was about $6,000,000.) Technically, Riverside County was probably correct. However, if you took an expanded view, there were other avenues we could pursue.

The idea of suing the county under the California Environmental Quality Control Act (CEQA) was brought to the board by Marshall. After many agonizing discussions, the board decided they had no alternative but to give the lawsuit a try. We sued Riverside County on six different points under CEQA. The school district lost in district court and we moved to the Appellate Court. The Appellate Court found in Murrieta's favor on all six counts. Riverside County then appealed to the State Supreme Court.

The Supreme Court upheld the findings of the Appellate Court and then did something extraordinary. They published their decision. That meant that the decision did not apply just to the Murrieta School District. It meant that it applied to each and every one of 1056 school districts in the state of California. It became the "Murrieta Decision". Based on the

Southwest Area Plan, SWAP, which had been adopted by the county as the new general development plan, build out of the Murrieta community in 10 to 20 years would require school construction expenditures of $1,000,000,000. That is billion with a B! After the favorable decision, Murrieta started collecting fees of $6,000 per house on average. The money spent on the lawsuit was money well spent.

Marshall's aggressive stance paid off in many ways for the district. One action that potentially backfired revolved around the bowling alley in California Oaks. Marshall had contacted them and demanded builder's fees. Their rejoinder was that they were not contributing any children to the school enrollment and they were not going to pay any fees. If fees were imposed, they would take their project elsewhere. I got wind of the altercation, told Marshall to back off and then called Chicago to advise them that no fees would be imposed.

One amusing incident occurred when we hit our first 100% plus enrollment figure. We sent in our figures to the State Department of Education and they returned them to us and asked us to correct them. Surely, we must have got the decimal point in the wrong place. We sent the document back and said the numbers were correct and asked them if they had any ideas to share with us as to what to do. Their rejoinder was that they had never seen figures like that and they had no idea what to do.

The high school bond election had met the needs for school facilities for our older students, but the elementary and middle school construction situation was getting worse and worse. We decided to try for another bond election. The need was enormous and the size of the necessary bond was too large for some in the community to swallow. This 1991 effort was approved by the voters at the 58.5% level, but that fell short of the 2/3 requirement set by Prop. 13. State funding was desperately needed. The voters of California had approved some state school bonds and the behind-the-scenes infighting was on big time because the needs statewide exceeded funds nearly 10 to 1.

Tom Tooker joined the fray. Once again he did himself and the district proud. With his high intellect and quite persistence he dogged the powers that be in Sacramento. Arguing that we were entitled to funds that at least matched the $38,500,000 high school bond, he pressed his case. What other district had stepped up to the plate and passed a school construction bond? Tom's tenacity paid off. He did not garner a one for one match, but he did secure $26,000,000 for the district. In my opinion, Tom never did receive the credit that this accomplishment deserved.

Although the board spent a lot of time on facilities and personnel, the heart of our effort was expressed in Planning for Excellence. There were many different initiatives. One that was probably unique was the board's decision to require every graduate from the Murrieta district to be literate and fluent in Spanish. By literate and fluent in Spanish, the board meant that each student would have the ability to read, write, speak and think in Spanish. This was not an elective; it was a requirement for every student. This decision was not discussed in advance with the staff or the community. I am sure that the main impetus for this was having board members who were not native English speakers. The board directed Van to come up with a plan to implement the Spanish language decision.

Van proposed and the board accepted the idea that we hire a teacher for each elementary school in the district who would not have a classroom assignment. This teacher would be fluent in Spanish and would rotate among all classrooms teaching Spanish. The classroom teacher was also expected to learn Spanish. There were six elementary schools in the district when this plan was started.

After establishing graduation requirements for the first high school class that followed traditional lines and UC requirements, the board created Task Force 2000. The charge to Task Force 2000 was to develop the curriculum, the means and the timeline for implementing the vision enumerated in "Planning for Excellence." This group was composed of parents, community members, teachers and board members and was ably chaired by Guy Romero. I do not know what happened to Task Force 2000 because I left the district and Murrieta in 1991. I will leave that story to those who followed to tell that tale.

A few parting observations. At the end of nine years on the board, I thought I had done my civic duty and it was time for someone else to take up the task. Having seen many board members come and go, I understood that the learning curve for a new board member was two years before they could really become a contributing board member. I also realized the turmoil that lay ahead for the district. Times of great change also create times of great opportunity. I decided to stand for reelection with the intent of making as large an imprint as I could. During the following three to four years I spent an average 30 to 40 hours a week on school affairs and an additional 20 to 30 hours a week on cityhood, SWAP, MECCA, CRWM, POP. That last stint burnt me out as I'm sure it did Van, Donna and many others. I think I can say for all of us: "It was a glorious fight."

12. Cindy Crismon

Accounts Payable
January 23, 2006

It was August of 1980 when I first walked into the office of Murrieta Elementary School to register my daughter Amy for the fourth grade, and Marie Curran was the first smiling face I saw. I remember it like it was today because life-changing moments stay locked in your memory to be recalled in later years when one yearns for the "good ole days." Little did I know then that a few short months later I too would be working in that office along side two women, Donna Brantly and Marie Curran, who would become not only co-workers but life-long friends.

I plan to retire this June, 2006, so perhaps it's fitting that I write down some of my memories to share with those who come after me. I hope they won't bore you. After all, we were a small community and not nearly as sophisticated as we are today. Times were simpler and so were the people. We had no computers or cell phones, and getting a new electric typewriter for the office was worth fighting over. After all, the new typewriters actually had correction tape. Amazing! (Sorry, didn't mean to sound like Huell Houser.).

When I was interviewing for the part-time secretarial position, I failed to ask about the work schedule. Imagine my disappointment when I found out that it was a twelve-month position. No summer, Christmas, or Easter vacation other than the allotted holidays and requested leave for earned vacation. I thought that when the kids were gone that there would be nothing to do. Wrong! In a one-school district there is plenty to do during the times when the students and teachers are away-- like cleaning out the refrigerator. If you think your home refrigerators are scary to clean, try cleaning an office refrigerator. Marie and I would pull the large trash can over and simply dump everything into it. We didn't even bother to save the plasticware. Yuk! The plasticware contained horrible green stuff and we were afraid to open the containers fearing that our lives would be snuffed out by the bacteria that might fly out from them.

There were lots of fun times too when everyone except the office staff and custodians were gone. For example, placing the annual school supply order and distributing it when it came in, which usually was the day before the students were due to come back. One year Marie and I actually worked on Labor Day distributing the supplies. Oh, by the way, we didn't get double time for working the holiday. We never even thought to ask for it. We simply did it out of the goodness of our hearts so that the teachers and students would have what they needed to start off another successful year at Murrieta Elementary. By the way, this was the year that I dropped a box on Marie's sore toe. Oops! No workers' comp. Well, there may have been workers' comp but Marie never asked for it.

Delivering school supplies was a highlight in Marie's and my summer duties. The supplies would be delivered to a large classroom, usually the science room because it had such nice large tables, and then using the supply request list from each of the teachers, Marie and I would fill a shopping cart full of what the teacher ordered and deliver them to the teacher's classroom. The piles would be waiting for the teachers to sort through and put away on their first day back. Little did we know that a few of the teachers were sending excess writing paper to the large storage barn located near the cafeteria. Teachers were supposed to store the supplies in their classrooms.

We found out about the stored paper one summer when we were writing up the year's annual order and Wayne Jones, our custodian/bus driver, asked us, "What about all the paper stored out in the barn. When is that going to be used?" Marie and I looked at each other and jointly said, "What? Show us!" You cannot imagine what years and years of stored paper looks like. Two whole walls of boxes stacked so high that we could not even reach the top. But then Wayne said, "And what about the storage room." "Storage room?" we ask. Yes, the storage room was full of boxes also. Marie and I spent about a week going through all the boxes. Opening them, inventorying the types of paper and pulling a sample to give to the principal, Susan Reynolds, so that she could present the samples to her staff. I don't think that we had to buy writing paper for the next three years. And to Susan's credit, all the paper was used. Marie, Wayne Jones and I all learned several lessons such as, always check the storage areas before placing an order, always spray the storage areas for black widow spiders, and never wear white on the days you're cleaning out the storage areas. These are smart lessons for anybody, right?

The times when the students and teachers were present were never boring either. There were unique personalities and needs that made Marie's and my life rich and rewarding. For example, dearly loved Mr. LaValley would scream and hang up on us when we rang him on the intercom. He did not like to be disturbed while he was teaching. The first time it happened to me, Marie laughed and said, "Don't worry, he does that to everyone." Needless to say, I hated to call him but sometimes I just had to do it. We all loved him. He was a wonderful teacher who loved his students and gave so much to the community. There were so many wonderful teachers then, and I'm sure there still are

226

today.

Scheduling the parent conferences twice a year was fun too. I don't know how it's done today, but when there were no computers it was a two-person job. The rules were that we had to schedule conferences at the parents' and teachers' convenience. In other words, for parents who had more than one student in our school, we had to schedule their conferences so that they did not have to come to the school more than once. Now remember, we also had the teachers' schedules when they would be available. Add to this the fact that some of the students don't have the same last name as the parents and you've got yourself a three-ring circus. Oh, and what fun it was when a teacher would suddenly remember a forgotten appointment after we had done the scheduling. Computers would definitely have made our lives easier back then. Not to worry though-- somehow everything seemed to work out fine. I don't remember any complaints from the parents or teachers, and if there were, Van handled them.

One year we had a lice infestation at school. Yes, I know. No one likes to talk about such things but it was a memorable experience. Van told Marie and me and several others that we would be checking each and every student's head in the school for head lice. Marie balked and refused. I smoothed it over by saying that we really needed Marie to keep track of our findings. Everyone was happy-- well maybe not happy, but willing to do their duty. On the day that the head exams were to begin, as a joke and to break the tension we were all feeling, I wore my youngest daughters' Halloween costume to school. I wore a nurses' cap and small blue cape with red trim. We all had a good laugh, head exams were completed, and, after several weeks, we finally got rid of the horrible lice infestation.

The days I worked directly at a school site are long gone. For the last eighteen years I've worked in the district office, or support center as it is now called, with little or no contact with students, teachers or parents. Many of the people that were working when I first came here are either retired, working at a location I rarely see, or worse, deceased. Now I'm in my own little cubicle working with a machine that I only dreamed about in the "good ole days."

There are so many things that I could and would like to share about those long ago days, such as the wonderful pot lucks and birthday parties in the office, memories of carnivals, PTA meetings, late-night Board meetings, and interesting, colorful people, but I really must stop. And then too, there are memories that cannot be shared except between good friends.

So in closing, it is the people that have always been the most important asset of Murrieta's School District. The district has always been lucky in hiring the best at any given moment in time. Each person that worked or is still working here has brought their own uniqueness, making an indelible impression on all whose lives they touch directly or indirectly. There are students and co-workers that I will always remember, and yes, some that I will probably forget. But even the ones I might forget have enriched my life while working here at Murrieta and for this I would like to thank everyone for passing through my life. I know that many will become fading memories like those in a school annual that you pick up, read what is written, and then wonder "who was that person?" Others will remain engraved in my memory forever.

Thank you all so very much for being a part of my life.

13. Guy Romero

Interim Assistant Superintendent of Educational Services
January 4, 2006

Opening Avaxat School was an experience not many administrators will have. I say this not because it was a new school, it is because of the conditions we were operating in. Even though some would consider the conditions similar to what you find in only remote areas, we opened with incredible teachers and staff and our students excelled well beyond what most students were doing in Riverside County.

228

Avaxat opened in August 1987 with 77 students in the Multipurpose Room at Murrieta School. Both Avaxat and Murrieta were K-8 schools (Avaxat had only K- 6 the first year), so Elementary School was not part of the title. The same was true for Rail Ranch, Alta Murrieta and E. Hale Curran. It was only with the opening of Shivela, which was intended to also be K-8 that we moved to the middle school format – due to the pressure by parents.

Operating in the Multipurpose Room was not too difficult. With partitions and utilizing the previous year's science project boards, we created classrooms. We even had some room left over for a lunch area. This was our first dilemma. Since Murrieta was also operating, it meant that Avaxat was in class while Murrieta students ate lunch. We had an awful lot of growling stomachs during the first few months.

On October 13, 1987, we bussed approximately 85 students (yes, we had started to grow) and staff to the Avaxat campus and occupied eight relocatable classrooms. In the days leading up to the opening of the school, the developer of "Las Brisas" was forced to lay asphalt in the rain on Las Brisas Road. No houses had been started, so it looked a bit odd to see these eight classroom buildings out in the middle of nowhere. Since water and power had yet to be installed, the developer gave us the use of a large generator that powered our school for a few weeks. We did have water, but the pressure was so low that toilets would not flush. The health department was ready to "red tag" us, which meant we could not occupy the school. Quick thinking brought "porta-potties" onto campus and so we were able to cut the opening day ribbon and start classes. Ironically, we did have phones, but only due to temporary wires strung on poles for about ¼ of a mile.

It didn't look like the water pressure issue was going to be resolved for months since it was due to a pump house that needed to be built and was not in the developers timeline until spring. Board member Patty Julian's husband, who dug wells and installed pumps and tanks for a living, came to our rescue. After using the porta-potties for one month and storing drinking water in the office, we finally had enough pressure by "sucking" the little water that was in the water lines into tanks and pressurizing it enough to flush toilets. By Christmas break we were becoming a real school with real toilets and by then, the power had come to us!

The only challenge was accessing the school in rainy weather. Some students had a hard time getting to school. And then there was Arnold, a kindergartener, who arrived at school on the last day before the Christmas break by helicopter – much to the chagrin of the other 90 students who thought I had arranged for Santa to visit.

Growth that first year was not tremendous. We ended the year with 127 students. Over the summer, we welcomed an additional 300 students and the growth in Murrieta began. The rest is history.

14. Christy Goennier

Principal, Diamond Valley Elementary School, Hemet
May 1, 2006

My first contact with the Murrieta Elementary School District was when it was a one-school district and I was as an eighth grade student in 1984. After graduation, I completed my education and returned to Murrieta when I was hired as an eighth grade teacher science teacher at Thompson Middle School in 1995.

Many of my students were kids that I had coached through the years or had waited on at my parents' restaurant, the Windmill Restaurant, at the corner of Jefferson and Ivy. Many of my "colleagues" were past customers and had watched me grow up. For me it was an honor to come back and teach in the district that served me as a student.

Guy Romero visited my class on the very first day I taught in Murrieta. This may not seem like much but he was my 8eighth grade science teacher and here I was teaching eighth grade science.

15. Elizabeth Ellsworth

Coordinator, BTSA
(Beginning Teacher Support and Assessment Program)
November 21, 2005

I came to Murrieta because my stepfather was diagnosed as having cancer and my mother's subsequent difficulties prompted my re-location from Northern California. I had just finished a teacher preparation program at Stanislaus State University while teaching middle school in Lodi and secured interviews with Fallbrook, Lake Elsinore and Murrieta. All offered teaching jobs, but Murrieta offered the desired kindergarten assignment.

I began teaching at Murrieta Elementary September 1985, as the district's second kindergarten teacher, the other being Lois Shumway. My classroom was the original cafeteria / multipurpose room and for a few months I had to vacate the room at 11:30, as lunch was served there for another two months. The new multipurpose room was dedicated in November.

Of course, the perk that offset the inconvenience was the stage! I soon secured a piano and the kindergarten class began a tradition of presenting songfests and plays to community organizations, such as the Murrieta Garden Club. It was a wonderful time to be a teacher in MVUSD. Van was transitioning to a full-time superintendent and Susan Reynolds was assuming a role as a full-time principal. We knew all our colleagues, having only one K-8 school, with the school being the heart of the community. Social events were plentiful and gave us the opportunity to mingle with few demarcations between board members, administrators, classified and certificated. Most problems could be settled with a personal talk and paperwork was almost non-existent.

I helped open Thompson Middle School in 1994 as a sixth grade Language Arts/ Social Studies teacher. I worked there for three years until I returned to Murrieta Elementary School as a fifty percent second grade

231

teacher. The other fifty percent of my job was as a Teacher on Special Assignment overseeing the Beginning Teacher Support and Assessment Program (BTSA). Over a three-year period that assignment evolved into a full-time coordinator position.

Like all the veterans from the 1980's, I have stories about school board meetings lasting until 1:30 a.m. and three-hour employment interviews. My initial interview started at 7:00 p.m. with eleven people on the panel. It continued until 11:00 p.m....I was called at 1:00 a.m. and offered the job. Whew!

I was the Murrieta Teacher's Association (MTA) representative to the Board of Education in the late 1980's and attended all functions, such as Board retreats and State School Board Association meetings. Austin Linsley was elected to the Board the year that I was MTA rep. At that time relations between the Murrieta Teachers' Association and the District were informal, cordial, and definitely student focused. Consensus was not yet a buzz word, but accurately described the negotiating relationship. Our contract was short and simple, yet met the needs of the time.

16. Ron Peace

Director of Construction Finance
May 23, 2006

I was hired by Elsinore Union High School District in 1985. The High School District served Lake Elsinore, Murrieta and Temecula Elementary Districts. When the voters chose to create three unified school districts, the administration of the elementary districts basically remained intact to administer the newly-created unified districts, and the district administration employees of the high school district were offered jobs at the newly created districts. So, I served the students of Murrieta since 1985, but didn't actually start working in Murrieta until 1989, when the district became the Murrieta Valley Unified School District.

17. Jack Isslib

Maintenance III, Security and Communications
March 20, 2006

Jack started with the school district at Murrieta Elementary as a night custodian in September 1988. After a little over a year on the job, he remarried and his wife said it would be nice if he were home evenings.

The district maintenance man at that time also served as bus mechanic, and decided that doing both jobs was too much, so he talked to Superintendent van de Wetering and became the bus mechanic only. When Jack learned that the maintenance job was available, he talked to Van and said he'd like that job, and so he became the first full time district maintenance man, working days.

In those days, everyone who worked for the district took on any duties that needed doing. When Jack came to work in the morning, if no one else had arrived he took over answering phones and welcoming students to school. One little boy, when Susan Reynolds introduced herself to the class as principal, told her he thought Jack was the principal.

Jack met his wife Shari through the community theater. She directed local plays and had a large collection of costumes. One year at St. Patrick's Day, she told Jack "You're going to wear the leprechaun costume to work," so he did. That started a district tradition, with Jack dressed up as a leprechaun, going to all the kindergarten and first grade classes, talking to the students. One little girl wanted to know how Jack got into the classroom, and Jack told her he sprinkled himself with fairy dust, shrank down, and came in through the keyhole. Asked how he got big again, Jack grinned, put his thumb to his lips, and blew, simulating blowing up a balloon. The students and adults loved it.

Jack recalls another costumed character, Smokey Bear, who used to visit the school each year. On this particular year, after the ranger had gotten into his bear costume, he stood too near the gas panel heater in the superintendent's office and the bear suit caught on fire. This gave a new meaning to "only you can prevent forest fires."

As the district grew larger, maintenance became too much for one person, and the district hired Stu Read to help out. Stu was primarily a locksmith, and the district by now had so many doors with locks that this was a big job. Stu went on to become the first Director of Food Services. Ed Riscen was the third man hired to handle maintenance, and he and Jack worked together for a long time.

Jack still meets people who say, "Hey, I know you—you used to wear that leprechaun costume on St. Patrick's Day."

18. Gary Farmer

Principal, Shivela Middle School
December 14, 2005

I had been commuting to Baldwin Park High School for ten years after moving to Temecula in 1979. Initially the traffic was not a problem – there was no I-15 and no traffic – so getting to and from work was actually a very relaxing time for me, especially on the days when I rode a motorcycle (yes, I really did). After ten years, the I-15 corridor was open all the way to I-215, Moreno Valley was/had exploded, flooding Highway 91 with more cars than anyone would have ever believed could be on the same freeway, and a seventy-five minute commute became a two-hour commute. It was time for a change.

I saw an ad in EdCal for counselors in Murrieta at all of their K-8 schools – totally unheard of. I had to call to make sure it wasn't a mistake. When I called, Assistant Superintendent Arvo Toukonen answered the phone and asked me to stop by on my way home the next evening, which I did. I had to knock on his window in his office on Ivy Street. We talked for about an hour and a half and he concluded by saying he thought we could work something out with my pay difference by having me work as a counselor and as an admin designee at Curran due to the double session schedule. All he needed to do was to have me interview with the principal. The next evening I met with Principal Charlie Riendeau and Counselor Betty Nead. I was hired the next morning, resigned in Baldwin Park and was on the job less than a week later (Betty later told me that she informed Charlie that if he didn't hire me it was the biggest mistake he would ever make). This is why I came to Murrieta, but the real question is why did I stay? Read on...

When I arrived on scene at E. Hale Curran Elementary School in November of 1989 the school was truly on double sessions – not just sharing a campus with two schools like Rail and Alta, but actually split into two schools in one. Charlie told me that since I was used to getting up early to commute to Baldwin Park, I could have the morning shift as the administrator. That meant being on site before 6:00 a.m., as school started before 7:00 a.m. Buses and cars would start arriving at about 6:30 a.m., in the dark. What a trip that was. We had students lined up outside of the K-6 classrooms waiting to go inside at 12:00 p.m. At 12:05 p.m. the morning students would walk out and the afternoon students would walk in. They would get to walk out at 5:15 p.m. Overlapping this schedule was the seventh and eighth grade students starting at 9:00 a.m. and leaving at 3:00 p.m.

The year was a success in so many ways, and we kept it going against all the odds. It became clear to me by the start of the second semester that I was in the right place at the right time. I told Arvo I wanted to be in a growing district and be a part of what would make it a great place for kids, but I had no idea what I was saying.

The high school was under construction. Lucinda Brouwer was already hired as principal to open Shivela as a K-8 school. Shivela was a bunch of buildings sitting on a vacant lot on Lincoln Avenue, with houses springing up all around it. Parents started coming to Board meetings demanding that we move into a true unified district with a middle school, not K-8 schools.

Eventually the Board made the decision to do just that and Shivela would be the middle school. So we started the transition to middle school. The sixth and seventh grade students were excited to be making the first move, but they lost some of their enthusiasm when they realized that Murrieta Valley High School was also going to have their first year at Shivela – two principals, a shared assistant principal, one counselor each and shared teachers.

Shivela opened in September of 1990. Murrieta Valley High School was not finished, so the first ninth grade students were placed at Shivela. To make room, Rail Ranch remained K-8 for two more years. I was still at Curran.

Principal Guy Romero left Avaxat later that year to fill the vacancy as Director of Curriculum and Instruction when Assistant Superintendent Karen Lynch left. Butch Owens, Betty Nead and I were interviewed by the staff and parents of Avaxat (three interviews in one afternoon – one each with teachers, classified staff and parents) to take Guy's place for the rest of the year. Butch won!

In the spring of 1991, Shivela, (and MVHS) had a "riot" according to the newspaper headlines. It was actually a sit-down demonstration by the students (one of them on top of a basketball backboard) against Principal Lucinda Brouwer. As the lead person of the district's Emergency Response Team I was called on to lead a delegation of counselors and psychologists to go to Shivela to determine what happened and what needed to be done. The next morning we met with the students and then Candyce Julian, MVHS Counselor, and I met with Lucinda, MVHS Principal Dan Burch, and MVHS Assistant Principal Shelly Weston to debrief them on what we found out – not the most positive place for someone who wanted to be an administrator in the district.

During this time it also became apparent that we would have to start looking at multi-track programs. I had the pleasure of working closely with Guy Romero evaluating the different programs and making recommendations to the district and Board. We attended seminars and conferences, visited schools in the area already on multi-track, held parent meetings and moved onward and upward. The two-year project culminated with one giant lottery at the Murrieta City warehouse to determine who would be on what track. We created four tracks of students at three schools, E. Hale Curran, Alta Murrieta, and Avaxat. Murrieta Elementary held off for a year, as did Rail Ranch.

Students at Shivela with high school students as siblings had first priority for "B" track to match families as much as possible. It wasn't close. So many parents protested (over 200 weren't matched up) that Superintendent Tate Parker directed us to fix the problem. With some very creative scheduling, a large number of teachers and students were rescheduled at Shivela (after the school year had begun) to match up as many as physically possible. Another lottery had to take place for those SMS students involved. We were able to reduce the number of unmatched students down to about fifty.

Lucinda Brouwer left in the spring of 1992 and Frank Passarella was hired as the principal of Shivela in July. He hired Sandra LeBaron as his assistant principal. David Lindsey was still on board from the previous administration, but he was on leave. I was the full-time assistant principal at E. Hale Curran Elementary School. In December of 1992, Al Ross left Rail Ranch to open Creekside Continuation High School. I applied for the principal position at Rail Ranch, but lost out to Shari Fox. In January of 1993, I moved to Shivela as an assistant principal.

In July of 1994, Thompson Middle School opened on the Shivela campus (hosting another school one more time). Manny Valdes was the first principal (I lost again) and we quickly exceeded 1800 students on one campus.

In June of 1995 Frank Passerella left to go to San Jacinto as the Director of Personnel and I was appointed to the principal position at Shivela in August. We were still on multi-track scheduling and still growing. Thompson Middle School was still on our site and it was a crazy place to be. Bonds were defeated by the voters, preventing completion of our regular campus. We were able to start the construction of our PE building during the 1995/96 school year.

Bonds were finally passed and Shivela was completed in April of 1998.

Big Day – June 30, 2000 – no more multi-track schedules. We moved to the common calendar in August of 2000, just before it killed us all off!

May 2001 – VERY BIG DAY – Shivela receives California Distinguished School recognition.

From 1995 to now I have been proud to serve with the greatest staff, helping the greatest students as they move on to high school. It has been a ride of memories that will never go away. As I write this I realize that, in comparison, the last five years have been rather easy. From 1989 to 2000, those eleven years were horrendous in comparison to what we do now, yet what we do now is just as important. I never realized until I put this on paper how much we've been able to focus on education and not schedules, bonds, and the crazy world around us. Thanks for asking us to do this – it has been a lot of fun.

19. Judy Gould

Operations Technician, Civic Center, District Support Center
January 20, 2006

I was living in Temecula, working part time without benefits, saw a newspaper ad that said Murrieta School District was hiring new clerks, and I decided to apply. I wanted full-time work and benefits since I had growing children.

I think one of my more memorable moments was actually when I was being interviewed for the clerk position. When I went to the District Office location on Ivy in 1991 and asked for information on the clerk position, the receptionist directed me to where all of the job descriptions were. I asked whether or not the health clerk job description was the same as all of the other clerks and was told 'yes.'

When I went to the interview I was shocked (if there were a stronger word for shocked I would use it!) to walk into a room that had about 16 people sitting around a group of tables. I was being interviewed for a health clerk position (which by the way was not a full time position but at least it had benefits!!). When Nurse Cathy Owens' time came to ask a question, she asked me to describe what you do in CPR. I looked at her and said – "HUH?" I told her I didn't have a clue. She looked strangely at me and said that First Aid and CPR are two of the requirements for the position. I kind of laughed and told her what the receptionist had told me about the job descriptions "all being the same" and said, "ask away," even though I didn't have much of a clue about what the answers would be.

I was asked a lot of questions and answered to the best of my ability, and somehow I got hired. Gary Farmer and Lynn Shockley (Farmer) were on the interview panel and said they liked my honest answers and knew I could get the certifications to bring me in line with the job requirements. So – the bottom line is, thanks to Gary and Lynn, I've now been in the district for 14 years!!

Many of us have lived through the changes, from a normal school schedule to multi-track and back, and have grown with all of the changes. I think one of the biggest changes is our incredible growth. We started out in the District Office on the corner of Plum and Ivy Street and now have a beautiful District Support Center that we are already outgrowing. It is phenomenal how many schools we have added and how many more employees we have. I used to know at least 90-95% of all the classified people and with our growth I now know maybe 60%.

People come and go in this district but I can really say that I have been lucky to find my niche and am very happy to come to work each day. There are an awful lot of people in this world that cannot say that, which is very unfortunate.

20. Doug Highlen

Social Science Teacher, Murrieta Valley High School
November 16, 2005

When I came to Murrieta it wasn't a real city yet. It was just some homes and businesses north of Temecula. Some people had decided to build thousands of new homes in Murrieta, because the new freeway (I-15) had been completed all the way to Corona. The completed freeway made it possible to live in Murrieta and drive to work in Orange County.

The first day I started teaching in Murrieta there were only five schools and two were brand new! Murrieta Elementary was the original school and everybody was a little jealous of them because they had "real" buildings. Avaxat Elementary and Alta Murrieta Elementary were completely portable classrooms. Rail Ranch Elementary wasn't built yet but was open anyway! This was done by having the Alta Murrieta students attend school from 7 a.m. till noon and then the school magically changed its name to Rail Ranch and that school went from noon to 5 p.m. in the same building!

I started teaching at E. Hale Curran Elementary. I arrived and found out that they didn't have a classroom for me. The school was grades kindergarten through grade eight and was so crowded that half of us went to school from 7:00 a.m. to noon and the other half from noon to 5:00 p.m. For the first six weeks, I taught Math and History to 7th and 8th graders using the cafeteria as my room.

We had no books, no desks and only first/second grade chairs, so the students either sat on the floor and used a chair as a desk or sat in a little chair and used their notebooks as desks. I had no white-boards, so we taped butcher paper to the walls and I used a felt tip marker to write. When we filled up the butcher paper we took it down and put more up. We had no grass fields so everybody played on dirt. Every day was an adventure. We made the schools up as we went, and we were having a great time doing it.

About half way through the first year the District started planning to build a middle school named Shivela and a high school, which was to be called Murrieta Valley High School. I was one of five teachers selected from those already in the district to go and start the high school. In the spring before we opened we asked the eighth graders what the high school colors should be and what they wanted as a mascot. There was a long list of colors, but we cut it down to five or six choices. Black and red was popular that year so it won.

We also had a few mascot choices. I remember Mustangs, Marauders and Nighthawks. I don't think anybody knew what a Nighthawk was, but it sounded tough so the kids went with it. We opened with about twelve teachers and 300 ninth grade students in fifteen portables on the Shivela campus. Later that year we bused all the students to the high school site and had a groundbreaking ceremony. It was a very proud time for Murrieta.

It was a special time for me as a teacher. As the schools grew, I moved up the grades along with the kids. I taught many of the same students 8th grade history, 9th grade world history, 10th grade history elective, 11th grade US history and 12th grade government! I believe the students enjoyed this as much as I did. Some of those students have come back to MVHS as teachers. Once in awhile I'll forget for a moment and wonder just what they are doing in the faculty room!

There are more students and teachers at MVHS today than there were in the entire school district when I started. Like me, MVHS is getting older and showing signs of wear, but I don't see that. I look back fondly on my early years at Murrieta Valley Unified School District as a time when I made a significant impact on how our schools are today.

21. Buck DeWeese
Interim Superintendent
April 25, 2006

I came to the District in January 1989. When I went to Avaxat Elementary School for the first time, Principal Guy Romero walked me down to a room to introduce me to the Alta Murrieta faculty. As we walked into the classroom where the staff meeting was going to be held, Charlie Riendeau and Bonnie Cringan were standing on opposite sides of the room yelling at each other about some teaching technique. As they stopped to catch a breath, Guy interrupted and introduced me, and then left with a "Good Luck" and a sly grin on his face. Charlie and Bonnie went right back to yelling for a few more moments, and when they paused to take another breath I took that opportunity to introduce myself and continue talking. They sat down and the meeting went on......I thought "Welcome to Murrieta, Buck!"

We shared the campus with Avaxat for a few weeks. Classes and teachers were already set up for Alta, but the rain had delayed our move to the portable buildings. When we did move, I believe it was in early February, I remember riding a bus over to Alta with students and stepping off into a mud puddle as I exited the bus. I really didn't notice because we were all so excited to moving into our new school/portable classrooms.

We were growing very fast...I mean over 100% per year. I recall coming back from spring break the first year and having a line of more than 30 students with their parents waiting at the door to register. Needless to say, I was hiring new staff from the time I arrived in Murrieta!

22. Jeanne Nelson

Library/Media Services Coordinator
November 23, 2005

My husband and I moved to California from Colorado in 1987 and purchased a home near Murrieta in 1988. At that time, it was a very small town with a gas station, the Murrieta Country Market, two bars (Joanie's Cantina and Ray's Murrieta Café), Post Office, hardware store, do-nut shop, pet store, and some other small shops. It was not quaint, it was country. We lived two miles east of Highway 215, and in those days, there were very few cars on this highway, or Highway 15. We went to Lake Elsinore for groceries, that being the closest large grocery, but purchased meat from the Murrieta Country Market, which had the best meat in the area and a great butcher, Harry.

In Murrieta there was only the small Murrieta School, definitely not big enough to hire a school librarian, so I got a job in Perris as the librarian for the two middle schools there, Perris Valley Middle School, and soon to be opened Pinacate Middle School. In those days it took me eighteen minutes to drive from my house to work at Pinacate in Perris, and there was very little traffic. There were no stoplights in Murrieta, and few stop signs.

My son Johnny was starting his senior year in high school when we moved here, and Murrieta students then had their choice of going to Temecula Valley High School or Elsinore Union High School. Temecula High School did not have a senior class yet, so Johnny ended up going to high school in Lake Elsinore. Later on I learned that our house was in the Perris Union High School District (and the Menifee Elementary School District), but our rural mailbox was across Los Alamos Road and inside the Temecula school district boundaries, so apparently that counted.

This was in 1987, and Murrieta slowly started to grow. The school district unified, breaking away from Temecula and Lake Elsinore and building their second elementary school, Avaxat, in all portable

243

buildings, led by Principal Guy Romero. Three hundred eager students and ten teachers opened this new school, proudly wearing sweatshirts with the Avaxat Warrior emblazoned on them.

In the summer of 1989, I saw an ad in the local *Rancho News* (which came out once a week) for a district librarian for the Murrieta School District. I immediately went to the district office, at the corner of Plum and Ivy, and filled out an application. I got a phone call soon after asking if I knew it was a classified position, since I had a teaching certificate and library services credential. I said "no" and asked them to discard my application.

A day or so later, I was asked to come in for an interview. I was confused, and asked if they knew that I had a teaching certificate, and was not interested in a classified position. They said they understood, but to come in for an interview anyhow. Well, okay....and I did. Karen Robertson was on the interview panel with Assistant Superintendent of Educational Services, Dr. Karen Lynch. When they asked me about my ideal high school library, I had definite ideas, and they exchanged startled looks. I left, thinking that was the end of that.

The following week, I got a call from Dr. Arvo Toukonen, Assistant Superintendent of Personnel, who asked if I would take the job if it were upgraded to a professional position. I was dubious, but said "yes." He asked me to attend the School Board meeting that week, and I did. I sat for what seemed like hours outside while the Board was in closed session. Afterwards Dr. Toukonen came out and said they had agreed to make the position professional, and that I was hired!

This was scary! I'd been told that this fledgling school district was probably going to fail, and discovered there were no written contracts for any employees, though there was a salary schedule. Further, I would have to take a cut in pay since they would not give me as many years' experience as Perris had. However, I decided to go for it, and have never regretted it. I started working on November 1st, 1989.

Since Murrieta had not expected to hire me, they had no place for me to work, but Karen Robertson, Technology Coordinator, graciously shared her office in a former storage room at Murrieta Elementary School. She even found me a computer.

I spent a lot of time in the Murrieta Elementary School Library, talking with Dorothea Tiss, who had worked there for many years. She wasn't sure if I was a good idea or not, and many of the teachers had the same doubts.

As a brand-new library coordinator, my first task was to hire personnel for the three new elementary schools that had just opened and oversee setting up their libraries. Karen Robertson and I worked together on the interviews, since my library folks would also be her computer techs. These new libraries would be half bookcases (with books), tables and chairs, and half computer lab. The job description at that time was "Library/Lab Technician."

Lee Titford was the first of the new library staff hired, and started working at Avaxat, reopening the library (in a classroom) that had been closed the previous year because it was needed as a classroom again for students. The library also housed Joanne Abrassart, the speech therapist, and special education teacher Anne Hosford. This was not an ideal situation for anyone. Lee had a huge job, getting all the books organized and cataloged, while also reading to classes, checking out books, and managing the computer lab. She could handle this, and the kids loved her, coming into the library whenever they could.

Alta Murrieta and Rail Ranch elementary schools opened next sharing a campus and operating on double sessions due to the facilities crisis. The Alta students arrived early, before sunrise, and the Rail students arrived in the afternoon and stayed until after dark. The afternoon students were incredibly quiet—it was like a zombie school, with students who had worn themselves out playing in the morning before school, and then faced a long, long day.

Susan Fralick was hired for the Rail Ranch library and Judi Rightmire for Alta Murrieta's library, sharing the classroom-sized library/computer lab facility during that first year. To avoid combining and then dividing two library collections and card catalogs (real card catalogs!), the Rail

Ranch books were kept in boxes hidden behind a divider wall, and students from both schools checked out the Alta Murrieta books. There was some unhappiness about this arrangement as the Alta books started showing signs of heavy use, while the Rail Ranch books stayed new in boxes.

Rail Ranch moved across town into their new school, again all portable buildings, in mid year. The new Rail library was a triple-wide portable building and seemed huge in comparison.

E. Hale Curran Elementary School also opened that year on their own site in portable buildings. The school opened with a very small number of students and teachers in what seemed like a large school, until students started arriving. This was the year of over 100% growth, and a new teacher and classroom of students was added almost weekly. By the end of the year, Curran was as large as the other schools, with around 500 students. Robyn Norland was hired as the first Library /LabTechnician at Curran, and like the others, her biggest task was putting the library books in order and starting a card catalog.

Dorothea Tiss had ordered books for these new school libraries, but when the ordering was being done, nobody was sure Curran would open. So, no books were ordered for this school. Some last minute scrambling resulted in a very small collection on the shelves, all paperback, and soon showing signs of heavy use.

After Curran was several years old, some of the land it was built on started slipping down the hill toward the gully behind the school. Cracks opened up in sidewalks and grew larger. Some rooms, including the library, had to be vacated. Robyn spent part of a year taking books to classrooms on a rolling cart so students would have books to read.

Each library occupied a portable classroom and was set up as half library, half computer lab. Karen Robertson, the Technology Coordinator, set up the Apple II labs herself, with help from an Apple consultant.

Because money is this growing district was always short, there was never enough funding to fill new library shelves. I made the decision that we would provide as many books as possible for students to read, and that meant paperback books. These new libraries opened with mostly paperback collections. Some of those books would still be on the shelves a decade later, still being checked out by students, and often heavily taped and glued to keep them going.

When it became evident that the district was indeed going to have a high school and a middle school, Dan Burch and Lucinda Brouwer were hired as principals, and spent a year preparing to open their campuses on a shared site. Shivela Middle School and Murrieta Valley High School, which housed only freshmen, opened on the Shivela campus in the fall of 1990. Initially there were not enough portable classrooms, and two classes shared the library under the able management of teachers Maureen Lorimer and Stacy Tumlin (Swenk). Two library/lab technicians were hired, Cheryl Dufresne and Cheryl Brummett.

Cheryl and Cheryl not only had to set up the library and create a card catalog, but they also faced stacks and stacks of textbooks from the other schools, for grades six through eight. Initially they had many more textbooks than library books. Again there was the question of how to combine and then separate library books when the other school moved? This time all books were put on the shelves, but tagged, so they could be separated again. Not easy, but it worked.

The following year MVHS moved to their permanent campus and added the sophomore class. The high school site included classrooms only, with the library occupying one classroom, where Cheryl Brummett provided library staffing. Heavy equipment, jackhammers, concrete trucks, and chain-link fence surrounded the school.

Murrieta Valley High School added a group of classrooms and a class of students each year, until there was finally the first graduating class. The current library opened for the first junior class, with 4,000 books on shelves planned to hold 30,000. It looked like miles of empty shelves. Reporter Carl Love took photos and wrote an article for the newspaper, and the community was generous with donations.

Facilities issues mandated that all the schools except MVHS go to a multi-track, year round schedule, which often meant that one school year ended on a Friday, and the next school year started the following Monday—hardly long enough to get ready for students! In the library, this meant getting all library books and textbooks returned, an overwhelming number of books. However, the teachers liked the year-round scheduling, saying students didn't require as much re-teaching when school started up again.

Thompson Middle School opened next, sharing the Shivela campus. Thompson's first library/lab technician was Pat Raether, who had worked half time in the library at Shivela with Cheryl Dufresne until her position was cut.

It was around this time that we started to automate circulation and textbook distribution. We chose the Follett software program because it was the program used in neighboring school districts. This was a difficult transition, especially at Murrieta Elementary School, with 12,000 books. Each book had to be barcoded and entered into the database. Later on, the process would be much easier, but during these first few years, it was manual data entry, by people who were also doing many other tasks.

Creekside Continuation High School opened sharing facilities with MVHS. When they moved to their own campus, there was no library for many years, and no library technician.

Thompson moved from Shivela's campus to their own campus across town, and like the other schools, this happened in the rainy season. Pat reported lots of mud and dampness. The new library, a mirror plan of the Shivela library, started out with very few books, and Pat worked very hard to stock the shelves with quality hardback books.

Tovashal Elementary was the next school to open, and for a year it shared the Avaxat campus. Jackie Katz was hired as the Library Technician. Tovashal parents were generous with book donations, and stuffed animal donations, and the library soon had full shelves and a welcoming look. Jackie started wearing funny hats, or theme hats, when she read to the kids, and soon there were lots of donated hats.

248

Tovashal was followed by Cole Canyon, and Debbie Foster was hired as the first library technician. Like everyone else, she faced the prospect of cataloging and organizing this new library.

An Eagle Scout provided some help organizing the textbooks. Over the years, the libraries have enjoyed help from many volunteers and organizations. Joe Matthews, a retired administrator, spent many years helping catalog books and sharing fascinating stories of the old days with our student helpers. The Murrieta Garden Club, the Friends of the Murrieta Library, Rotary, and the Ladies Relief Society helped out at different times., to name just a few.

The next school to open was Daniel N. Buchanan Elementary, and Jan Lauletta, who had worked in the library at MVHS, transferred to Buchanan Elementary to open the library there. Changing from a school of teenagers to one with much smaller students was a challenge she gladly took on, and soon had things organized.

Monte Vista Elementary School, with Barbara Vogel as the library technician, followed Daniel Buchanan School. Barbara had worked in the Thompson library, and knew what needed to be done. However, she preferred working with older students, and transferred back to Thompson when the opportunity arose.

That same year Vista Murrieta High School opened, and Debbie Jacobs, the first credentialed librarian at MVHS, transferred to Vista Murrieta High School to open the new library. Working with her was Jeanne Russell, library technician. Susan Cline, from Oceanside, was hired to take Debbie's place at MVHS. Susan's library support crew included library technicians Susan Fralick , Sharon Haubrick, and Peggy Buechler. Pretty awesome team.

The following year yet another elementary school opened, Antelope Hills Elementary, just across Highway 215 from VMHS. Cindy Lee was hired to work in the library (she said it was her dream job!), and that first year dealt with hundreds of donated books along with regular classes of students.

Murrieta Mesa High School opened in 2009 during an economic

recession. We had been able to plan ahead and buy books in anticipation of other schools opening, but for this school, no. New schools in other districts asked for donations of money, but when $100,000 will only buy 4,000 books, that is not a good solution. I set as my *only* goal for the year the collection of 5,000 books for this new high school, a $125,000 value. I asked Carl Love, teacher and reporter, to write an article for the paper, which he had done when MVHS opened. His earlier article had garnered a lot of books, and he came through for us again.

We collected over 12,000 books during that year. Lisa Rivera, the Mesa library technician, had her hands full running the library and processing a seemingly endless supply of books. Because of the recession, for the first time ever there was facilities and construction money left over, money that could be spent on library books. I reminded them of this, and the district was generous in allocating $100,000 to the Mesa library. What started out the year as a skeleton library became a real library in a fairly short time, thanks to so many generous donations.

When I first started out in the district, the only school library was Murrieta Elementary School, with around 12,000 books, many of them very old. Currently there are over 350,000 books in the 16 district libraries, and the 20,000 plus students check out around 40,000 books each month.

23. Lorena Beckwith

Rail Ranch Custodian
February 27, 2006.

I remember when Rail Ranch Elementary School students shared the Alta Murrieta campus and the Rail students went to school in the late afternoon and evening.

On one of my first days as the new campus custodian, I had to call in because of illness but there was no district phone number to call in those days. I had Superintendent Charles van de Wetering's number as an emergency, so I called it. I woke him up around 5:00 a.m. and he went to unlock the school, apparently without wasting any time, so he was quite scruffy – hair needed combing, etc. When childcare aide Leslie Rothrock came in to open up at 6:00 a.m. she assumed that he was the day custodian. Principal Al Ross, needless to say, was not pleased. I was very embarrassed, but back in those days the superintendent could even be called on to be the day custodian.

I remember when Rail Ranch was K-8 and grew beyond the capacity of the portable classrooms. Teacher Ron Pickrahn had to conduct class in part of the multipurpose room portable building while lunch was being served on the other side of temporary partitions.

There was a time when space was so limited that the RSP room shared a portable with K-5 Special Day Class (SDC) classes.

For a while, former Board of Education member Patty Julian Powers (current Health Technician at Rail) used her home to store the basketball equipment for Rail until they had a place to put it.

When the school district started on year-round, multi-track scheduling, we moved entire roomfuls of materials up and down the line of portables (Rail's portable's were on a hill). All curriculum, teacher and student personal items, and furniture if it related to grade level changing, had to be moved 4 times a year.

24. Judi Rightmire

Library Technician, E. Hale Curran Elementary
March 16, 2006

What a morning November 13, 1989 was! Newly hired, I arrived at Murrieta Elementary School and met Dorothea Tiss in the library. We started talking and figured out I had been sent to the wrong site. I was the new girl at Alta Murrieta Elementary School. Imagine my surprise at

251

finding my new library…a portable classroom filled with boxes of books, computers, tables, chairs and shelving units.

I wasn't there too long before learning that Alta and Rail Ranch Elementary School would be sharing a school site. Alta would start around 7:00 a.m. and go until a little after noon and then Rail students would arrive and stay until around 5:30. What a schedule! It was also there that I met a wonderful woman, Susan Fralick, who was the Rail Ranch Library Technician. She had come from the Lake Arrowhead School District and her work background was very similar to mine. We plunged right in and got to work making cards, pockets and spine labels for boxes and boxes of books. Half of the portable classroom was the library and the other half was a computer lab complete with 20 Apple computers.

We were able to get the Alta/Rail library/lab up and running by January of 1990 when everyone came back from Winter Break. What a thrill it was to see the excitement on the faces of the students when they came in for the first time. We worked double time doing both library and computer lab. Teachers brought their classes in once a week for computer and once a week for library. Thank heavens for Karen Robertson, who was there for those of us with less than perfect computer skills and Jeanne Nelson who gave us all tremendous support in those early days.

In 1990, the permanent buildings for Alta were finished and we moved from our small portable classroom to a larger room. We still had the computer lab and library together. It was a job moving all the books and computers. My husband and sons came in on the weekend to move carts and carts of books. Students were still coming in once a week for either the library or the computer lab and much of our time was spent running back and forth between the two.

In 1995, I transferred to the E. Hale Curran site. Library Technician Robyn Norland was leaving and moving to Idaho, and I felt it was time for a change. Curran library was much larger than Alta and I had the fun of revamping it to suit Curran needs. That was the year that we became "automated" in the library. What a job to put bar codes on all the books and enter them into the system, but how great it was when it was all finished. We currently have over 20,000 items for student, teacher and parent needs.

25. Tim and Lavinia Tikasingh

Music Teachers
February 5, 2006

Murrieta Music Memories!

Tim and I came to Murrieta to visit my sister and family in their new home. My niece told me that they needed teachers and that we should apply, so we did. We returned to northern California only to return a month later for an interview. We interviewed for the position of music teacher on the Friday of Labor Day Weekend in September 1989, were both offered positions and started a week later.

Karen Strauss interviewed and was hired at the same time and started in September 1989. The first few days we sat in the old district office on the corner of Plum and Ivy and went through applications and résumés of other music teacher candidates. Most of the applications were from Bowling Green University in Ohio. We came across the applications of another married couple, Kirk and Mary Green. We decided to call them and invite them to fly out and interview for the district.

Finally after day three, Arvo Toukonen, Assistant Superintendent, decided to take us on a tour of the elementary schools and introduce us to the principals. Arvo, who was fairly new to the district, got lost and could not find one of the schools. Needless to say we made several U-turns that day. At that time we visited Murrieta Elementary, with Susan Reynolds, Principal, Alta Murrieta, Buck DeWeese, Principal, Avaxat, Guy Romero Principal, Rail Ranch, Dr. Al Ross, Principal, and E. Hale Curran, Charles Riendeau, Principal. Rail Ranch was sharing the Alta Murrieta campus at that time.

The fall of 1989 the district hired five music teachers, one per elementary site.

Alta Murrieta – Tim Tikasingh
Avaxat – Mary Green
E. Hale Curran – Kirk Green
Murrieta – Karen Strauss
Rail Ranch – Lavinia Tikasingh

Being first hired we had our pick of school sites. Tim and I decided to start teaching at Alta & Rail Ranch School which shared the Alta Murrieta Campus on double sessions. Alta Murrieta started school at 6:00 a.m. and Rail started at 12:00 noon. It was amazing to watch the "changing of the classes" as the Rail Ranch students lined up and waited for the Alta students to be dismissed before entering their classrooms. The music room was also the lunchroom. The Alta/Rail kids would enter in and get their hot lunch while Tim was finishing his last classes of the day on the other side. We felt lucky to have a little space to call a music room complete with a spinet piano donated to the school and a set of Macmillan Music Textbooks that someone in the district had ordered. Trying to sing over the noisy lunch crowd was challenging at times, but the lunch servers enjoyed listening to Tim play the piano.

Every week there were new students enrolling at both Alta and Rail Ranch. In the spring of 1990, Alta added several new portable classrooms for growth. One of the portables was designated as a music room that Tim and I shared. That year we did an 8th grade classroom musical production of "Alice in Wonderland" at Alta, and a patriotic musical "My Country 'Tis of Thee" with the Rail Ranch students. We also started an elementary children's choir – grades 2-5. Due to facility constraints, concerts and performances had to be held at either Murrieta Elementary School Multipurpose Room or the Murrieta Town Hall.

The Alta Murrieta and Rail Ranch choirs performed for the school board meeting one night at Murrieta Elementary School, and in the middle of the song, a dog entered the back stage door and upstaged the kids as they sang. The newspaper photographer took a picture of the kids standing on the stage with the dog in the middle. Through the giggles and smiles the kids kept singing. By combining the two school choirs we became jokingly known as the "Tikasingh Family Singers" by a few district employees.

The following year 1990-1991 was the opening of Shivela Middle School/Murrieta Valley High School ninth grade sharing the campus at Shivela. Mary Green was assigned to start the instrumental band program and Tim Tikasingh was assigned to start up the vocal music. This lasted for a week. The music teachers met with Superintendent van de Wetering and were reassigned to schools to accommodate the growth and the addition of new schools.

Mary Green stayed at Shivela/MVHS to begin both the vocal and band programs.

Karen Strauss was assigned to teach instrumental band to 5th grade students at all elementary sites as an itinerant band teacher.

Tim Tikasingh and Lavinia Tikasingh were assigned as itinerant music teachers K-5 at Alta Murrieta, Avaxat, Murrieta and Rail Ranch. We traveled to one elementary school each day Monday – Thursday, and on Friday, we returned to each elementary campus to teach 4th/5th grade choir.

In 1991 – 1992, with the completion of the Murrieta Valley High School campus, teachers were shifted and reassigned again. All 6th graders except Rail Ranch attended Shivela and needed a full-time music teacher. Tim Tikasingh was assigned to Shivela to fill this position as a roving teacher to provide 6th grade music prep time for the teachers. Mary Green split her time between Shivela and Murrieta Valley High School to continue developing the instrumental band program. Lavinia Tikasingh stayed at Alta Murrieta and Rail Ranch teaching general music to grades K-8. Karen Strauss continued to teach 5th grade instrumental band music.

In 1992, to accommodate rapid growth, the school board approved a year-round multi- track schedule for all K-8 sites. This presented the challenge of offering music to all students and all tracks in a fast-growing district. Again to accommodate growth, Lavinia Tikasingh was assigned to Shivela Middle School and this ended general music classes in grades K-5. The classroom teacher was expected to provide music instruction. Fifth grade students could sign up to take instrumental band music with Karen Strauss who continued to be the itinerant elementary band teacher in the district. She served all five elementary schools: Alta, Avaxat, Curran, Murrieta, and Rail.

Murrieta Valley High School stayed on a modified year round schedule, adding a grade each year and developing both a band and choir program. This required a full-time music teacher at that site, and Bryan Boos was hired to fill this position.

At the middle school level, music teachers were assigned to a track or modified track schedule. Mary Green was assigned to Shivela to continue developing the instrumental band program. Tim Tikasingh stayed at Shivela and assigned to C-track as an exploratory music teacher and Lavinia Tikasingh was assigned to D-track at Shivela as an exploratory teacher.

1992-1995 was a period of rapid growth, changes and transition

There was a developing and growing high school, multi-track elementary and middle schools, and a second middle school opening. Rail Ranch school lost the 6-8 grade students who transferred to the middle school. In June 1993, Mary Green left Shivela and Joe Beneshan was hired to replace her. In 1994, Thompson Middle School opened as a modified single track-school and shared the Shivela campus. Joe Beneshan was asked to start the band program at Thompson but due to the different track schedules of Shivela and Thompson, it was decided to hire a separate band instructor instead. Jennifer Tan was hired to take over the band program at Thompson and assigned to that site once the school was built. Joe Beneshan left in June of 1995 and Bruce Davidson was hired to take over the band position at Shivela.

As the MVHS music program continued to grow, they needed a full-time vocal instructor and in 1995 John Byun was hired to fill this position. In 1996, Lavinia Tikasingh was assigned to start a vocal/choir program at Shivela. Jennifer Tan took an administrative position in the district and Ed Wentz was hired to take over the band program at Thompson. After a year or so, Ed Wentz decided to help Karen Strauss out with the 5th grade elementary band program, and Craig Moore was added to teach the band program at Thompson.

With growing music programs in grades 5-12 and the additional teachers, schools, and programs, we needed more funds to purchase instruments and music. We started to meet a few times a year and with the help of Jeanne Nelson, our district Library/Media Services Coordinator, the district began to allocate a music budget. This helped us build our programs and help the music thrive through out all 5-12 schools.

1995-2005: Expansion and Continued Growth

The next ten years was a period of continued expansion and growth for the music programs in the Murrieta Valley Unified District. With two strong and successful directors, Brian Boos and John Byun, the instrumental and vocal music programs at MVHS received many honors and accolades. Bryan Boos decided to transfer to Thompson Middle School to start the vocal/choir music program to feed into MVHS. Ken Mello was hired to take over the instrumental band program at MVHS.

The elementary population continued to grow and four new K-5 elementary schools opened, Buchanan, Cole Canyon, Monte Vista, and Antelope Hills. The district's commitment to continue offering elementary instrumental music to 5th graders resulted in teaming Craig Moore with Karen Strauss and Ed Wentz. They divided the elementary schools between them and continued developing a strong 5th grade instrumental band program.

257

After twelve years of teaching high school band in Moreno Valley, Kirk Green returned to Murrieta and took over the instrumental band program at Thompson. In 2002, Warm Springs opened and Tim Tikasingh was transferred there to begin the vocal music/exploratory music program along with Trent Newton who was hired to start the instrumental band program. In 2003, Murrieta opened its second comprehensive high school and hired Donald Wade to begin the instrumental band program and Jennifer Page to start the vocal/choir program. The district generously adjusted its music budget to meet the needs of thirteen music teachers and strong instrumental and vocal music programs in grades 5-12.

In June, 2005, John Byun, after of ten years of service to MVHS as vocal/choir director, left to take a position at Riverside Community College. The district hired Chad Zullinger to fill the position as vocal/choir director of MVHS.

2005- Present: New Challenges and Changes

Projected enrollment figures will put all three middle schools at maximum numbers. Plans are currently underway to open the fourth middle school and fourth high school and the eleventh elementary school.

26. Patrick Kelley

Interim Assistant Superintendent, Human Resources
January 06, 2006

I was first hired in Murrieta in August of 1991 as a teacher at Shivela Middle School. Since then I have been the activities director, a teacher on special assignment, Coordinator for Child Welfare and Attendance (the first such in the district), Assistant Principal at Rail, Principal at Rail,

Principal at Buchanan, Director of Human Resources, and now Interim Assistant Superintendent for Human Resources (following Dr. Chet Francisco's resignation, and pending his replacement).

The opening of Buchanan Elementary School was, I believe, significantly different than the opening of any other school in MVUSD. It couldn't have gone more smoothly. The building was done early and ahead of schedule, allowing us the opportunity to leisurely move in and get settled starting June 21, 2001. All furniture, equipment, and staff were in place early in the spring. There was a tremendous sense of being prepared and having some wonderful programs and focuses in place.

A large group of teachers transferred from Alta Murrieta and Rail Ranch, so the beginning staff was made up of 34 veterans of the district and 1 new teacher, Gus Bonilla. Some of the long-term employees that were first year teachers at Buchanan Elementary School were Lorie McKenzie, Jill Buschhausen, Garry Zajec, Kristin Richardson, Debbie Saldivar, Mary Mikolich and Amy Montgomery. The group of teachers that started was extremely talented and dedicated in everything they did. It was a great time because of the excitement of starting something new, yet the staff was experienced and confident. It was truly a time that highlighted the exceptional quality of education in Murrieta.

Estelle Jaurequi was the first Assistant Principal, coming from Shivela Middle School. Cathy Diyorio was the first secretary, having started out at Rail Ranch Elementary.

We anticipated and were staffed to start with approximately 650 students. On the first day, we had 725 show up. By the end of the year, we were over 900. Buchanan grew at a faster rate in this year than any other school year. We ended up adding more teachers and buildings to accommodate the fast growth.

On the second day of school, we had to hire five new teachers due to greater enrollment than projected. So, we had four portable buildings rolled on to our new campus during that first week of school. There was some sadness that this beautiful facility had to immediately add portables.

We were without our field for five months. The workers who had done the cleanup after the construction had used the field as the dumping ground. A week prior to school opening the field was seeded. We had a long time to wait before the grass grew and it could be used.

Many of our 5th grade students were challenging this year. They had gone to elementary school someplace else. We worked hard to help them develop pride in a school that they didn't have history with and would be leaving in ten months.

The dedication of Buchanan occurred on Thursday, September 13, 2001 – two days after the World Trade Center 9/11 attacks. The staff and community were still in shock over this tragedy. The students, however, had a real innocence about the magnitude of the events of that week. They were extremely excited about their new spirit t-shirts and the pride of being part of this new school as the first students. The dedication took on a beautiful and somber air of patriotism and gratefulness for the opportunities our nation provides, as evidenced by the opening of the school. I remember Californian reporter John Hunneman writing a great article for his column on the sadness and optimism of this dedication ceremony.

27. Jeff Boone

Administrator, Risk Management
November 15, 2005

Thanks for asking the question
The time is right for me
You must know where I'm at here
Where I was in the District
Over time
When we had our cake and ate it too
How parts of me ache for those times now

Way sentimental
So melancholy
Such Honesty
I could scour my old Daytimers to pick out the morsels
What made them so magical?
I think a combination of Chuck Depreker
And the need to produce schools
He was new to this construction stuff
I was eager to get after it
Every site has stories
Starting at Murrieta Valley High School....just thinking how my
    recollections
would be made truer with others that were there. Lori Noorigian, Kelly
    Webster, Randy White.
There is so much good stuff
I am inspired greatly
Where to start?
The precious unknown of it all
Pulling, pushing and prodding out resolve
Never did we falter in our effort
All pure
So this pours out of me
I'm ready to relish those memories
I will be your archive boy, digging up those golden nuggets of
    crystallized recall
Be amazed that the people along the way
How forging ahead was simply what we did
Take the plans off the shelf and dust them off
Build an Avaxat or Alta for under 4 million
All the IOR's--- Fernando, Gary, Leonard, Norman
Such respect, engagement by our forces
Establish District Standards
Ask the pointed questions

Challenge ourselves
There was only one road
Full of potholes and sinkholes
Such a passion for the bottom line$
Always asking why
Why so much grass? Why all this tech?
So many great forged relationships
Such awesome in-house ability
Remember when Charlene Stone projected
Exactly the CBEDs number?
And we dreamed hard about CAD,
Getting Randy White set up right
Library Internet
Do us all proud
The relentless plan review
What worked, what didn't
Right from the source
Don Burkes, Jim McLeod, Therese O.
A form of exhilaration
That the pioneers must have had
So these stories I share
On the fly will certainly seed a multitude of others.
MVHS—wow—no plan review here
Deb would run right over us
Steve Profit (Edge), Deb Framer
I think Jeff Hale too (J&B Concrete)
Hebranser (IOR)-- Taking codeine for a bleeding ulcer
RAP (Ralph Allen and Partners) retrieving his custom lights
Mike Blazek—architect—but mostly
comedian—his story while out at EHC where he wanted to drive
out into the desert with just him, his wife and a <u>shovel!</u>
Jimmy Johnson, an Iwo Jima veteran
Running Rail Ranch with such authority

And Lori Nooriegan, expertise I marvel
Ask what Charlie Riendeau said about those flies at Creekside.
The WWII form work for the bridge at MVHS
How Tate Parker did not want to
Raise the MVHS parking lot
How we salvaged eight classrooms at E. Hale Curran off the collapsing
    alluvium
Brilliant solution by Mike Blazek with light weight skylight
How Karen Robertson introduced me to Toastmasters
The mastodon bones at Thompson Middle School
The green slime causing a landslide at Cole Canyon elementary
Our custodian who helped the construction at Rail Ranch and died
The two boulders at Avaxat
Wendy and Al—the Architects
Those old school architects, not proponents of CM
How the groundwater would not stop at the drilled footings at Avaxat
How I thought I had the best job in the District
How did he do it?
Pull the best out of us
Us wanting to be our best.
The ultimate leader
Thanks.

28. Linda Diaz

Coordinator, Certificated Personnel, Human Resources
District Support Center
January 23, 2006

I have always felt my situation was somewhat unique in the Murrieta Valley USD. My family moved to Murrieta in November of 1988 and my three children registered at Avaxat Elementary School in a temporary

263

school facility. In February 1989, they moved to the newest "temporary school" in Murrieta, Alta Murrieta Elementary School, (K-8 setting, prior to unification). In March of 1989, I was hired as an instructional assistant at Alta Murrieta Elementary School. The following school year, Alta Murrieta shared their campus with Rail Ranch Elementary School and went on double sessions until Rail opened the next year on their own site.

A few years later, Julie April, newly hired Purchasing Agent for our district, hired me to be her clerk in the Purchasing Department. Bill Racz, Marie Curran, Julie and I were located on Hobie Circle in a warehouse that housed purchasing, reprographics, and district mail services. During this time, the district purchased their first mega-reprographic copier with a variety of capabilities, including tabs and binding. We also established the first district warehouse supply facility. The four of us enjoyed working there.

A few years later, Frank Passarella, new principal at Shivela Middle School, hired me as his Secretary. By this time, two of my three children were attending Shivela, too. Shivela was on a multi-track calendar, in a temporary school site housing approximately 900 to 1200 students every day, depending which track was "on," (A, B, C, or D). Teachers worked three months on, one month off; classified employees worked every day except their vacation days.

There were so many daily happenings during this time: staff coming on-track and going off-track with students doing the same; "mobile" teachers roving from one classroom to another (with the ongoing assistance of Bill Cammell, site Custodian). Rainy-day schedules were unique days that included changing the bell schedule, keeping students in classrooms, and providing classroom supervision utilizing all office staff members. Frank, Sandra LeBaron, Gary Farmer, Jan Danker, Roxanne Stearns, Sue McGoldrick, Bill, and I were the "guts" of the operation and every day gave our best effort to meet the needs of students, parents, and staff.

A few years later, I was hired to the Personnel Department as a Personnel Analyst to work with the certificated staff members monitoring their credentials. By this time, my three children were at Murrieta Valley High School, along with some of my nieces and nephews. My oldest niece, Nicole Diaz, was part of the first graduating class at Murrieta Valley High School. To date, our district has graduated my three children, two nephews, two nieces, and the youngest niece will graduate June 2006.

About five years ago, the Personnel Department changed its name to the Human Resources Department, and Payroll Services was reassigned to the Business Services Department. As student attendance has grown, our department has grown from nine people in 1995 to seventeen as of 2005/06. The district office has moved from leasing a building on Beckman Court to building our own two-story District Support Center facility on McAlby Court.

The Murrieta Valley USD has afforded my children and me a variety of experiences and valuable educational opportunities. Over the years, staff and students have come and gone, but occasionally we have prior graduates returning seeking teaching positions. And I am proud to say, we have hired quite a few.

29. Deborah Jacobs

Library/Media Teacher, Vista Murrieta High School
March 8, 2006

Murrieta Valley High School

My earliest memory is when Jeanne Nelson took me to look at the library at Murrieta Valley High School and informed me that "when it rains, you can't get to the school." And it truly was an adventure when it did rain. The "bridge" at Adams Street seemed on the verge of washing out any time any moisture fell from the sky. Cars and busses alike rumbled over the bridge, with water lapping at the edges. It took several years, but improvements were finally made.

Yes, of course we had tons of empty shelves in the library, but I also remember the room of "donations" that needed sorting. And some of the donations were very interesting indeed.

I remember very tall carts with TV/VCR's going out and about the campus from the library, and just knowing that they were going to crash! And they did, at least one turned over, especially as I watched the student transporting it back to the library racing across the cement quad area and jumping on for the ride!

The cement, the cement, the cement! Aluminum too. There were lots of discussion about the architecture of the building, and the absence of shade for students. Trees were planted several times before they finally survived the heat, and shade structures were added too.

Vista Murrieta High School

We started out with just a few buildings being released two days before school started. We used the Dance room to process the incoming textbooks. Power and water supplies were continually interrupted – and staff would take "breaks" at the McDonald's on Los Alamos.

We moved the library into temporary quarters for the first year, and had a wonderful floor plan all ready-- until Jeanne, Butch and I walked into the room and found an 8 foot octagonal planter smack dab in the middle of the floor, and no ceiling at the top. The circular area opened up to teacher offices up stairs. It took awhile for staff to realize that during their breaks and lunches, all the students in the library directly below them could hear their conversations. The planter made for great conversation, as it was empty of plants, but it did make for a nice display area for new books. We were staffed only by the Library/Media Teacher for the entire first year. Jeanne Russell, Library Technician, was hired the second year.

We moved into our new completed library the second year. It had quirks, like columns that block the view of the library, sagging books shelves, and a lack of computer seating, but adjustments were made.

Again, we needed books for our many shelves. PTSA sponsored a "Kiss the Bronco" contest with proceeds going to the library. Judi DeWeese was a great sport, and kissed our Bronco Horse.

30. Kate Hamaker
Family Services Director
May 11, 2006

In 1992, Murrieta Valley Unified School Board learned about the working concept of a parent center at a California School Board Association workshop. They visited the Long Beach Parent Center, which at that time was funded through Title 1 and focused on computer training and computers. Upon returning to Murrieta the Board and Murrieta Council PTA Parent Involvement Committee decided to open a Parent Center in the district, and hired Kate van Horn (Hamaker) to plan and manage it. When Mrs. Hamaker was hired, there were no facilities, and funds were set aside to help with startup expenses. From the beginning, it was planned to be self-supporting.

Originally the staff consisted only of Mrs. Hamaker, who was given the responsibility of creating the parent center, finding funding to continue programs and facilitate the programs. After the first year, she was able to procure funds to hire a Parent Center Assistant to provide child care.

Through Mrs. Hamaker's efforts, the Center was furnished by collaboration with Riverside County Office of Education-Children's Services Unit, Murrieta Valley Unified School District, and Hughes Aircraft, San Diego. One year after the Parent Center opened, the Murrieta Valley Unified School District Board of Education received the *American School Board Journal*'s Magna Award. This award is given for the School Board's programming excellence and was received for the Parent Center project.

267

The Parent Center has had several locations throughout the district. In 1994, it was located at Murrieta Valley High School. As the student population grew at MVHS and Thompson moved from Shivela to its own campus, the Parent Center found space at Shivela. After being located at Shivela for two years, the Parent Center had to move again, this time to Creekside High School, where once again rooms were available because the school was so new. As the school grew, increased demand for classroom space forced the Parent Center to find a new home. For one year operations were moved to the district office while the search for a new location continued.

In 1999, Tovashal moved to its permanent location, vacating the original portable buildings on the Avaxat campus. The Parent Center has continued to be located at the Avaxat campus for the past six years.

The original funding for the Parent Center came from a generous donation from American Industrial Manufacturing and an annual $40,000 General Fund commitment from the MVUSD Board. The first year's budget for the Parent Center was $86,000. Over the years, the Parent Center has received grants and awards from City of Murrieta Community Development Block Grant, County of Riverside Community Development Block Grant, Riverside County Probation, Department of Social Services- Child Prevention Intervention and Treatment; Department of Social Services -; American Industrial Manufacturing; GTE; City of Temecula Community Services; First Five Riverside and private donors. The budget in 2005-06 was $316,500.00.

Services provided by the Parent Center have changed over the years. The Center has been providing the parenting classes, support groups, referral services, and child care job training since February 1994. Parenting classes offered by the Parent Center now include:

- Parenting with P.R.I.C.E. (Positivity, Responsibility, Influence, Consequences, and Encouragement)
- Co-Parenting with P.R.I.C.E. (with a divorce counseling component)
- Parenting with P.R.I.C.E.- Spanish

268

- Systematic Training for Effective Parenting- Basic, Teen, and Early Childhood
- Parent Project for Strong-Willed Adolescents
- Parent Project for Strong-Willed Adolescents-Spanish
- Loving Solutions for Strong-Willed School Age Children
- Los Niños Bien Educados
- Parents as Teachers
- Parent and Me.

To help meet the child care needs of the community and area, the Parent Center provides first aid, CPR training, and Child Health and Safety Training. Support groups that operate out of the Center include: Alanon; Alanon-Spanish; Rape Crisis Center; Family and Friends of Murder Victims; and Walden Foster Care.

Child Care staff cares for children during these classes and a clerk provides office support. Family Services Director, Kate Hamaker has been with the program since its inception in February 1994. She developed and implemented the program and continues to administer the program, train and supervise class facilitators and facilitate a small percentage of the classes offered.

Family Services now also offers a State Preschool Program and continues to provide the before and after school child care program originally started by Susan Reynolds in 1985.

31. Tim Custer

Principal, Warm Springs Middle School
January 24, 2006

I was one of the eleven original teachers at Thompson when it opened in 1994-1995 on the back of Shivela's campus. In 1994-95 we moved to our new permanent campus, which was only half completed. Over the next several years the campus was completed in phases.

It was a fantastic experience being a part of opening a new school – an experience that prepared me for opening Warm Springs as the principal in 2002. Of the eleven original teachers at TMS and seven are still employed in the district. That first year we had 250 kids, that grew to 350, and then slowly grew over the years to the 1,800 students there today.

After three years as a teacher and four years as Assistant Principal at Thompson Middle School, I went to Murrieta Valley High School as Assistant Principal for one year (2001-2002), and was then named principal of Warm Springs Middle School. We opened WSMS with 750 kids, have grown to 1,500 and expect to top 2,000 before the next middle school opens.

While opening a new, small, school is awesome because you get to know students very well, being the principal of a large school is also very exciting. I'm looking forward to the next few years leading the charge as we grow into one of the largest middle schools in the country.

While I could share many stories about staff and students (some stories should probably best be forgotten), there is a theme that clearly runs throughout my experiences here in Murrieta and my life in general: *It's all about relationships*. I can't tell you how many former students are still in my life: They work for the district (need something painted? – the entire MVUSD paint crew are former students). They are completing their student teaching and looking for jobs. And they are in my life in numerous ways, such as the young lady who works as a clerk at Barnes and Noble in Oceanside. I've even run across former students on the beach in Hawaii!!!

32. Jennifer Tan

Principal, Rail Ranch Elementary School
January 11, 2006

270

I was hired in Murrieta in 1995. I had taught Elizabeth Ellsworth's daughter in Bonsall and she encouraged me to apply for the new band teacher job at a "new school" (Thompson Middle School) in Murrieta. I taught at Thompson three years, was a district GATE (Gifted and Talented Education) specialist for 1/2 year, Assistant Principal at Rail Ranch Elementary for 2 1/2 years, and now am in my 5th year as Principal at Rail Ranch Elementary School.

I remember parking in the dirt and rock parking lot when Thompson Middle School shared a campus with Shivela Middle School. How fun it was to trudge through the mud when it rained! None of us had clean cars. I had to change classrooms annually (sometimes 2-3 times during the year) because the school was growing so quickly. The exploratory (elective) department consisted of only 3-4 teachers, including Tim Custer and me. Because there weren't many band students the first year, I had to also teach four periods of exploratory (art, music appreciation, careers, crafts, communication). As a department, we created our own curricula in these exploratory areas!

Each year, the band grew, more periods of band were added, and we had an after-school jazz band and dance team. I took the band and dance team (they performed with poms and flags) to march and perform in the Temecula Light Parade during our off-track time. I often had to call Bryan Boos at MVHS to borrow band instruments because we had so few in the beginning.

Thompson Middle School changed from less than 500 to 800 students within 3 years. I had some classes that first year with 20 students, and by my third year, I had 40+ in every period! I never had a classroom computer or email during those early years at Thompson. The staff was only 18 teachers my first year. All of us chaperoned the dances! When the new campus opened up, we all packed up, moved and unpacked over a weekend. That was just how things were done in those days.

The GATE program has changed over the years. Bonnie Cringan created a "GATE Seminar" program for elementary students in 1997. She and I were teachers on special assignment together, coordinating and teaching this program in 1998. We created our own seminar curriculum, picked students up from each elementary site on a bus, and did our "seminar" at Thompson Middle School so that we had access to their brand new computers!

33. Karen Briski

Principal, Antelope Hills Elementary School
January 6, 2006

I was hired in May 1996 at Avaxat Elementary School as the Principal. Before coming to Murrieta, I was an assistant principal in Lake Elsinore as well as a teacher.

My first year in the district was very unique because Tovashal Elementary School was sharing our campus as a brand new school. Chuck Jones, the new Tovashal principal, was hired at the same time as I was, and was also new to the district. We were "thrown together" as colleagues sharing a campus and we still laugh about what a disaster it could have been, but how great it actually turned out to be.

When Antelope Hills Elementary (2005) was planned, I had the opportunity to open a new school. It was exhausting and exciting to start from scratch. The most exciting part still is to have a vision and to watch that vision develop and materialize; not just the buildings but actually the people and the plan.

One of the biggest challenges we faced was that we did not have desks assembled two days before the start of school. Teachers were in classrooms putting desks together. That was interesting!

We all wore pith helmets on the first day as part of our *Join the Adventure* theme for Antelope Hills.

34. Chuck Jones

Administrative Facilities Planner
April 26, 2006

I was hired in May of 1996 to open Tovashal School on a section of the Avaxat Campus. We started school in July of 1996 with just 13 teachers, 240 students, a secretary, a half- time attendance clerk/half time health clerk, two aides and one custodian on tracks A and B. Over the next two years we added six classrooms and increased our enrollment to 680 students. In September of 1998, after two months of instruction, we moved into the new campus. The students took buses from Avaxat on the Friday before the opening to carry their books and personal belongings to their new classrooms. Teachers and staff were allowed on campus just three days before we opened school. The staff worked long hours all day Friday, Saturday, and Sunday to get ready and provide a smooth opening of school.

Tovashal PTA was selected as one of the top ten PTA's in the state on three separate occasions during my tenure at Tovashal. We were also recognized as one of the top ten PTA's in the nation and received recognition at the national level in Chicago, Illinois. Our focus was on providing educational materials, library books and family activities. Because of our efforts, the Tovashal library became the largest elementary library in the district in just five years. Our family nights included activities that centered around curricular topics like reading, phonics, and math as well as the arts. We hosted Fall Fairs, Arty Parties, Dances, and Astronomy Nights that were extremely well attended.

I left Tovashal in 2002 and opened Monte Vista that same year. Monte Vista opened at capacity with 790 students. There were construction glitches that added to the challenge of opening a new school. The office carpet was completed at 5:00 P.M. Sunday evening, the day before student registration. The multipurpose room and cafeteria were completed in December. Students ate lunch in their classrooms on inclement weather days or "bee days" (days when there were so many bees on campus that it became dangerous) for four months. Seventeen classrooms did not have air conditioning for the first week. The alarm tests took place the morning before school started. Frequent "bugs" were found in the system tripping the alarms as many as five times during a day for a period of three weeks.

Despite all of the inconveniences, the staff handed out leis and dressed in Hawaiian attire the first day of school and greeted the students with warmth and excitement. The PTA was formed five months prior to the opening of the school and a full complement of activities was developed for students as well as evening family events.

References

Austin, Michael. Fostering A Feeling Of
Connection Guides Vista Murrieta. *Coach and Athletic Director*,
November/December 2013. Retrieved December 11, 2013 from
http://www.coachad.com/pages/Program-Of-Excellence-Vista-
Murrieta-High-School.php

Avants, Maggie. Murrieta Mesa's Walters Promoted to District Level;
Interim Principal Announced. Murrieta Patch, June 20, 2013.
Retrieved February 27, 2014, from
http://murrieta.patch.com/groups/schools/p/murrieta-mesas-
walters-promoted-to-district-level-interim-principal-announced

Azar, Lara. Murrieta school district drops Town Square plans. San
Diego Union Tribune, March 29, 2001. Retrieved July 10, 2013
from www.utsandiego.com/news/2001/mar/29/murrieta-school-
district-drops-town-square-plans/all

Barnett, Malcolm. *History of Old Temecula's Schools*. Temecula Valley
Historical Society website, 2002.
http://www.temeculahistoricalsociety.org/schoolhistory.html
Retrieved June 25, 2013.

Boyce, Mary Alice Rail. *Murrieta: Old Town, New Town*. Murrieta, CA:
Rosemar Publishing Company, 1995.

California Department of Education. Distinguished School Awards.
Retrieved from http://www.cde.ca.gov/ta/sr/cs/distinguished.asp
August 20 2013.

Dodge, Richard V. The Fallbrook Line. Printed in *DISPATCHER*, April
10, 1958 Issue 17. Retrieved from
http://www.sdrm.org/history/cs/calsouth.html June 23, 2013.

Downey, Dave. "High school laboratory figures prominently in
survival of endangered butterfly." *San Diego Union Tribune*, May 1,
2005. Retrieved November 29, 2013, from

http://www.utsandiego.com/news/2005/May/01/high-school-laboratory-figures-prominently-in/2/?#article-copy

Garrison, Arlean. *My Children's Home.* Lake Elsinore, CA: Mayhall Print Shop, 1963.

Gerstbacher, Emily. *Temecula History: A Chronology 1797-1993* http://www.oldtemecula.com/history/history1.htm

Hunneman, John. "More than two decades after it burned, Murrieta Grammar may have to be leveled." *The Californian,* May 21, 2006.

Lake Elsinore Historical Society. *Lake Elsinore.* Charleston, SC : Arcadia Pub., 2008.

Murrieta Fire Protection District History. Retrieved from http://www.murrieta.org/services/fire/info/history.asp

Murrieta Valley Unified School District. "Keeping our landscape looking first-class." *The Inside Connection* (1,1), December 2001.

Pechanga Band of Luiseño Indians. Retrieved June 7, 2013 from http://www.pechanga-nsn.gov/page?pageId=8

Proximity: Resources to create and apply insight. *School districts by geographic size.* Retrieved April 4, 2014. from http://proximityone.com/schooldistrict_size.htm

Rail, Floyd. *Elsinore-Temecula History: Stories and Experiences.* Unpublished manuscript, 1990.

Railroad map. Wikipedia http://en.wikipedia.org/wiki/California_Southern_Railroad Article: California Southern Railroad. Rothwell, Christine. School Nursing: More than Just Bruises and Band-Aids. *NurseZone,* 2001. Retrieved July 11, 2014, from http://www.nursezone.com/nursing-news-events/more-features/School-Nursing-More-than-Just-Bruises-and-Band-Aids_21764.aspx

Temecula Valley Historical Society. http://www.temeculahistorialsociety.org/schoolhistory.html January 16, 2013

School Addresses

Alta Murrieta Elementary
  School
39475 Whitewood Road
Telephone: (951) 696-1403

Antelope Hills Elementary
36105 Murrieta Oaks Avenue
Telephone: (951) 445-4110

Avaxat Elementary School
24300 Las Brisas Road
Telephone: (951) 696-1402

Buchanan Elementary School
40121 Torrey Pines Road
Telephone: (951) 696-1428

Cole Canyon Elementary
  School
23750 Via Alisol
Telephone: (951) 696-1421

E. Hale Curran Elementary
  School
40855 Chaco Canyon Road
Telephone: (951) 696-1405

Lisa J. Mails Elementary
35185 Briggs Road
Telephone: (951) 304-1880

Monte Vista Elementary
  School
37420 Via Mira Mosa
Telephone: (951) 894-5085

Murrieta Elementary School
24725 Adams Street
Telephone: (951) 696-1401

Rail Ranch Elementary School
25030 Via Santee
Telephone: (951) 696-1404

Tovashal Elementary School
23801 St. Raphael
Telephone: (951) 696-1411

Dorothy McElhinney Middle
  School
35125 Briggs Road
Telephone: (951) 304-1885

Shivela Middle School
24515 Lincoln Avenue
Telephone: (951) 696-1406

Thompson Middle School
24040 Hayes Avenue
Telephone: (951) 696-1410

Warm Springs Middle School
39245 Calle de Fortuna
Telephone: (951) 696-3503

Murrieta Valley High School
42200 Nighthawk Way
Telephone: (951) 696-1408

Murrieta Mesa High School
24801 Monroe
Telephone: (951) 677-0568

Vista Murrieta High School
28251 Clinton Keith Rd.
Telephone: (951) 894-5750

Creekside High School
(Continuation)
24150 Hayes Avenue
Telephone: (951) 696-1409

Tenaja Canyon Academy
(Independent Study)
24150 Hayes Avenue
Telephone: (951) 304-1661

District Support Center
41870 McAlby Court
Murrieta, CA 92562
Phone: (951).696.1600
www.murrieta.k12.ca.

Postscript

For whoever steps up to write the rest of the story, and I hope you include photos, maps, and documents. I will be happy to share notes, resources, and what I've learned along this fascinating journey to publication.

Every effort was made to check dates, name spellings, and other facts, but with so many details, there still may be errors. My apologies for those.

It has been an honor to be part of this Murrieta story.

Made in the USA
Charleston, SC
26 August 2016